P9-AQX-969

03/24
STAND PRICE
$ 5.00

Alger Hiss, Whittaker Chambers, and the Schism in the American Soul

Edited by

PATRICK SWAN

The imprint of the Intercollegiate Studies Insitute
Wilmington, Delaware

Copyright © 2003 ISI Books

All rights reserved. No part of this publication may be reproduced or transmitted in any form or by any means, electronic or mechanical, including photocopy, or any information storage and retrieval system now known or to be invented, without permission in writing from the publisher, except by a reviewer who wishes to quote brief passages in connection with a review written for inclusion in a magazine, newspaper, or broadcast.

Cataloging-in-Publication Data:

Alger Hiss, Whittaker Chambers, and the schism in the American Soul / edited by Patrick Swan. –1st ed. –Wilmington, Del. : ISI Books, 2002.

    p. ; cm.

Includes bibliographical references and index.

    ISBN 1-882926-85-4 (cloth)
    ISBN 1-882926-91-9 (pbk.)

        1. Hiss, Alger. 2. Chambers, Whittaker. 3. Communism–United States. 4. Spies–United States. 5. Subversive activities–United States–History–20th century. 6. Treason–United States. I. Swan, Patrick.

E743.5 A44 2002   2002107930
364.1/31–dc21   0210

Interior book design by Claudia L. Henrie

Published in the United States by:
    ISI Books
    Post Office Box 4431
    Wilmington, DE 19807-0431
    www.isibooks.org

Manufactured in the United States of America

Acknowledgments

THIS ENTERPRISE OWES its existence to patience, persistence, and patronage. Patience, because I recognized its value nearly fifteen years ago while providing research assistance to Terry Teachout for his volume of Whittaker Chambers's collected journalism, *Ghosts on the Roof*, and am only now seeing it published. Persistence, because, despite being rejected by publisher after publisher (including three "with great regret" over the years from the friendly publishing house, Regnery Gateway), I never gave up my belief that this was a workable project and a constructive contribution to the Hiss-Chambers record. Patronage, because of the unselfish assistance of four great men. First, Al Regnery, who on my last pitch to him, graciously recommended that I contact ISI Books. It turns out, as the saying goes, that I had been walking on the right street all along, but had been knocking on all the wrong doors. Second, William F. Buckley Jr., who helpfully referred me to a historical foundation that helped fund the project. Third, Terry Teachout, who offered encouragement and whose short biographical narratives ensured that I became well-versed on the stature of the authors featured in this collection. And finally, Wilfred McClay, who kindly shared his unique insights about the historical impact of the Hiss-Chambers case for the book's introduction.

I am also indebted to a number of friends and family members in this endeavor. Dr. Jeremy Beer, my editor at ISI, provided critical guidance and perspective, and Mark Henrie of ISI came up with the elusive title for this book, one that had escaped me these many years. Anne Krulikowski tirelessly tracked down authors, publishing concerns, and estates to obtain timely reprint permissions. Many of those authors, such as Sam Tanenhaus, Hilton Kramer, Ron Rosenbaum, and William F. Buckley Jr., graciously waived or steeply discounted their fees so this project could move forward. Thanks are due all the authors included here (or their estates) for permission to reprint their pieces. The *Atlantic Monthly, Esquire, New York Times, Partisan Review, Harper's, New York Observer, New Republic, New Statesman, Saturday Review, New Leader, American Spectator, New York Review of Books, New Criterion, Commentary,* and Random House are also to be thanked for granting the necessary permissions. The copyright for each piece remains in the hands of its original owner. In each essay, any footnotes that appear have been added by me for purposes of clarification or identification. Any endnotes are those of the author.

My sister, Lisa M. Swan, tenaciously re-typed many of these articles from dog-eared photocopied versions, and also proofread the final galleys. Throughout this lengthy odyssey, the unconditional love of my daughters, Amy and Stephanie Swan, and my parents, Harry and Marilyn Swan, sustained me, especially during its darkest periods. Finally, I want to show gratitude to Linda Jones, my former companion, who kept after me to get this work published (even if for no higher reason than that it would remove one more box of what she saw as clutter from our home).

TABLE OF CONTENTS

PREFACE
Patrick Swan ... XI

INTRODUCTION
Wilfred McClay ... XXV

1. HISS, CHAMBERS, AND THE AGE OF INNOCENCE
Leslie A. Fiedler
Commentary, August 1951 ... 1

2. A MEMORANDUM ON THE HISS CASE
Diana Trilling
Partisan Review, May-June 1950 ... 27

3. THE COMPLEX ISSUE OF THE EX-COMMUNISTS
Arthur Koestler
New York Times Magazine, February 19, 1950 ... 49

4. WHITTAKER CHAMBERS'S TESTAMENT
Granville Hicks
New Leader, May 26, 1952 ... 57

5. THE FAITHS OF WHITTAKER CHAMBERS
Sidney Hook
New York Times Book Review, May 25, 1952 ... 69

6. GOD, MAN AND STALIN
Irving Howe
Nation, May 24, 1952 ... 81

7. HISTORY IN DOUBLETHINK
Elmer Davis
Saturday Review, June 28, 1952 . . . 91

8. THE WITNESS
Kingsley Martin
New Statesman and Nation, July 19, 1952 . . . 101

9. WHITTAKER CHAMBERS
Rebecca West
Atlantic Monthly, June 1952 . . . 107

10. THE MISFORTUNE OF A NATION
Mark DeWolfe Howe
Nation, May 18, 1957 . . . 127

11. OF GUILT AND RESURRECTION
David Cort
Nation, March 20, 1967 . . . 133

12. THE END OF WHITTAKER CHAMBERS
William F. Buckley Jr.
Esquire, September 1962 . . . 139

13. A NARODNIK FROM LYNBROOK
Murray Kempton
New York Review of Books, January 29, 1970 . . . 165

14. WHITTAKER CHAMBERS
AND *THE MIDDLE OF THE JOURNEY*
Lionel Trilling
New York Review of Books, April 17, 1975 . . . 179

15. THE STATE OF THE ART OF ALGER HISS
Philip Nobile
Harper's, April 1976 . . . 201

16. WHY HISS CAN'T CONFESS
Alfred Kazin
Esquire, March 28, 1978 . . . 213

17. CHAMBERS' MUSIC AND ALGER HISS
Hugh Kenner
American Spectator, June 1979 . . . 221

18. THE TWO FACES OF WHITTAKER CHAMBERS
John Judis
New Republic, April 16, 1984 . . . 235

19. ALGER HISS: A GLIMPSE BEHIND THE MASK
Eric M. Breindel
Commentary, November 1988 . . . 253

20. WHITTAKER CHAMBERS, MAN OF LETTERS
Sam Tanenhaus
New Criterion, April 1990 . . . 265

21. SIFTING THROUGH THE EVIDENCE
Sam Tanenhaus
Appendix to *Whittaker Chambers: A Biography*, 1997 . . . 285

22. MY LUNCH WITH ALGER:
OH NO, NOT HISS AGAIN!
Ron Rosenbaum
New York Observer, April 16, 2001 . . . 293

23. THINKING ABOUT *WITNESS*
Hilton Kramer
New Criterion, March 1988 . . . 303

A HISS-CHAMBERS BIBLIOGRAPHY . . . 325

NOTES ON CONTRIBUTORS . . . 339

INDEX . . . 349

PATRICK SWAN

Preface

F IVE YEARS AGO IN THE *New York Times*, Arthur Schlesinger Jr. affirmed the continuing relevance of the twentieth century's most famous trials in America. His list included the trials of John T. Scopes, Sacco and Vanzetti, Leopold and Loeb, Bruno Richard Hauptmann, and (he reluctantly added) O. J. Simpson.

As important as those cases were, however, Schlesinger explained that, for people of a certain age and political concern, "the trial of Alger Hiss remains paramount."

That trial (more accurately, trials, as there was more to this case than the simple criminal indictment for perjury) exposed to the public for the first time the tragic, unlikely figures of Alger Hiss and Whittaker Chambers and gave us the infamous spy case that bears their names. The narrative snaked a tortuous, often perplexing path, one that left an indelible mark on the American political and cultural landscape.

It began on a sweltering August day in 1948, when Chambers, a senior editor at *Time* magazine with a shadowy past as a communist agent, reluctantly testified to a House investigating committee that a number of former government officials, including a highly regarded one named Alger Hiss, were secret Communist Party members. When pressed further by House investigators, Chambers later admitted that he, Hiss, and others had engaged in espionage for the Soviet Union against the United States during the 1930s. Thus began the great case.

A spellbound nation watched breathlessly as the drama unfolded. The committee summoned Hiss. Hiss denied the allegations. The two were brought together and confronted each other. Chambers recognized Hiss. Hiss emphatically denied knowing Chambers. Hiss challenged Chambers to repeat his charges in public. Chambers obliged on a radio broadcast. Hiss sued Chambers for slander in civil court. In the criminal court, a grand jury convened. Chambers produced additional evidence. Hiss was indicted. A trial was held. A mistrial was declared after the jury deadlocked. A second trial was held. In January 1950, Hiss was convicted of perjury for lying about his relationship with Chambers and his covert actions. He was sentenced to five years in a federal penitentiary. A judge then threw out Hiss's slander suit against Chambers.

Hiss completed his sentence, began a career as a greeting card salesman (as a convicted felon, he was disbarred from practicing law), published his first memoirs, *In the Court of Public Opinion*, essentially a pedestrian lawyer's brief, and continued defiantly declaring his innocence until his death in 1996.

In 1952, Chambers wrote his memoirs, the modern biographical classic titled *Witness*, detailing his life with the Communist Party and the challenges America faced with communism in mid-century. Chambers succinctly summarized those challenges by asking the rhetorically profound question: "Faith in God or Faith in Man?" He believed the fate of Western Civilization rested on the correct answer ("Faith in God"). By presenting the stakes in such stark terms and by in effect putting secular liberalism on trial, the soft-spoken Chambers had inadvertently fired the opening salvo in the modern American political discourse between Left and Right. With his career at

Time ruined by the case, an exhausted Chambers retired to his farm in Westminster, Maryland, writing sporadically and publishing commentary in William F. Buckley's fledgling *National Review*. He died in 1961.

As is well known and oft repeated, Hiss and Chambers were two men scarcely cut from the same political or personal cloth. Hiss was tall, handsome, well pedigreed and highly credentialed. He had graduated from Harvard with a law degree and had clerked for Supreme Court Justice Oliver Wendell Holmes. He had served in the Agriculture and State Departments, ultimately advising President Franklin Roosevelt at Yalta. Later, in 1945, Hiss served as the secretary-general of the United Nations Conference on International Organizations (UNCIO), where he presided over the negotiations that led to the ratification and signing of the UN Charter. When the case broke, Hiss was working as president of the Carnegie Endowment for International Peace, and many believed he was a strong contender for Secretary of State in a future Democratic administration.

Hiss was also an undercover operative supplying intelligence information for the Soviet Union.

In contrast, Chambers was short, squat, and rumpled in both attire and demeanor. In the essay included here, Rebecca West noted incredulously that "[i]t is one of the great jokes of history that the dragnet of a Washington committee should have fetched up this man of all men to take part in a dervish trial." Chambers was a Columbia University dropout. A gifted writer, he had penned stirring essays for the communist *New Masses* magazine and *Daily Worker* newspaper in the early 1930s before going underground to do "special work" for the Communist Party. Emerging in 1937 after becoming disillusioned with Stalin's purges and what he saw as the diabolical true meaning of communism, Chambers informed the government (in 1939, one day after the Nazi invasion of Poland) of his activities, alerting adminis-

tration officials to the spy network operating from within the government, and waited for action. None ever followed. He subsequently
landed a job with *Time* magazine, where he wrote thoughtful, sometimes moving, and often provocative book reviews. He later stepped
up for a controversial stint at *Time*'s Foreign News desk, where he
employed his editorial perch weekly to sound the alarm about the
not-so-friendly intentions of America's not-so-trustworthy ally, "Uncle
Joe" Stalin and the Soviet Union. Because *Time* did not assign bylines
to its writers and editors in those days, Chambers remained a relatively unknown figure to the American public until the House Un-
American Activities Committee subpoenaed the former communist
agent to testify in the summer of 1948.

The Hiss-Chambers case was a trial in more ways than the traditional courtroom trappings would suggest. True, there were congressional hearings and grand jury indictments. A young U.S. representative from California, Richard M. Nixon, would cut his political
teeth on the case, earning as his reward a national reputation (and the
Left's undying enmity).

There were distinguished prosecutors and defense attorneys. Tom
Murphy, a New York City prosecutor, had compiled a 99 percent
conviction record in the U.S. Attorney's Office. For the defense, the
renowned trial lawyer Lloyd Stryker, the Johnnie Cochran and Alan
Dershowitz of his day, earned Alger Hiss a mistrial in the first prosecution, but took a pass on a second Hiss defense. That subsequent
jury convicted Hiss of perjury (the statute of limitations for espionage having passed).

In addition, there were the witnesses—many, many witnesses.
Fifteen character witnesses vouched for Hiss, either in person or in
writing. These included Supreme Court Justice Felix Frankfurter, Il-
linois Governor Adlai Stevenson, and 1924 Democratic presidential
nominee, John W. Davis. Familial witnesses for Chambers included
the singular figure of his wife, Esther, who after sustained badgering

by Stryker, exclaimed to the jury, "My husband is a decent citizen, a great man!"

And there was the evidence: the prothonotary warbler, a rare bird Hiss had confided sighting to Chambers in the 1930s and the occurrence of which Hiss later unwittingly divulged to congressional investigators seeking to verify a relationship between the two men. There were the purloined secret State Department memos and documents Hiss passed to Chambers. There were the additional copies Hiss had keyed overnight on his Woodstock typewriter. Most famously, there were the "Pumpkin Papers," actually rolls of incriminating microfilm Chambers had photographed from secret documents Hiss had removed from State. Chambers spirited away these canisters when he made his break with communism, and later stowed them away for safekeeping in a hollowed-out pumpkin on his farm at the height of the investigation's furor. *Pre-medeated Framing*

This recitation of the sensational twists and turns behind the Hiss-Chambers case leads us to this anthology, which consists of a representative collection of essays about the case's continued importance to the American body politic. To paraphrase an assertion made by Whittaker Chambers himself (published posthumously in *Cold Friday*), every serious political essay, like every life, is issued ultimately, not to those among whom it initially appears, but to the judgment of time, the sternest umpire. What serious man, he added, could wish for a judgment less final? These essayists, all serious men (and women), influential as public-opinion shapers, would surely concur.

Each essay in this collection examined, for its own contemporary audience, the impact of the Hiss-Chambers case on American political culture. What sets these essays apart from most of the hundreds of other lesser pieces is that their unique observations have best withstood the judgment of time.

In general, the passionate convictions manifested in these essays fall into one of three categories. First, there are those who believe

Alger Hiss testified truthfully that he was not a communist and did not engage in espionage for the Soviet Union; those who subscribe to this conviction see Hiss as perhaps the most wronged man in U.S. history, a man victimized by an unjust judicial system (such is the *Nation*'s long-time position).

Thus, in a 1952 *Saturday Review* critique of *Witness*, law professor Charles Alan Wright complained that the case was "too complex for either reporters or the jury to understand properly. . . . The burden of proof was on Hiss to prove his innocence, rather than on the government to prove him guilty. . . . [W]e seem deliberately to make it as difficult as possible for a jury to reach a rational verdict." And in a 1957 review of Hiss's *In the Court of Public Opinion* (included here), legal scholar and historian Mark DeWolfe Howe wrote that Hiss had satisfied him that "abuses of congressional power, supplemented by the excessive zeal of the prosecutor, go farther to explain the second jury's verdict than does any presumption that twelve jurors who heard the witnesses accurately measured the conflicting testimony." Howe concluded with this bitter prediction: "Whether the tribunal of history will accept or reject the jury's verdict we cannot say. It seems clear, however, that it will condemn the action of those who converted an investigating committee of the Congress into a prosecuting agency of the government."

Hiss personally advanced this line of attack as late as 1986, when, in the *New York Times*, he wrote that his case was

> tried in the hysteria of the early cold-war year of 1949 after sensational hearings by the House Committee on Un-American Activities. Those documents showed that the prosecution had withheld exculpatory evidence, misled the judge and jury on the identity and authenticity of the typewriter that was the crucial exhibit in the case and committed other transgressions. . . . Anyone can examine this proof of my assertion that the conviction was a miscarriage of justice. The issue presented is one of fact and common-sense judgment. Any reader can determine whether

or not to agree with the judge, himself a Nixon appointee, who denied my petition. Once more, I assert that I did not engage in espionage. It is still simply Whittaker Chambers's word against mine. In calmer times my word has been accepted, and it will be again. My case seems to be a barometer of the cold war.

Over the years, Hiss's aggressively unyielding stance has led advocates of his innocence to swear themselves to something of a loyalty oath. William F. Buckley Jr. noted that Hiss's innocence had once been "a fixed rational conviction, then blind faith, and now was rank superstition." Chambers wrote to Buckley that Hiss was vindicated every time "one of the most respectable old ladies (gentlemen) says to another of the respectable old ladies (gentlemen): 'Really, I don't see how Alger Hiss could brazen it out that way unless he were really innocent.' All Alger Hiss has to do for this victory is persist in his denials." Such tenacity seemed persuasive to both Hiss's diehard and lukewarm supporters, who can be heard to exclaim in exasperation at times, as we read in Philip Nobile's essay, that Hiss must be telling the truth because "[n]othing else makes sense."

In a review of Allen Weinstein's *Perjury* published in 1978, Garry Wills would have none of it, giving Hiss's game away, as he sees it: "Hiss's strategy of total and universal denial and forgetfulness from the very outset, his refusal to volunteer autobiography, make sense if Hiss had more to hide than the Chambers documents. This is why I would not pay him the insult of believing him. I would rather think he has been serving his own gods with hidden gallantry. It is only as a secret foe that he regains the integrity people have always sensed in him."

The *New York Observer*'s Ron Rosenbaum didn't accept the "nothing else makes sense" reasoning of Hiss's defenders, either. Instead, Rosenbaum, writing just last year, articulated a more novel take on the case, namely, that Hiss's defense is best served by readily and proudly admitting his guilt. He argued that Hiss's defenders adopted the values of Hiss's accusers when they committed themselves to the idea that, if Hiss did do it, there is no defense for it. Rosenbaum implied that Hiss's actions were, in fact, defensible if one saw them as those of a true believer, working for the salvation of mankind through communism. "Perhaps Hiss loyalists should consider whether they are in fact no longer defending Hiss at this point, but rather perpetuating a cover story he no longer needs—at the cost of denying him a truly principled defense, a defense, at least, of the person he really was," Rosenbaum concluded.

Occupying the second category of argument in this compilation are those who trusted the veracity of Whittaker Chambers's testimony (and who, in fact, were profoundly moved by it). Those supporters believed that Chambers had sacrificed his reputation, career, and health with his willingness to swear that, in the 1930s and 1940s, agents of a hostile foreign power had infiltrated some of the highest levels of the U.S. government, and that among those agents was a man named Alger Hiss. In this view, Chambers's solitary struggle personified the "mystery of human redemption" in the epic twentieth-century struggle between freedom and totalitarianism (*National Review*'s position). Commenting on the awful, agonizing paradox that was Whittaker Chambers's witness, Murray Kempton writes, "(His enemies) condemn him to the degradation of having lied, while he writhes in the degradation of having told the truth."

Unhappily, this category attracted a few of the more unappealing supporters of anticommunism, such as Senator Joe McCarthy. But one should remember this: Although McCarthy embraced Chambers, Chambers in quick order denounced McCarthy, repudiating his tactics as counter-productive to the political goals they appeared to share. ("For the Right to tie itself in any way to Senator McCarthy is suicide," Chambers advised. "He is a raven of disaster.") And, in retrospect, although American leftists have for more than fifty years routinely issued shrill cries of McCarthyism as a convenient shorthand for any conduct they perceive as a politically intolerant "witch hunt" (by the American Right), McCarthy's actual disruption of civilized U.S. political debate was rather short-lived.

Chambers also attracted some unlikely liberal allies. One such latecomer was John Kenneth Galbraith, who wrote in a 1970 "revisionist" review of *Odyssey of a Friend: Letters of Whittaker Chambers to William F. Buckley, Jr., 1954–1961,* published in the *New Republic,* that in time he had come to accept Hiss's guilt, and to some degree even to blame Hiss (rather than Chambers) for Joe McCarthy. He then added, with regret, "(But) I never got around to forgiving Whittaker Chambers." He wrote that he had dismissed *Witness* because he "did not care for the author or his political associations," and conceded that this was not the best foundation for literary or artistic criticism. He concluded, "It is not news that Chambers destroyed Hiss. But these letters show that Hiss also destroyed Chambers."

What Hiss did not destroy, as John Judis claims in a 1984 *New Republic* treatise reprinted here, was Chambers's far-reaching influence, which Judis wrote was clearly of "more than passing contemporary interest." Judis reminded readers that after Chambers wrote *Witness,* he dedicated the remainder of his life to working with "a new generation of American right-wingers trying to develop an American conservative movement." Mary McCarthy recognized immediately the threat to the American Left, which was why she, among many others, wanted so badly to exonerate Hiss and to discredit Chambers. "The great effect of this new Right," she advised a friend in 1952, "is to get itself accepted as *normal,* and its publications as a *normal* part of publishing . . . and this, it seems to me, must be scotched, if its not already too late."

It was.

Although Lionel Trilling had written in 1950 that liberalism was the sole intellectual tradition in American society, that was all about to change, thanks in large part to Chambers, whose *Witness* provided much of the intellectual foundation for conservatives' defense of the West. He brought conservatives, who had been fairly anti-ideological until the 1950s, into the national argument. Chambers, a self-described "man of the Right," gave conservatives a voice, even as he himself remained uncomfortable with the term "conservatism." His encouragement nurtured the growth of what Mary McCarthy famously had hoped to "scotch"; a successful and influential conservative American political movement.

One of the so-called right-wingers whom Chambers's worldview profoundly influenced was the youthful conservative pundit and publisher William F. Buckley Jr., with whom Chambers struck up a lengthy and remarkable correspondence. Buckley's fortnightly *National Review*, established in 1955, has influenced generations of conservative intellectuals, activists, and pundits. In turn, the anticommunist, pro-freedom embers Chambers fanned in the late 1940s and early 1950s inspired a grass-roots movement in the Republican party to first nominate a conservative, anticommunist presidential candidate in 1964 (Barry Goldwater), and then to elect a conservative, anticommunist president in 1980 (Ronald Reagan), one who could quote passages from *Witness* by memory.

The battle lines drawn between the political Left and Right, as revealed in a substantial portion of this collection, should dumbfound no one. What *should* surprise those unschooled in American political alignments of the 1950s is the appearance of a third faction; namely, anticommunist liberals who found themselves uncomfortably caught in the middle of an ideological blood battle. These liberals typically conceded that Whittaker Chambers *was* right, but nonetheless found him an unsympathetic (and unsavory) character who must be kept at arm's length (for, among other reasons, because he was *of* the Right). One aspect of this position is best summarized by a former communist correspondent of Arthur Koestler's, who thought that "Whittaker Chambers is the real villain because he didn't keep his mouth shut about things past and done with." In the article reprinted here, commentator Elmer Davis reflected another component of this position when he wondered impatiently, "How long will these ex-Communists and ex-Sympathizers abuse the patience of the vast majority which had sense enough never to be Communists or sympathizers at all?"

The most thoughtful members of this category are Lionel and Diana Trilling, two of the country's most influential liberal intellectuals at mid-century. The Trillings realized that if it was believed that communists were dedicated to overthrowing the American democratic political system with a tyranny of the Left, then a liberalism that stood too close to communism was a liberalism in mortal danger. After all, as Terry Teachout has observed, Alger Hiss seemed the very personification of the fervent left-liberalism of the 1930s, and if he could be a Soviet agent, perhaps there really wasn't much difference between liberalism and communism after all (one recalls Eleanor Roosevelt's remark that she had always thought communists were simply "liberals in a hurry").

The Trillings therefore worried that the clear, but subtle, distinction between genuine liberalism and communism might be lost on the general populace. Hence, they counseled, although both liberalism and communism could be said to be on the left side of the American political spectrum, liberals could not afford to associate themselves with the communists. Leslie A. Fiedler also acknowledged the liberals' predicament: Either one must lump together as "Reds" everyone who is left-of-center, or one must refuse to recognize as a communist anyone who denies it. "The one kind of Communist likely to be missed by both approaches is the genteel Bolshevik who keeps his nose clean and never even reads the *New Republic*."

That left these anticommunist liberals in an awkward position: They absolutely abhorred the American Right, and what they saw as both its opportunistic embrace of anticommunism and its long-stand-

ing reactionary response to all liberal "good government" social policies and goals—the very policies and goals championed by Alger Hiss.
As Diana Trilling wrote, "It has always been true that politics makes
strange bedfellows, but never so horribly true as in these last decades
in which Communism has not only split the liberals among themselves, but also time and again thrown the anti-Communist liberal
into the same camp with forces he detests, or should detest, as much
as he detest Communists." They were agonized by the realization
that British leftist journalist Christopher Hitchens articulated many
years later, "If Hiss was wrong, then Nixon and McCarthy were right.
And that could not be." Thus, the challenge to the anticommunist
liberals was to balance (and advance) the seemingly contradictory view
that Hiss *and* Nixon *and* McCarthy were all wrong. For they knew in
their hearts that an Alger Hiss, stubbornly maintaining his innocence,
in the face of all logic and evidence, would irreversibly corrupt a fair
understanding of their liberal beliefs.

Thus, the Hiss-Chambers case played a major role in defining
the post–World War II political battle lines between the emerging
anticommunist conservative movement of the Right and the nascent
anti-anticommunist reactionaries of the Left (with beleaguered establishment liberals struggling in between for a middle ground). Its
revelations about communism's undemocratic intentions and desire
for global domination provided Republican Party candidates, office-
holders, and activists a key component of their political worldview for
nearly fifty years. In a sense, the Hiss-Chambers case was a mirror
held up to America's collective face. The ugly reflection—the picture
of Dorian Gray, if you will—that revealed in Alger Hiss an all-Ameri-
can boy, dedicated government servant, and communist spy caused
many to wince, others to hang their heads in shame, and some to
attack the man holding the mirror.

The scope of the literature on Hiss, Chambers, and their conflict
makes it impossible for this anthology to impart an exhaustive exami-

nation of all viewpoints. (See the bibliography for further investigation.) However, this compilation does provide a representative sampling of all three perspectives, presenting a balanced spectrum of opinion on the case and its significance to the continuing American political dialogue.

It may strike one as oddly ironic that the initial essay—Fiedler's, originally published in 1951—should begin, in a collection that spans fifty years of reflection and conjecture, with the remark, "It is time, many of us feel, to forget the whole business. . . . [T]he prison doors have closed [on Alger Hiss]; let us consider the question also closed." But then, this is a tale wrapped in irony of the strangest sort. "History is not so easily satisfied," Fiedler reminded his readers. "Like some monumental bore, it grabs us by the lapels, screaming into our faces the same story over and over again."

In his foreword to *Witness*, Chambers might well have been addressing succeeding generations, as well as his children, when he wrote sorrowfully: "As long as you live, the shadow of the Hiss Case will brush you." He was right, no matter which side of the great debate one champions.

Alexandria, Virginia
July 2002

Fu
8/30/13

WILFRED McCLAY

Introduction

FOR MANY READERS, particularly those under the age of twenty-five or so, an encounter with the contents of this book may feel rather like the discovery of a time capsule, filled with the brilliant fragments and curious remains of a singular world that has all but vanished. This will seem a surprising assertion to those who were mature and politically aware adults in the early years of the Cold War, when the Hiss-Chambers case was literally inescapable, and when every sentient person was expected to have an opinion about the furiously contested question of Alger Hiss's guilt or innocence. Yet the memory of those turbulent times has faded, and so too, perhaps, has the historical awareness and imagination of those who would preserve their memory. Those of us who make a living teaching American history to young people know all too well that it is becoming increasingly difficult to get them to grasp what the Cold War was even about—its high stakes, its issues, its hatreds and pathologies, its immense psychological intensity.

This is not an entirely unfortunate state of affairs. Indeed, it is probably one of the inevitable wages of victory. Once-fearsome dangers come to be retrospectively downsized, and even pitied, once they have been vanquished. And immunity from a certain kind of idealism can also provide immunity from a certain kind of corruption. But something is inevitably lost, too, as our sense of the Cold War fades into cliched obscurity. A sense of gratitude, for one thing, gratitude to those who struggled and prevailed. And, even more fundamentally, a sense of what the fighting was all about. For better or worse, today's young people, whose principal examples of ideological passion come from the hapless hippie retreads of the anti-globalization movement, or the murderous nihilism of Timothy McVeigh and al-Qaeda, cannot quite conceive of what might have motivated intelligent and highly educated Western men and women to embrace the Communist cause with a fervor that can only be called religious—or to resist it with a fervor of equivalent power. It all seems so bombastic, so terribly overwrought, overblown, and uncool, in the eyes of a generation accustomed to breathe a more relaxed moral atmosphere, a generation more comfortable (at least on its uneasy surface) with the self-defensive pose of irony and parody, rather than the more robust and dramatic impulse toward heroism and idealism. How can such a generation, a generation most decidedly *not* on trial, begin to comprehend what Chambers meant when he wrote that "life is pain," and "each of us hangs always upon the cross of himself"? What will keep them from saying of Chambers, as one of my students did, that "the dude needed to chill"?

This book cannot pretend be a remedy to that problem, but it can be a beginning. It doesn't propose to give a full account of the Cold War. But as a way of jumping in, and sampling the reactions of intellectuals to the Cold War in the writ-small form of their unfolding reactions to the Hiss-Chambers case, it succeeds admirably well. Those who take the plunge into these pages will find themselves pulled irresistibly into the whirl of a heated debate, or set of debates, that has coursed around and through the past half-century of American history. The ideological element in the struggle between the United States and the Soviet Union is here miniaturized and personalized in the improbable encounter of these two strange and enigmatic men, and in the endless debates that their encounter left in its wake. It was a case of genuine world-historical importance; but it also was an intensely personal psychological drama. As these essays show, the Hiss-Chambers case quickly became one of those iconic moments of symbolic politics, like Jackson's Bank War or Bryan's "free silver" campaign or the Sacco-Vanzetti case, that endure and come to define the landscape of American history—events which may or may not be important in their own right, but which are chiefly significant for the way they reveal and embody the grand social forces and larger meanings that stand behind them, straining for expression. As such, the conflict between Hiss and Chambers was not merely a cynosure of history, as the self-dramatizing Chambers was so eager to portray it. It also was a puzzle, even to the convinced. It posed a near-endless set of riddles, whose precise answers remain to this day a subject of endless dispute.

Therefore it was not a coincidence, one might say, that the case has proved the source of some extraordinarily inspired and stimulating prose. How could it not be? Psychological complexities (and historical cynosures) draw talented writers the way mountains draw climbers. Chief of those prose works is Chambers's own masterpiece *Witness*, which even Arthur M. Schlesinger, Jr., who differed from Chambers in so many ways, rightly credited as one of the greatest of American autobiographies. No one has done a better job of conveying the psychological and moral appeal of Communism, and the metaphysical stakes involved in accepting or rejecting it. *Witness* forms the object, direct or indirect, of a great many of the essays reprinted herein. Those who have not read it before, or have not reread it for many decades, will feel compelled to do so, and make up their minds for themselves what manner of man Chambers was, and how prophetic his vision may have proved to be.

Even so, in many respects these essays give one a more adequate historical introduction to the era, and provide a valuable framework for thinking about Chambers's book. For one thing, they give one a better sense of the extent of the "uproar" (Hilton Kramer's word) that the publication of *Witness* caused, and the diversity of reactions it produced, then and now. One runs the whole gamut here, from the dismissive personal assault of Kingsley Martin to the stiffly reserved "yes, but" of Diana Trilling to the tender recollections of William F. Buckley, Jr. These essays offer a kaleidoscopic overview of the historical situation, fragments of a large and complex story that one has to piece together for oneself, like the perspectives of a hundred partial witnesses, in order to gain some independent sense of the truth of the matter.

More importantly, readers of these essays will find themselves tantalized by the case's unresolved mysteries, which run through these pages like haunting Wagnerian leitmotifs. Even those who are firmly convinced, as the overwhelming body of evidence by now clearly indicates they ought to be, of Alger Hiss's guilt, will find themselves bothered by certain enduring questions. At their core, nearly all of these questions involve mysteries of the human psyche, mysteries that revolve around the interplay between loyalty and truth-telling.

To be sure, there are elements in the drama that, though they struck many contemporary observers forcibly, seem far less significant now. For example, there is the vivid class contrast between the protagonists—the handsome, elegant, and impeccably pedigreed Hiss against the disheveled and unprepossessing Chambers, with his ever-remarked-upon bad teeth. Chambers himself commented on the bad casting choices that history seemed to have made in this case. But the casting seems less suspect today, when the term "the best and the brightest" can hardly be uttered without overtones of sarcasm, and when the role of accredited elites in American life seems more morally problematic than ever.

But the psychological mysteries are, if anything, more unfathomable to our confessional age. Chief among these is the matter of Alger Hiss's demeanor, an issue that comes up again and again in these pages. How is one to account for his equipoise and his silence, by which is meant his dogged refusal to confess, or provide even so much as a scintilla of corroboration for the charges against him? Was outward serenity a sign of his innocence, that he seemed so unruffled, so completely remorseless and unbowed, because his conscience was so completely clear? Or was it paradoxically a sign of his guilt, that he never behaved as one would expect a man who had been so comprehensively wronged—that he was in fact secretly satisfied with what he had done, that he had been loyal to the only "truth" that matters, and that his martyrdom only added to his sense of smug moral superiority? Neither explanation, if truth be told, seems entirely satisfactory.

How, too, to account for the passionate and enduring loyalty shown to Hiss by his followers? Of especially perplexing interest is what Leslie Fiedler calls "the half-deliberate blindness of so many decent people." (21) The problem invites—indeed insists upon—a psychological explanation. Was there simply too much at stake—politically, intellectually, emotionally—for Hiss's guilt to be an admissible thought? Was there, as Sidney Hook claimed, "no arguing with symbolic allegiances"? Was it so important to defeat the Right that it could not be allowed a victory, even when the Left was clearly at fault? Was the disagreeable shiftiness of Chambers, and the seeming venality of Hiss's other foes (such as Richard Nixon) to be taken to be sufficient evidence of Hiss's righteousness? Were Hiss's alleged crimes to be understood as acts that, to a committed person of the left, were comparatively trivial, particularly compared to the patent monstrousness of the right-wing foe? Was it the case, then, that it didn't really matter whether or not he was a spy—just as it didn't really matter whether or not Bill Clinton had sex with an intern, and if asked about it, he was entitled to lie? Or is it possible that they were, and are, honestly and rationally convinced of Hiss's innocence, partly swayed by Hiss's unflappable demeanor? No one explanation seems to dispel the mystery. As was demonstrated by the O.J. Simpson case—another of the American "dervish trials" that Rebecca West so aptly describes herein—there will always be a constituency of those convinced by a man who stubbornly refuses to admit his guilt, particularly if there is a "symbolic allegiance" that can be played upon.

Some of the essays have worn the passage of time better than others. Leslie Fiedler's "Hiss, Chambers, and the Age of Innocence" is as fresh as if it were written yesterday, and it reminds us of what a powerful and imaginative literary and cultural critic he could be. The same can be said of the nearly forgotten Granville Hicks, whose generous examination of *Witness* is full of sympathetic insight, and much superior to the formulaic put-down of Irving Howe. Yet both Hicks and Howe, and nearly all the critics herein, seem to agree in one respect: that Chambers's book, even if it is to be accounted a magnificent achievement, goes too far in asserting that the Cold War was ultimately a theological struggle, against those who have perfected "the vision of man without God," and who see "man's mind displacing God as the creative intelligence of the world." Even Hicks, who openly admired Chambers, even considered him a "great man," nevertheless felt it necessary to say emphatically that "I reject Whittaker Chambers's conclusions," so far as the ultimate meaning of the Communist experiment was concerned.

Were they right to do so? Until recently, it might have seemed that they were. Yet, as Hilton Kramer's superb concluding essay hints, the cultural upheaval of the Sixties reintroduced the problem of faith in a form that the liberal mind found much harder to answer. And the same question, of the primacy of man or God, now poses itself to us in an entirely new form, with the advent of biotechnologies that, literally, place in human hands the power to make over the human condition.

Suddenly Chambers's rhetoric does not seem so extreme. When he spoke of "the vision of man's liberated mind, by the sole force of its rational intelligence, redirecting man's destiny and reorganizing man's life and the world," (59) he was speaking specifically of Communism. But he was also, perhaps without having known or intended it, addressing himself to something like the very prospect we now face, not because of some foreign threat, but because of the flourishing of certain aspects of our own victorious civilization. Even if he did not know specifically what was to come, he clearly understood that Communism was not something alien to the history of the modern West, but represented the purest and most logically consistent expression, in political and economic terms, of one of the most powerful and distinctive strains in that Western history. Communism was, he argued, merely "the next logical step which three hundred years of rationalism hesitated to take, and said what millions of modern minds think, but do not care or dare to say: If man's mind is the decisive force in the world, what need is there for God? Henceforth man's mind is man's fate."

Such a statement may well have seemed overdrawn a half-century ago. We will see if it seems less so in the half-century to come.

1

L E S L I E   A .   F I E D L E R

Hiss, Chambers, and the Age of Innocence

C O M M E N T A R Y ,   A U G U S T   1 9 5 1

You will either aid in moulding history, or history will mould you, and in the case of the latter, you can rest assured that you will be indescribably crushed and maimed in the process. . . . History is not a blind goddess, and does not pardon the blindness of others.

— Whittaker Chambers in 1931

ALGER HISS IS IN JAIL. The last legal judgments have been passed. The decision of the courts stands: guilty as charged— guilty in fact of treason, though technically accused only of perjury. It is time, many of us feel, to forget the whole business: the prison doors have closed; let us consider the question also closed. But history is not so easily satisfied. Like some monumental bore, it grabs us by the lapels, keeps screaming into our faces the same story over and over again. The case of Judith Coplon, the case of William Remington, the case of Julius and Ethel Rosenberg,* the inevitable case of tomorrow's

---

* *All were convicted of either espionage or perjury about espionage for the Soviet Union.*

Mr. X—the names change but the meanings are the same, and we protest that we have long since got the point. But have we? Of what was Alger Hiss guilty anyhow?

The statute of limitations protected Hiss against the charge of having passed secret material from State Department files to his accuser Whittaker Chambers, of having placed in the hands of agents of the Soviet Union documents which, whatever their intrinsic value, enabled our present enemies to break some of our most important codes. The transaction had taken place in 1936 and 1937—a war away, in years we ourselves find it difficult to remember, in years some of us don't want to remember. It is a painful thing to be asked to live again through events ten years gone, to admit one's identity with the person who bore one's name in a by now incredible past. It is hardest of all to confess that one is responsible for the acts of that past, especially when such acts are now placed in a new and unforeseen context that changes their meaning entirely. "Not guilty!" one wants to cry, "that is not what I meant at all!"

And yet the qualifying act of moral adulthood is precisely this admission of responsibility for the past and its consequences, however undesired or unforeseen. Such a recognition Hiss was called upon to make. Had he been willing to say, "Yes, I did these things—things it is now possible to call 'treason'—not for money or prestige, but out of a higher allegiance than patriotism—"; had he only confessed in the name of any of the loftier platitudes for which men are prepared publicly to admit the breaking of lesser laws, he need not even have gone to prison. Why did he lie?

* * *

Had Hiss told the truth, the whole meaning of the case might have been different, might have attained that dignity for which Alistair Cooke[1] looks through its dossiers in vain. The defenders of Hiss, and of the generation they take him to represent, would have been delivered from the intolerable plight that prompted them, during the trials, to declare at one and the same time that (a) Hiss was innocent of the charges, the victim of a malevolent psychopath and (b) even if he was technically guilty, he had the moral right, in those years of betrayal leading to Munich, to give his primary loyalty to the Soviet Union. Why did he lie, and lying, lose the whole point of the case in a maze of irrelevant data: the signature on the transfer of ownership of a car, the date a typewriter was repaired . . . ?

The lie, it is necessary to see, was no mere accident, but was of the essence of the case, a clue to the deepest significance of what was done and to the moral atmosphere that made the deed possible. We can see Hiss's lie now in a larger context, beside William Remington's even more vain denials of Elizabeth Bentley's charges, and the fantastic affirmations of innocence by Julius and Ethel Rosenberg. These were not, after all, common criminals, who plead innocent mechanically on the advice of counsel; these were believers in a new society, for whose sake they had already endangered their closest friends and endangered the security of their country. In the past (and even yet in the present—the Puerto Rican nationalists, for instance)* such political idealists welcomed their trials as forums, opportunities to declare to the world the high principles behind their actions, the loyalty to the march of history and the eventual triumph of socialism that had brought them to the bar. They might have been, in some eyes at least, spectacular martyrs; they chose to behave instead, before the eyes of all, like blustering petty thieves.

Not that the avowals of innocence, especially in the case of Hiss,

---

* *Two Puerto Rican nationalists, Oscar Collazo and Griselio Torresola, attempted to assassinate President Truman on November 1, 1950. They thought the assassination would advance the cause of Puerto Rican independence.*

were not affecting. Despite the absurdity of his maunderings about "forgery by typewriter," there was something moving—for a generation brought up on stories of Dreyfus and Tom Mooney, and growing to social awareness through the Sacco-Vanzetti trial and the campaigns to free the Scottsboro boys—in Hiss's final courtroom pose as The Victim. Even now, it is hard to realize how little claim he had to the title. For here was no confessed revolutionary, marked by his avowed principles, his foreign accent, his skin color, as fair game for the frame-up; here was a supereminently respectable civil servant from the better schools, accused by the obvious outsider, the self-declared rebel and renegade, Whittaker Chambers. Hiss seemed to desire both the pathos of the persecuted and the aura of unblemished respectability. His is, as we shall see, the Popular Front mind at bay, incapable of honesty even when there is no hope in anything else.

. . .

After the hung jury, the second trial, the reams of evidence that frittered away the drama in boredom, one thing is perfectly clear. Twenty of twenty-four jurors, presumably twenty of twenty-four of us, believed that Alger Hiss was guilty of the perjury with which he was charged, of the treason with which he could not be charged.

For many, that verdict may be sufficient; for some, it is not enough. These cannot help feeling that the total issue of the guilt or innocence of Alger Hiss remains still to be solved. The verdict of the courts applies only to the "facts" as defined by precedent and law, a few fragments torn from their rich human contexts and presented to a group of men deliberately chosen for their relative ignorance of those contexts, and for the likelihood of their not being sympathetically involved with the passions and motives which underlay them.

Is there any sense in which Hiss is *symbolically* innocent—in which he may, indeed, have made the mistake of having passed certain papers via Chambers to the Russian agent, Colonel Bykov, but out of such naive devotion to the Good that it is a travesty of justice to find him on merely technical grounds "guilty"? It sometimes seems possible that when a Remington or a Rosenberg or a Hiss speaks publicly of his "innocence," he is merely using a convenient shorthand for an account of motives and actions too complex to set before an ordinary juryman without completely re-educating him. One of the distinctive features of the recent series of "spy" trials has been that the accused and the chief accusers have been intellectuals, whereas the jury, the lawyers on both sides, even the judges, were not. And since in this country the intellectuals have been notoriously set apart from the general public, living, especially since the Russian Revolution, by different values and speaking a different language, communication is difficult. How can people who do not read the same books, and whose only relationship is one of distrust, arrive at a common definition of innocence and guilt?

One might argue on these grounds that what a jury could have meant by voting "guilty" is ridiculously far from the truth; that Hiss is not what the average mind, brought up on E. Phillips Oppenheim and pulp fiction, means by a "traitor"; that he can surely feel himself neither venal nor skulking, for he has always been faithful in intent to his true fatherland, Humanity; that if in fact he has ended up by helping the interests of just another imperialist power, the Soviet Union, it is not his crime but that of the Soviet Union, which he took in good faith to be the deputy of mankind's best interests.

This was Henry Julian Wadleigh's defense: a minor source of information for Chambers in the pre-war years, and a witness at the Hiss trials, he attempted to declare his innocence and guilt at the same time. With no sign of contrition, he admitted passing secret documents to Chambers but insisted that his course had been justified in history; it had not even struck him, he explained condescend-

· 5 ·

ingly, as a matter of conscience—though merely joining the Communist party had, and he had finally *not* signed up.

The comic aspects of Wadleigh strike one first—the cartoonist's pink-tea radical, with his thick glasses, disordered hair, and acquired Oxford accent. The articles which he wrote for the New York *Post* are classics of unconscious humor, monuments to smugness and self-pity, and trailers for the novel which (of course!) he was busy writing about his Experience. When Hiss's lawyers found they could not pin on Wadleigh the stealing of the papers Chambers had disconcertingly produced, they were content to make him the butt of their jokes. At several points during his questioning, the judge had to cover his mouth with his hand to preserve the dignity of the court. Wadleigh is the comic version of Alger Hiss.

The clowning of Wadleigh reveals what is not so easily read in Hiss: a moral obtuseness which underlies the whole case. Mr. Cooke tries to make of Wadleigh his tragic figure, but the true protagonist of tragedy suffers and learns. Wadleigh has learned nothing. He cannot conceive of having done anything *really* wrong. He finds in his own earlier activities only a certain excessive zeal, overbalanced by good will, and all excused by—Munich. Was he not a better man for having tried to counter, however ineptly, the shameful appeasement of Hitler? That the irony of events had made him, just insofar as he was more idealistic and committed, more helplessly the tool of evil, he cannot conceive. In the end, his "confession" is almost as crass a lie as the denial of Hiss—a disguise for self-congratulation, a device for clinging to the dream of innocence. He cannot, even in the dock, believe that a man of liberal persuasion is capable of wrong.

It was this belief that was the implicit dogma of American liberalism during the past decades, piling up a terrible burden of self-righteousness and self-deceit to be paid for on the day when it would become impossible any longer to believe that the man of good will is identical with the righteous man, and that the liberal is, *per se*, the hero. That day came at different times to different people: for some it was the Moscow Trials, for others the Soviet-Nazi pact, and for a good many—including a large number who had, during the war, regained lost illusions—it came on August 17, 1948 when Hiss and Chambers were brought face to face before the House Committee on Un-American Activities.

· · ·

The facts were clear from the moment of confrontation, but for many the facts did not matter. Chambers stated flatly that Hiss had been a Communist, his associate in the "underground"; Hiss as flatly denied it. Simply to ask *cui bono* would have been enough: which one of the men stood to gain by lying? But somehow such a common sense approach seemed excluded. The most fantastic psychological explanations were dredged up. One heard via the intellectual underground the unlikeliest, proto-Dostoevskian stories to suggest reasons for Chambers' self-vilifying testimony. *Psychopathia Sexualis* was hauled out, and Freud quoted glibly by the same skeptics who had laughed at the psychologizing explanations of the Moscow Trials.

But there remained still the detailed circumstantiality of Chambers' memories, the documents stolen from the office in which Hiss had worked, the microfilms taken from the dusty dumbwaiter in Brooklyn and hidden in the famous pumpkin on Chambers' Maryland farm. For all the theatrical instincts of Chambers, who seemed to possess a flair for adding one artistic touch too many to any situation, out of God knows what compulsion, the documents were there—the undeniable goods.

An unbiased look at the proceedings of the House Committee reveals that from the start Hiss quite apparently lied, or more precisely, half lied and equivocated with the canniness of the trained lawyer. During the trials his version of the events was delivered with great aplomb, but before the Committee one can see him uncertainly feeling his way into the situation, cautiously finding out at each point how much he will have to admit to escape entrapment.

At first, he said simply that to the best of his knowledge (the qualifying phrase hardly seemed significant, a lawyer's habit) he had never met the man Chambers who had named him as one of a Washington cell of infiltrators. There was no mention of espionage, it must be remembered, until Hiss had forced Chambers' hand. Then, advised perhaps of the convincing nature of Chambers' testimony, he began slowly to shift ground, first, however, taking the initiative and charging with increasing surliness that the Committee had been leaking back to Chambers everything he said. At this point the Committee, which had handled him until then with more than normal sympathy, began to press him hard. He could not say for sure, Hiss now testified, but he thought that certainly he had known no one who called himself "Chambers," or anyone who looked very like the photographs he had been shown. They were, however, not very good pictures, so he could not be positive. Indeed, the face on the photograph before him might be that of the chairman of the Committee. It was his last joke.

Finally, he admitted that he had, after all, known the man in question, under a name he had written down on a pad in front of him. It was "George Crosley" (Chambers was later to say that, although he had used many names, he was quite sure he had never used that one), a dead-beat writer whom he had known casually, and with whom he had occasionally talked over possible story material, though he had really found the man despicable. As a matter of fact, he had even once, for certain obscure reasons, let the dead-beat move into his apartment for a couple of days, or was it weeks; and when Crosley had welshed on the rent, Hiss, for reasons even more obscure, had given him a car—just a little old car, it must be understood, with a "sassy" rumble seat, though one, Hiss admitted, to which he had been sentimentally attached. It is a fantastic story, enough to send anyone less well placed to jail without any ado. Later, there was to be a good deal of trouble over the dates of this strange transaction—and records were to turn up proving that the car had never been presented to Crosley-Chambers at all, but apparently to the Communist party!

. . .

All the while this amazing farrago was being served up by Hiss, Chambers was patiently building up the story of their actual relationship, born in intrigue and common devotion to an ideal, and destined to end in bitterness and mutual accusation. They had been comrades and close friends, Chambers said, he and the promising young lawyer whom he was still able to describe as "of a great gentleness and sweetness of character." At first, their dealings were concerned only with dues and reports, but they had quickly grown closer together, in the sort of relationship hard to parallel outside the party, the two of them utterly dependent on each other's loyalty, and both betting their self-esteem on the truth of the Marxist-Leninist dream.

They are men who could never have met outside the Communist movement, and even as Communists they were utterly different: Chambers the romantic recruit of the 20's, hating a world that had rebuffed him at every encounter, and choosing the movement as an alternative to suicide; Hiss, universally respected, and by nature an opportunist, but with a streak of social conscience (personified in his earnest wife, who could not even let a casual visitor call the day "fine" without reminding her of the plight of the sharecroppers), choosing the party to protect himself from a merely selfish kind of success. Different as they were, Chambers had found Hiss a "real Bolshevik," perhaps sensing in him a kind of hardness to which he himself could only aspire, and had defended him against the sneers of their Russian boss, Bykov, who always referred to Hiss condescendingly as "our dear lawyer."

The quality of the feeling that must have existed between the two men is revealed by Chambers' last-minute attempt to draw Hiss with him out of the party, after he himself had become convinced that the Soviet Union was serving not justice but her own selfish national interests. Feeling that he might well be killed by party agents after his desertion (such political murders have occurred even in America), Chambers, nevertheless, risked exposing himself by a final visit to Hiss's home. But Hiss had stood firm, scarcely listening to the arguments of Chambers, though he had finally wept a little (the scene stays in the imagination, the completely unexpected, uncharacteristic tears), and had given to Chambers a trivial Christmas present for his daughter—"a little rolling pin."

Perhaps, even before the break, Hiss was already tired of Chambers as a person, a little ashamed of his admiration for the shabby writer who wrote nothing, and who had a tendency to remake his experience as he told about it, retouching and bringing up the highlights here and there. Mrs. Hiss had distrusted him from the first, finding him, with a strange inconsistency for a genteel internationalist, "too foreign." They had pretended, finally, Alger and "Crosley," that "Crosley" was a Russian which made him all right, of course; and Chambers had played up to it with all his love of subterfuge.

. . .

Whatever the status of their personal relations, when Chambers had come to Hiss with his talk about the Moscow Trials and the betrayal of the revolution, Hiss already could not afford to listen to him. He had by then too much to lose; for, without ceasing to be a Bolshevik, he had become a "success," a respectable citizen. To acknowledge that Russia

could be fundamentally wrong would have changed the whole meaning of his own life, turned what had perhaps seemed to him his most
unselfish and devoted acts, the stealing of State Department documents, into shameful crimes—into "treason"! Only the conviction that
there was no final contradiction between his activities, public and
private, could have made Hiss's life tolerable. He must have felt that
what he had done as a New Deal lawyer, helping to expose the
"munitions makers" in the Nye Committee, or working for the AAA
in the Department of Agriculture, did not contradict what he tried to
do as a member of a left-wing faction in the State Department, urging
certain attitudes toward Chiang Kai-shek; and that what he had sought
in both these capacities was merely completed by his "secret" work as
a purveyor of information to warn the Soviet Union—his Soviet Union,
mankind's Soviet Union—of the forces that worked for and against her
in the inner world of diplomacy.

He was not a "traitor"! What the Un-American Activities Committee could not understand, what the two juries were certainly not
able to comprehend, is that to Hiss, his service to the party and the
Soviet Union is an expression of "loyalty," not "treason." Before con-
senting to marry him, Remington's former wife had made him sol-
emnly pledge "not to succeed"; to so many of the generation of
Remington and Hiss, the bourgeois success of the American Dream
was the final treachery, and each step forward in their personal careers
had to be justified in terms of opportunities provided for infiltration.
Hiss offered his "espionage" as an earnest to the inner few whose opinion mattered to him (in those days chiefly Chambers, and always
himself) that he had not "sold out" to the bourgeois world in which
he was making a splendid career.

No wonder Hiss was inaccessible to Chambers' arguments against
the party! No wonder he seemed scarcely willing to admit his existence, refusing him his very name! It was as if Hiss had wanted to
shrug off his accuser, not like a real being in the outside world but like

a nightmare. Indeed, the persistent voice of the man he had once admired must have seemed to him to possess the quality of a nightmare, speaking in its characteristic half-whisper the doubts, thrust down in himself, that could destroy his self-esteem.

And so Hiss had spoken out over the condemning voice, protesting his innocence with a vigor that contrasted oddly with Chambers' quiet tone. All the accounts speak of the voice of the accuser as one that, symbolically enough, could scarcely be heard. There is, even in the printed testimony, a sense of a counter-desire not to be heard along with the resolve to speak out. Far from seeming the vindictive persecutor of some accounts, Chambers strikes us as oddly reluctant, willing for a long time to risk perjury rather than reveal the full guilt of his former comrade. What Chambers really seems to be after is a confession of the truth from Hiss; he does not feel he can hide forever what Hiss had done, but he would prefer him to speak out himself.

Hiss, on the other hand, baits Chambers furiously, daring him to become the complete "rat," as if knowing Chambers will suffer in speaking out, as if wanting to shame and punish him. He seems to have felt sure that Chambers could not really harm him. A man does not unflaggingly succeed from high school days to early middle age without losing something of humility, and forgetting that a single failure of the most superb luck is enough for destruction. When the end comes, when the threat of a suit for defamation against Chambers leads to the disclosure of the damning papers, to the trials of Hiss for perjury, and to the final conviction, one has the sense that both of the men are surprised.

. . .

Some of the commentators on the case have spoken of the anti-Red "hysteria" that prevailed at the time of the case, as if in such an atmosphere the cards were hopelessly stacked against Alger Hiss. But precisely the opposite is the case. He is just the type that does not normally get caught in the indiscriminate "witch hunt," which tends to pick out those who look like "witches," the visible outsiders. A woman like Assistant Secretary of Defense Anna M. Rosenberg, for instance, foreign-born and a Jew, is much more likely to be haled up without any evidence against her, while a man like Hiss can slip past the ordinary Congressman, to whom Red really means loud-mouth or foreigner or Jew (Rankin, who was on the Committee that examined Hiss, apparently spent his spare time thumbing through *Who's Who in American Jewry*, and turned all his fire on—Chambers!).

The Committee did not want to believe Chambers. They were convinced by his, and his wife's, astonishingly specific memories: though some members of the Committee had been eager to "get the goods" on the New Deal, to catch out the State Department at last, they had apparently found it difficult to put much faith in Chambers. It was impossible to like him, as one instinctively liked Hiss for the boyish charm we think of as peculiarly American. Chambers seems to have worn his prepossessing air (he is the sort of person of whom one believes immediately quite unfounded stories of insanity and depravity) deliberately, as if he had acquired in his revolutionary days the habit of rebuffing all admiration based on anything but his role in the party.

Every word he spoke declared him an ex-traitor, a present turncoat and squealer, and Hiss, sensing his inestimable advantage in a society whose values are largely set in boyhood when snitching is the ultimate sin, had traded on his role as the honest man confronted by the "rat." Really, Hiss kept insisting, they'd have to call the Harvard Club, say he'd be a few minutes late to dinner—after taking care of this unpleasantness. For a while it came off quite unsuccessfully, coming from one who visibly belonged, whose clothes beautifully fitted, whose manners were adequate to all occasions.

We learned later, of course, how much the genteel aspect of Hiss was itself a mask, imposed on a background of disorder and uncertainty not unlike Chambers': the suicide of his father and sister, the undefined psychological difficulties of his stepson, into whose allowance from his actual father, we remember, the Hisses sometimes dipped for contributions to the party. It was as if Alger Hiss had dedicated himself to fulfilling, along with his dream of a New Humanity, the other dream his father had passed on to him with his first name— from rags to riches. How strangely the Marxist ideal and the dream of Horatio Alger blended into the motives of his treason. . . .

· · ·

Any good bourgeois bristles when confronted with Whittaker Chambers. His years as an editor on *Time* (he is "brilliant," of course, but the adjective is itself ambivalent), his present role as a small farmer cannot conceal his real identity as the outsider: the "butterball who could not even learn to play marbles," the writer of poetry for little magazines, the obnoxious young radical expelled from college, the uncomfortable spirit that either blasphemes or is too religious for respectability. At one point, Chambers is asked by a Committee member how he spent his time during a week-long period when he had borrowed Hiss's apartment; and when he says, "reading..." one feels the troubled silence. How could someone read so long? It is the suspicious vagary of the kind of man who once believed in Stalin and now believes in the Devil.

After his years in the "underground," he still seems ill at ease in our daylight world; and beneath the guise of the magazine executive, assumed only, we remember, to establish an "identity" for himself as a protection against being murdered by the GPU, the old Chambers persists. Everyone who had known him in his revolutionary days— except Hiss, of course—had no difficulty in recognizing Chambers at the time of the trial.

The jowls and the new teeth do not fundamentally change the face we can still see on the inside back cover of the Communist literary magazine, the *New Masses*, for July 1931. After twenty years, the young Chambers looks up at us still with the sullen certainty of one who has discovered in the revolution an answer to the insecurity and doubt which had brought his brother to suicide, him to months of despair and near paralysis. In the movement he had found a way out of immobility, a way to join with the other insulted and injured of the earth to change the world which excluded them. To appear in the *New Masses* in those days was not merely to be a writer, but to subscribe to a new myth of the writer, summed up in the blurb under the photograph: "Youth as a periodically vagrant laborer in Deep South, Plains, Northwest. Brief Columbia College experience ending with atheist publication. . . . Joined revolutionary movement 1925. . . ."

Hiss, who really knew Chambers, of course, better than anyone else except Chambers' wife, put his finger on the sources of the myth when he told the Committee that Chambers thought of himself as a kind of Jim Tully or Jack London. To understand Chambers, one must understand the concept of the literary bum as hero that came out of Tully and London, a special Marxist class-angling of the old bohemian ideal. Chambers' once living in the same quarters as an old whore, and his stealing of library books of which Hiss's lawyers and psychiatrists were to make so much during the trials, his name-changing and wandering, were all standard procedure for the rebel-intellectual in those days.

. . .

The life style he adopted was perfected in the Communist "Third Period," in the years before 1935, and it is the Third Period we must first of all understand. The term is Lenin's, invented to describe that last stage of imperialism, the age of cataclysmic wars and revolutions, but it comes also to describe the way of life of those who believed themselves the sole carriers of the future in those final days. To the young comrades in their blue work shirts or flat-heeled shoes, there was no need to come to terms with the dying bourgeois world; Marx had told them that the point was to change it. They lived in a fine apocalyptic fury, issuing leaflets to ROTC units in Midwestern agricultural colleges, urging the "peasants and soldiers" to turn their guns the other way; they cried for an autonomous Negro republic to be carved out of the Deep South; and in the few cities where they had sufficient numbers, they were forever rushing "into the streets" to shout their resolve to "Defend the Soviet Union" against their own bourgeoisie in case of war. The only reality in their paranoid world was the Workers' Farmerland, still encircled and unrecognized by our own government. Here is a typical passage from an editorial that appeared in the *New Masses* in 1931, and which may actually have been written by Chambers:

> It is only a question of time until all the imperialist powers mobilize their manpower and hurl its bleeding masses in a rain of steel across the frontiers, to destroy the first Socialist Republic. In this situation what are the intellectuals to do? . . . They realize, however imperfectly, that the Union of Soviet Socialist Republics represents the advance guard, the hope of human progress and civilization. . . . And they desire, the most advanced of them, to employ their minds as weapons in the fight to save the Soviet Union from its reactionary enemies.

Reread in the pages of the old magazine, in the heavy black format that seems to shriek at us across the years, and surrounded by the pen and ink drawings with their incredibly depraved bosses and their unbelievably noble workers, the banal paragraph seems merely unconscionably funny, like a bad silent film. But when we remember the universal loss of faith in those years of mass unemployment and seemingly endless depression, we can appreciate the attractiveness of the Marxist answer, guaranteed by the miraculous existence of the

Soviet Union, the last best hope of human culture. We sense, too, the appeal of violence in a world of words—an instant of bloodshed and the whole golden future unfolds!

No Third Perioder could have become, like a later type of Communist, really a "traitor" as distinguished from a mere "spy." How could they betray a world they publicly disavowed? Romantic and ridiculous, they were still revolutionaries, their allegiance single and unconcealed. When such Communists went underground they hid, but they never pretended to be good bourgeois. When the call came in 1932 from Max Bedacht, asking Chambers to disappear as the individual he had been in order to take on "special" work, Chambers seems to have welcomed the chance. He had already sacrificed his will to party discipline, his fate to history. He had little more to offer up beyond his name and the small fame that had become attached to it in the movement: the praise he had received in the Russian press for his stories of Communist life, the popularity of the play *Can You Hear Their Voices?*, based on one of his works, already presented at Vassar and about to be produced in Russia.

Something in his temperament seems to have greeted the prospect of self-immolation; even before he entered what the Communists mean by the "underground," he had been, in the Dostoevskian sense, an underground man, his own enemy. It had apparently pleased him to take the final step, to become one whose death it would be forbidden to notice. What did Mundt* or Rankin or Nixon know of Dosteovsky, or those twenty-four jurors of the kind of alienated life that conditioned Chambers? What trick of history brought them and him into the same room, pushed them toward an uneasy alliance?

Karl E. Mundt was a Republican member of HUAC from South Dakota and an outspoken critic of the New Deal. He later became a U.S. senator. Rankin, a former Ku Klux Klan member, was a powerful Democratic member of HUAC from Mississippi.

It was Hiss—the embodiment of the subsequent Popular Front era, as Chambers was the embodiment of the Third Period—who provided the common link: Hiss who had as desperately to look respectable as Chambers had not to. The New Deal had moved American politics left, and had opened the doors of the trade unions and the Washington bureaus to the university intelligentsia at the very moment when that intelligentsia had been penetrated by the Communists, and Communism had undergone two decisive changes: first, the national Communist parties had lost all initiative and internal democracy, coming under the absolute control of the Russian bureaucracy; and second, world Stalinism had adopted the Popular Front line of collaboration with the bourgeoisie.

No longer was the ideal Bolshevik the open rebel, the poet-bum chanting songs of protest, but the principled government worker with the pressed suit and the clean-cut look. It was the day of "fronts" and "mass organizations," of infiltrating and "capturing" and "boring from within." As the headlines in the *Daily Worker* declared peace-with-capitalism, a new kind of underground Communist moved into Washington, unnoticed among the purer, pragmatic New Dealers.

Hiss is the prototype of the new-model Bolshevik (Lee Pressman and Henry Collins and John Abt, Noel Field and George Silverman were others) who was the more valuable as he seemed less radical. Far from being urged to sell the party press, he was even discouraged from reading it. These new secret workers had never been open members of the party; they did not merely hide, but pretended to be what they were not. For the first time, a corps of Communists existed for whom "treason," in the sense of real deceit, was possible. These were not revolutionaries but Machiavellians, men with a double allegiance, making the best of two worlds and often, like Hiss, profiting immensely within the society they worked so hard to destroy.

Doubtless some of these new Bolsheviks were able to deceive themselves into believing that there was no actual contradiction between their real allegiance and their pretended one. What helped the self-deception was the rise of Nazi Germany as the chief threat on the world scene, and the changing role of the Soviet Union in international affairs. The blanket phrase "anti-fascism" covered over conflicts as deep as life itself. On the one hand, the New Deal had finally recognized the new Russian regime; and on the other hand, Communist Russia had joined the fellowship of nations. In the League of Nations (which Lenin had long before called "a den of thieves"), Litvinov was calling for the unity of the anti-fascist world. The watchword was no longer "Defend the Soviet Union!" but "Establish Collective Security!" The Communists insisted that the interests of Russia and the United States were forever identical, and the majority of liberals collaborated in the hoax—which was to crash with the signing of the Nazi-Soviet pact, be ridiculously revived during the war when we were "allies," and collapse once more at the foot of the Iron Curtain. Here are the words of Earl Browder, written in the first blush of the Popular Front honeymoon:

> In this world movement, there stand out before the peace-loving peoples of the world two centers of resistance to the fascist flood, two points from which leadership and inspiration can be given to the majority of mankind struggling for democracy and peace, two rallying grounds for the hard-pressed forces of progress and culture—the Soviet Union and the United States. . . . The Soviet Union and the United States have common problems, common interests and common enemies. That is a central fact in the new world situation.

The platitudes, read in their context of rallies-for-Spain sponsored by the "big names" from Hollywood and Broadway, seem only a little less old-fashioned and absurd than those of 1931, but we must read them with attention, remembering that they made treason easy. The bureaucrat, busy making himself a niche in the government service while transmitting secret material to the Russians, didn't even have to pose to himself a moral "either-or"; in both his roles, he could consider himself serving what Browder liked to call "the spirit of Jefferson, Jackson and Lincoln."

. . .

Before the Popular Front Communist the ordinary Congressman is helpless, unless there is a "renegade" willing to make revelations. The average legislator pursues ordinarily one of two policies in regard to Communists, springing from his profound inability or unwillingness to tell a Stalinist from a liberal. Either he lumps together as "Reds" everybody left-of-center (and even an occasional right-winger by mistake), or he refuses to recognize as a Communist anyone who denies it. The one kind of Communist likely to be missed by both approaches is the genteel Bolshevik who keeps his nose clean and never even reads the *New Republic*.

That is why the Committee was at first so completely buffaloed by Hiss. When he thundered righteously, "I am sorry but I cannot but feel to such an extent that it is difficult for me to control myself that you can sit there, Mr. Hébert, and say to me casually that you have heard that man [Chambers] and you have heard me, and that you just have no basis for judging which one is telling the truth," Hébert could only stutter lamely about the degrading necessity of using low "stool pigeons" like Chambers and Miss Bentley.

It is easy enough to understand the shouts of "red herring!" raised in the earlier days of the case by certain old-line Democrats led by President Truman. They did not dissent on principle, but merely on party lines. If a venture sparked by Republicans is admitted to have succeeded, the Democrats stand to lose votes; and one denies anything that might lose votes. But the real liberals, in and out of the Democratic party, from whose ranks most of the actual believers in the innocence of Hiss are drawn, are a different mater. They had not even listened to the earlier testimony, out of a feeling that paying any heed to the House Committee on Un-American Activities was playing into the hands of the enemy, and that, in any event, the personnel and procedures of that Committee made it impossible for it to arrive at the truth. During the trials they paid attention for the first time.

Chambers' documentary evidence was still there, of course, and his circumstantial story was told again; but by this time Hiss was able to make a better showing than he had, taken unawares, before the Committee. He was imperturable and glib in his testimony; and his lawyers were able to make Chambers seem more than ever a "moral leper," turning his very virtues (the lies and half-revelations by which he had attempted to protect Hiss) against him, and mocking his new-found religion. All the world distrusts a convert, but no part of it does so more heartily than the liberals. Finally, there were the psychiatrists, prepared on the basis of courtroom observation to call Chambers seriously unbalanced.

But most important of all, there arose to stand beside Hiss, one by one, a series of respectable character witnesses, an elite corps, as it were, of the New Deal, distinguished civil servants and honored judges, until it seemed as if the whole movement that from 1932 on had swept the country out of fear and towards prosperity was staking its very reputation on the innocence of this single man. We know the character witnesses did not deliberately lie. But if they were not liars—as they certainly were *not*—they were, in some sense, fools. It is not an easy admission, certainly not for them, but not even for those (among whom I include myself) who have admired in them a vision of national life that still appears worth striving for.

· · ·

Even the wisdom of Franklin Roosevelt, the final culture hero of our liberal era, is brought into question. For he seems personally to have pooh-poohed the suspicions, relayed to him in 1940 by Ambassador Bullitt, about the reliability of Hiss. How could he have done otherwise? Was not Hiss one of those young men, mocked by the reactionary press as "brain-trusters," it had been his special pride to bring into political life? The big-city bosses, the unprincipled "experts," and the party hacks, he had been forced to carry with him for expediency's sake; but these young idealists he had supported for the sake of principle. Superficially, the history of Hiss is the prototypical history of the New Dealer at his best: the distinguished years at Harvard Law School, the secretaryship to the almost mythical Justice Holmes, the brilliant career that began in the Nye Committee and culminated at Teheran.

Certainly, a generation was on trial with Hiss, on trial not, it must be noticed, for having struggled toward a better world, but for having substituted sentimentality for intelligence in that struggle, for having failed to understand the moral conditions that must determine its outcome. What is involved is not any question of all or most of the younger New Dealers having been, like Hiss, secret agents of the GPU, but of their having been so busy denying that there was a GPU or that it mattered, that they could not identify an enemy of all the values in which they most profoundly believed.

They cannot even flatter themselves on having been fooled by master tricksters. Hiss was, perhaps, an extraordinarily accomplished dissembler, but what of the Pressmans, the Wadleighs and the Remingtons, more obvious in their intended deviousness? Lest the New Dealers seem "Red-baiters," they preferred to be fools. Even in the case of Hiss, disquieting reports were transmitted to his superiors from time to time, and it was noticed, on at least one occasion, that information which passed through his hands had an odd way of leaking out. At one point A. A. Berle, after a conversation with Chambers, had gone to Dean Acheson, then Hiss's immediate superior, to report the rumor that "the Hiss boys" were members of a secret Communist group, and Acheson called in Donald Hiss to ask him if he and his brother were really Reds.

The naivety of the thing is monumental! He asked Donald Hiss, and when Hiss said no, Acheson was "satisfied." After all, he had known "the Hiss boys" since they were children; they had gone to the same schools, belonged to the same clubs, could speak man to man. Dean Acheson simply could not bring himself to believe that if the Hisses, who were gentlemen, were also Communists, they would as a matter of course lie. One thinks of Mrs. Roosevelt, under somewhat similar circumstances, calling the leaders of the American Student Union into her drawing room, asking them please to tell her the real truth: were they Communists?

In part, the lack of realism shared by Acheson and Mrs. Roosevelt came from belonging to a world in which liberals and conservatives (and even radicals) are assumed to share the same moral values, the values of the old Judeo-Christian ethical system, however secularized; but in another sense it arises from long conditioning of the public mind by the "front organizations" of the late 30's, through which the bulk of the liberals learned to maintain the paradox that (a) there were really no Communists, just the hallucinations of witch hunters, and (b) if there were Communists, they were, despite their shrillness and bad manners, fundamentally on the side of justice. After all, the Communists are "left," and everyone knows that only the "right" is bad. This absurd metaphor of "leftness" managed to conceal from men of good will and some intelligence the essential fact that the Communists had ceased to subscribe to a political morality universally shared, whatever its abuses, until 1917. How many victims of this confusion were able to spend years moving in and out of Communist fronts and say blandly in the end, "To the best of my knowledge, I have never known an actual Communist"!

Seen in this larger context, the half-deliberate blindness of so many decent people, which is a vital part of the total Hiss case, explains itself. The erstwhile defenders of Hiss's innocence show a growing tendency to remain silent, but their silence does not mean, alas, that they are finally convinced. Looking through Carey McWilliams' recent *Witch Hunt*, for instance, one is startled to discover in a study of the rising tide of accusations of Communism, no mention of the name of Alger Hiss—nor, indeed, of Klaus Fuchs. So significant an oversight must mean, if not active skepticism about Hiss's guilt, a feeling that his case is somehow less relevant than those in which charges of Communism have not been substantiated.

We must clearly understand that the failure of Hiss to confess, far from casting doubt on his guilt, merely helps to define its nature. If Hiss's guilt is the sort I have tried to indicate, it is clear that, without some changes of heart or values, he could not possibly have confessed. One has only to think of the recent trial of the twelve members of the national committee of the Communist party. Even those avowed and open leaders of the movement, whom one had perhaps expected to cry out their faith proudly before the tribunal, could only plead— so ingrained had the Popular Front lie become—in the teeth of the evidence of their own early writings, that (a) they had never advocated revolution and (b) by God, it was their inalienable right as American citizens to do so. What could one expect from Hiss?

If there is a note of tragedy in the case, it is provided by Chambers, the informer driven to mortify himself and to harm those he still loves. The Third Perioder, still pursuing the absolute, makes a tragic final appearance as the scorned squealer; the Popular Fronter can only exit in the role of the hopeless liar. It is difficult to say what factor is most decisive in cutting Hiss off finally from the great privilege of confession; opportunism or perverted idealism, moral obtuseness or the habit of Machiavellianism; they are all inextricably intermingled.

In the end he failed all liberals, all who had, in some sense at some time, shared his illusions (And who that calls himself a liberal is exempt?), all who demanded of him that he speak aloud a common recognition of complicity. And yet, perhaps they did not really want him to utter a confession; it would have been enough had he admitted a mistake rather than confessed a positive evil. Maybe, at the bottom of their hearts, they did not finally want him to admit anything, but preferred the chance he gave them to say: he is, we are, innocent.

· · ·

American liberalism has been reluctant to leave the garden of its illusion; but it can dally no longer; the age of innocence is dead. The Hiss case marks the death of an era, but it also promises a rebirth if we are willing to learn its lessons. We who would still like to think of ourselves as liberals must be willing to declare that mere liberal principle is not in itself a guarantee against evil; that the wrongdoer is not always the other—"they" and not "us"; that there is no magic in the words "left" or "progressive" or "socialist" that can prevent deceit and the abuse of power.

It is not necessary that we liberals be self-flagellants. We have desired good, and we have done some; but we have also done great evil. The confession in itself is nothing, but without the confession there can be no understanding, and without the understanding of what Hiss case tries desperately to declare, we will not be able to move forward from a liberalism of innocence to a liberalism of responsibility.

NOTE

[1] Alistair Cooke, *A Generation on Trial*. In addition to Mr. Cooke's book, a thorough and scrupulous work, though one with many of whose interpretations I disagree, I have used for this article de Toledano and Lasky's *Seeds of Treason*, which is marred by a journalistic and melodramatic style, but contains much valuable background material and sets the Hiss case in illuminating context of Communist espionage on two continents. I have also consulted the newspaper accounts of the case, particularly those of the New York *Times*, and printed hearings of the House Un-American Activities Committee; while for further background, I have turned to the *New Masses* for 1931, and various other official Communist publications. I do not know personally either of the principals in the case, nor have I made any attempt to communicate with them. I have no private or special sources of information. What I have attempted in this piece is an analysis based on publicly available documents, considered in the light of my own experience and knowledge of that world of values and beliefs out of which the incidents of the case arose. It is the lack of such experience and knowledge which makes even Cooke's careful and subtle book miss what seems to me the essential point.

2

DIANA   TRILLING

A Memorandum on the Hiss Case

PARTISAN   REVIEW,   MAY-JUNE   1950

RALPH DE TOLEDANO AND Victor Lasky's *Seeds of Treason* is first to appear of the several forthcoming books on the Hiss case. Mr. Toledano is an editor of *Newsweek,* Mr. Lasky a *World-Telegram* reporter—both are experienced newspaper men and particularly knowing in the ways of Communist organization and intrigue. Frankly pro-Chambers, they devote a good part of their book to Chambers' personal history, from his youthful quest for a meaningful purpose in life, through his involvement with the Communist movement and his meeting and subsequent joint espionage with Alger Hiss, to the days of his ordeal in court. But they also amplify the court record with a variety of material gathered in extensive independent research and interviewing. There is an enlightening account, for instance, of Communist espionage throughout the world, similar to and contemporary with that in which Hiss and Chambers were engaged. And there is an instructive section dealing with the steady refusal of the Roosevelt administration to pay any heed to the knowledge constantly being pressed upon it, that there were undercover Communists in high government places, Hiss among them. Mr. Toledano and Mr. Lasky's actual recapitulation of the Congressional hearings and the two trials is perhaps too brief, but it is cogent. Certainly nothing which came out in court is not the more firmly established for being presented against the background they have so painstakingly built up.

I say "established" because I speak from the point of view of someone who agrees with the authors of *Seeds of Treason* that Chambers told the truth and Hiss lied. But what about the many people of good will who followed the case to a quite opposite conclusion—that Chambers is a vicious liar and Hiss the innocent victim of his persecution? Is there any possibility that they will change their minds just because they are freshly confronted with evidence and with the material Mr. Toledano and Mr. Lasky adduce in its support? I expect not. For such is the political and cultural context of the Hiss case that feelings have considerable precedence over reason, especially among Hiss's defenders. In addition, the tone of *Seeds of Treason* is of a kind that is likely to reduce the persuasive power of its facts for the very people it might have hoped to influence.

Where our emotions are involved—and wherever there are ideas there are emotions—we all of us tend to hear what we wish to hear, believe what we wish to believe. Evidence, in the sense in which it is sought by the law, is something to which we repair only as it supports our emotions, and it is one of the everlasting miracles of the American jury system, imperfect as it may be, that again and again twelve human beings can be brought together and be disciplined, discipline themselves, to *try* to free themselves of prejudice and reach a decision only on objective grounds. The effort of objectivity which we see demonstrated in a courtroom would probably not be possible were it not for the living presence of a defendant to remind the jury of its responsibility. The juror functions in direct and immediate relation to the object of his decision, and this is his great protection against self-delusion. An analogy to the juror at work might be the psychoanalyst at work—both have been warned of their need for an extraordinary consciousness of their unconscious processes. It is a caution that is reinforced for the juror by the judge's last words to him as he files out to make his decision: he is charged to his prime duty of self-awareness.

But we who are not in the jury box have no one to charge us to beware of our hidden motives. We are perfectly free to function in relation to ourselves, or to some prejudicial concept of mankind or progress, instead of in relation to immediate fact. Public opinion is seldom face to face with responsibility. Especially in a case like Hiss's, where there are so many historical and political ramifications, our awareness of our unconscious partisanships is likely to be in inverse proportion both to our passion and our pride of conscience.

If one dare measure the unmeasurable, I would offer it as my impression that as the public—the articulate public—has lined up for and against Hiss, there has been more conscience on the Hiss side, more consciousness on the side of those who think Hiss guilty. By conscience, I mean a formulated moral intention. By consciousness, I mean an awareness of subjective motive. It is those who believe Hiss, much more than those who believe Chambers, who are worried about the consequences of the case, fearful of the uses to which the retrograde forces in this country will put his conviction. Those who believe Chambers are turned more to the past than the future. Hiss's conviction represents a retroactive victory for them, the proof that they were right in their repeated warnings against Communist infiltration. (I am speaking here, obviously not of the reactionary section of anti-Hiss opinion, but of the anti-Communist liberals who believe Hiss guilty.) It is not that they are unconcerned about the future, but that they invoke it less frequently than they do the past, and less frequently than they do experience—experience of Communism's methods and goals. But in this very fact that they are so much turned to the past lies the source of their superior consciousness. Most anti-Communist liberals have been through the mill, or frighteningly close to it—which has given them a first-hand knowledge of the way political partisanship can blind one to glaring political fact. To be a decent person and to have had proof, in one's own political past, of one's power for self-deception is to be forever charged to self-awareness. It means that at least one tries to put evidence before prejudice.

But however much more reliable the anti-Hiss side may be in point of weighing evidence, it has not served its country well by its deficiencies of conscience. To hate and fear Communism, to see Hiss's triumphant public career as the triumph of a defeat of this enemy—this is not enough conscience. Not enough, at any rate, for a liberal. Whoever thinks Hiss guilty who would still think of himself as a liberal has the duty of bringing to the case his most finely tempered understanding of its complexities.

The first demand that conscience puts on him is that he separate himself from his undesirable allies, from those who think Hiss guilty because they believe that anyone who is on the side of freedom and change, of labor and internationalism, is guilty of subversion and unAmericanism. It has always been true that politics makes strange bedfellows, but probably never so horribly true as in these last decades in which Communism has not only split the liberals among themselves but also time and again thrown the anti-Communist liberal into the same camp with forces he detests, or should detest, as much as he detests Communists. In the Hiss case, this enforced alignment between anti-Communist liberals and reactionaries is particularly open and distasteful. Who brought Hiss's perfidy to public issue, except the one agency in Washington most suspect for its political motive, the un-American Activities Committee? What is the anti-Hiss press, except the usual rabble-rousers and Red-baiters? What party has the most to gain from his conviction, except the Republican Party, and the Republican party in its most retrograde wing? It is scarcely an attractive company, and the liberal must make a clean break with it. Just as the pro-Hiss liberal claims his right not to be smeared as a Communist just because the Communists agree with him in this case, so the anti-Hiss liberal must insist on his right not to be labelled a reactionary just because reactionaries agree with him in this case.

This voice of conscience is never heard in Mr. Toledano and Mr. Lasky's volume. There is no criticism of the un-American Activities Committee, no dissociation from its purposes or from the purposes of Hearst or the Republican Party. Nor do the authors of *Seeds of Treason* make any discriminations of judgment on Chambers. Mr. Toledano and Mr. Lasky go beyond believing Chambers told the truth. They apparently regard him as a hero of our times, a martyr to principle and to the security of the nation. Chambers is their hero, Hiss their villain.

It is an unthoughtful and dangerous attitude; in logic, an untenable one. There is nothing Hiss has done which Chambers did not do. It must therefore be Chambers' repentance which makes him a hero. But it would follow, then, that were Hiss to repent, he too would be a hero—unless Mr. Toledano and Mr. Lasky think it is too late for Hiss to repent. But if they think it is too late for Hiss to repent, would they be willing to name the precise date when it became impossible any longer to wipe out the sin of having been a Communist?

Naturally, where any crime has been committed—I am setting aside the whole delicate question of the moral difference between a crime committed for personal gain and a crime committed in devotion to a selfless goal—we are more sympathetic to the repentant person than to the unrepentant. But repentance does not retrospectively change a crime into a virtue, any more than our sympathy for a repentant person makes the unrepented crime any the more heinous. It is my sense of Chambers that this is his own moral attitude vis à vis Hiss. Certainly there is nothing in his conduct or in his public pronouncements calculated to assert a moral superiority to Hiss. And this does him much credit.

The defenders of Hiss have made Chambers out to be a sort of moral monster. They have dreamed up or transmitted on hearsay all manner of impalpable personal charges to explain away the palpable evidence of documents transcribed in Hiss's handwriting or on Hiss's typewriter from government papers available to Hiss. Some of these specific charges either backfired or threatened to backfire if used in court—the homosexual charge, for instance, of which Hiss's lawyers made so much in their pre-trial investigations. Only the general allegation that he was a psychopath was brought to court, and even this turned out to be more of a liability than an asset to the defense. For what Hiss's lawyers failed to realize is that you cannot have things like this only one way: if there are certain criteria for a psychopath, they are as applicable to the psychiatrist—or the defendant—as to the witness. Although the pro-Chambers people find it easy to understand this, they do not seem to understand its corollary in the moral realm— that if it is villainous for Hiss to have been a Communist agent, it is equally villainous for Chambers.

Better, of course, that the concepts of heroism or villainy be dropped from the discussion, for here they can only be concepts of journalism, not of serious thought. And not only the personal suffering of the chief protagonists in the case, two men whose lives have been ruined, but also and literally our fate as a nation requires that it be dealt with on a higher than merely journalistic level, like that of *Seeds of Treason*. Mr. Toledano and Mr. Lasky speak of the case as a tragedy. But the tone of their book is far indeed from the tone of tragedy which, it seems to me, would be bound to accompany any study of the Hiss case which proceeded from a wholesale political premise—the premise that for the case to have served any useful purpose there must be salvaged from it a better notion of liberalism.

• • •

A man in public life, like Hiss, is of necessity a man with many friends. Even among public persons, however, Hiss would appear to have had a special gift of friendship; everywhere one goes these days one meets someone who knew him, either at college or at law school, in Washington or through his work with the Carnegie Foundation—and evidently to know him was to admire him. And yet, when one inquires further into these relationships, it develops that most of Hiss's friends were not really friends at all, in the sense of being on frequent visiting terms with him or in relationships of evolving intimacy. In fact, Hiss seems to have had remarkably few friends, but a host of acquaintances and associates for whom he suggested the possibility of friendship. His looks, his manner, his career evidently symbolized for the men who met him or worked with him some principle of their own personalities which they would happily see fortified or multiplied in their social world. Every friend stands for something we either need or value in our own characters, supplements what we lack or reinforces what we already possess. For those who knew him Hiss apparently stood for a particular kind of practical idealism—an idealism not wasted in fantasy or in an acerbity of criticism of the status quo but beautifully assimilated to practical activity. Just as his good manners were a reminder that deportment can go along with intelligence, so his fine career was a reassurance that idealism can be made a worldly success.

It was also a reassurance that history was on the side of political idealism and that liberalism need no longer be merely an embattled sentiment. For a long time before the Roosevelt era the political idealist had been a very lonely man, and certainly had no hope of being able to shape policy. Now, in the Roosevelt years, this was changing. Government had raised the intellectual minority out of its isolation and placed it at the very center of power.

That, even in these circumstances, the intellectual liberal minority still needed even more reassurance than history was giving it; that it still conceived itself as an ineffectual little group buffeted about by the reactionary hordes; that it persisted in thinking itself lonely even while its ranks swelled, and isolated even while it stood at the apex of public life—this is one of the salient features of its psychology. Once unpopular, always unpopular; once weak, always weak—such is the informing feeling of modern liberalism, a feeling which has outlasted even the Roosevelt years. And it derives, I think, from the identification liberalism has made with Communism. The friends of the Soviet Union can watch it grow from one-sixth of the earth's surface to one-fifth to one-third and still persuade themselves that Russia is in as much need of protection as she was in the early days of the Revolution. Just so, even at the height of the Roosevelt era, when liberalism had achieved a hitherto unimagined power, it lived, not by the reality of its strength, but by the conviction of its frailty.

What forged or cemented the bond between liberalism and Communism, rationalizing this sentiment of liberalism's weakness was, of course, the threat of fascism. The economic depression had given a terrific jolt to liberal complacency and freshly thrust upon the intellectuals of this country the fact of the class structure of our economy; but it made revolutionaries only of those middle-class intellectuals sufficiently imaginative to make a very long-range association of their own fates and that of the proletariat. The middle-class liberal suffered a certain amount of personal strain in the depression but he was not really damaged to the point where the Soviet system presented itself to him as a fierce necessity. If he would make a revolution it would be for the immediate sake only of the working-class, not for his own imminent advantage or protection. It was Hitler's rise that swung the full tide of America's idealistic middle class; for a dominant fascism, it quickly became clear, directly and catastrophically affected the life of every member of society, whatever his class roots or profession. In fighting fascism, the liberal middle-class American was fighting in self-defense. He was fighting, not in the name of a remote ideal, but in the name of everything worth preserving in our own system—liberty, democracy, religious tolerance. And in the idea of self-defense, he had an excuse for a fervor, even a violence, which yet did no violence to the popular image of the liberal temperament.

After Russia had lost Germany to Hitler rather than have Germany fall to any left-wing party except the Communist Party, she was quick to recognize the hidden ally she had in fascism. The fear on which fascism had risen to power was the fear of Communism, and now Communism, thus established as the prime enemy of fascism, could represent herself as the prime friend of democracy. In the name of a military anti-fascism, the Communist movement could now organize and control the world over all the vagrant liberal and democratic forces which had previously eluded her solicitations. The League against War and Fascism was the best-known of these innocents groups, but there were many others—especially when the civil war in Spain further concretized the fascist menace. The conduct of England and America in relation to the Spanish War of course made it all the more natural for sympathizers with the Loyalist cause to look to Russia as the spearhead of anti-Franco feeling. The handful of liberals who had been close enough to radical politics before 1932 to understand the extent of Russia's betrayal of the German working classes, and who had sufficient political experience to follow the double game Russia was playing in Spain, might try to warn the innocents among the Russian-dominated anti-fascist groups in this country that they were being used, but their efforts were in vain. Not only were there few places where they could make themselves heard, most of the so-called liberal press having been completely won to this popular anti-fascist front, but also having no political party around which to group, they had no organization of their own with which to combat the highly-organized movement which the Communist Party had brought into being, all unknown to most of its participants.

One of Roosevelt's first acts when he had been made President had been to recognize the Soviet Union. It had been a gesture which had won virtually unanimous support from American progressives. Here was the perfect symbol of the new dispensation we could look to, and after so many years of Republican timidity and backwardness. The drastic domestic reforms of Roosevelt's first term, especially the new government attitude toward labor, further marked out the path of progress which this country was now to follow—suddenly American liberals could feel a real congruity of purpose with the administration. And if the price of this resurgent energy was the hatred of the reactionaries of the country, it was a price the liberal gladly accepted. Let the backward forces in American political and economic life call him Red, he could meet the charge head on, with the firm conviction of his Americanism. The word "patriotism" was not yet invoked on the side of progress; this was to wait a few years more. But to the concept of Americanism there were now assimilated all the good values which fascism attacked—freedom of speech and thought, freedom of religion, the right of labor to organize for collective bargaining. And expectably enough, whoever questioned a single attitude on the anti-fascist side himself fell under the fascist imputation.

Thus, not very slowly but very surely, the ranks of American liberalism were broken into two profoundly antagonistic groups—those whose only enemy was fascism; and those who had two enemies, both fascism and Communism. And if this division was clearly drawn even before the war, if the anti-Communist liberal found it hard to make himself heard even in peacetime, how much more difficult was his role after 1941, when Russia and America became military allies. The blow which the dominant liberalism of this country had suffered in the short period of the Soviet-Nazi pact would have appeared to be staggering. It has resulted in the disaffection of many intellectuals who had been able to overlook all the other threats to their faith in the Soviet Union. But the termination of the pact with Hitler's attack upon the Soviet Union brought most of them back into camp. For it gave American liberals just the excuse they had been seeking for Russia's unseemly alliance—it was clear Russia had just been temporizing to prepare for the fight. This, we must understand, was the *reality* of politics: even an ideal government had often to use un-ideal methods to achieve her goals. Means were justified by their ends, and only political dreamers measured an end by the methods used to attain it. It was the same argument that had been put forward to explain away so many contradictions between socialist theory and Communist practice, or to defend Roosevelt against the criticism that he had never broken with the Democratic Party bosses.

And the appeal to practicality became even more urgent once we were in the war. It was not practical to question the conduct of an ally, particularly of an ally who had so much reason in the past—intervention, non-recognition, cessation of trade—to be unsure of our friendliness. It was not practical to jeopardize Russian confidence by raising the question of peace terms while the fight was still raging. It was not practical to give a forum to dissident opinion on Russia's role in world affairs. It *was* practical to give Russia anything she needed which we had, with no strings attached to it—all the lend-lease she wanted, say, with no conditions imposed; indeed, to send Harry Hopkins to Russia with its offer, rather than wait for Molotov to come and ask for it. What *was* practical, when peace terms were at last under discussion, was the conciliatory spirit of Yalta, the reassertion of our faith that we had only to disarm ourselves in relation to Russia for Russia to disarm herself in relation to the world.

What was practical, in other words, was what was ideal. The Roosevelt administration was notable in history for having been able to resolve that age-old, apparently unresolvable contradiction in the minds of liberals—between what might be wished for, and what could be. In the space of a decade and a half, a paradox had become a simple working formula.

· · ·

This, sketched in haste, was the political background of Hiss's public career. Chambers has told us his ideological story. We have to guess at

Hiss's by understanding the external circumstances of his intellectual life, and by trying to fill in the gaps between the public and the private man.

I have said of both sides of the Hiss case, of both those who believe him guilty and those who believe him innocent, that they tend to neglect the evidence in the case because they are motivated by hidden preferences. But I have offered it as my impression that this is even truer of Hiss's partisans than of his accusers. And indeed perhaps the most striking aspect of the Hiss case is the passion of loyalty that has been roused on Hiss's side, not merely among people who knew him—that is readily understandable—but among men and women who would seem to have had no closer connection with him than with Chambers. How can we account for the unshakable faith people who never set eyes on Hiss have in him, so that they will go to any imaginative extreme to explain away Chambers's charges and evidence?

Some of these people think Chambers is a moral monster not only because he has called Hiss a Communist and a spy, but because he was himself a Communist and a spy. That is, they would be ready to think Hiss monstrous too if they believed him guilty. They point to Hiss's idealistic career, which was so much in consonance with their own idealism, as proof of the outrageousness of the accusations made against him. They do not recognize that idealism is the very nature of the Communist commitment—perhaps a misdirected idealism, perhaps an idealism carried to undesirable length, but an idealism nonetheless.

This, however, is a minority of the Hiss defense. Most partisans of Hiss take another ground. They admit that the Communist, even the Communist spy, is motivated by idealism, although it is an idealism different from that of the liberal. But reactionaries, they know, have a way of making an amalgam of the idealisms and of calling every liberal a Communist. And they believe that Hiss is an innocent liberal victim of this kind of slander.

This latter group is the most passionate and personal in its loyalty to Hiss. And the first thing we observe of its members is that they have certain shared social and cultural characteristics. Apart from the known fellow-travelers, most of Hiss's supporters are people of the middle and upper middle-class, of education, breeding, professional solidity and distinction; people of great probity; thoughtful and con-scientious citizens. Judged by the conventional criteria of class, Hiss's defenders come off rather better than his accusers. In contrast to the respectability of those who are on the Hiss side, those who think him guilty have a taint of the bohemian, of the unconnected. (It is the generalizing social distinction one might make, say, between Hiss's Harvard and Chambers's Columbia.) One wonders why the lines can be drawn in this curious fashion, by class. For surely it cannot be only class loyalty, in the simple snobbish sense, that has attracted such handsome support to the Hiss cause. In dealing with people of this much probity and intelligence and social conscience, it would be mani-festly unfair to ascribe to them an ingrained class-feeling which func-tions in despite of their educated democratic principles. No, on the contrary: people of this sort do not exist without their principles, and therefore it is to their principles that we must look for an explanation of their feelings about Hiss. What principles do they embody which are also incorporated in Hiss? What moral identification do they make with Hiss which makes it so imperative that Hiss not be condemned? Hiss's personal acquaintances defend themselves, or at least their abil-ity to judge people, when they defend Hiss—that is obvious enough. But do not the men and women who never knew him but yet stand by him so staunchly also defend themselves in defending Hiss?

The Hiss principle is, of course, a configuration not only of ideas but of social personality. Even the scantiest outline of the years be-tween 1929 and the present remind us of the new kind of figure which appeared on the American political scene during Roosevelt's administration. Wilson had been a scholar and a gentleman; Teddy

Roosevelt had been a person of good birth. But neither of them had the unmistakable marks of breeding, the amenity and grace, of Franklin Roosevelt, and neither had been able to bring his own kind into politics with him in any number worth notice. Before the Roosevelt era, politicians were a raffish company. Even at their best they must be condescended to by people of cultivated mind and habit. But when Roosevelt came into office, this changed overnight.

From his start in office and increasingly as the years went on, Roosevelt attracted to government men and women for whom, in an earlier day, the political life would have been unworthy—men and women whose professional competence had been established in fields far removed from politics and whose private ambitions were subordinate to a precise, conscious morality. Of this new kind of political man Hiss can be described as almost a prototype, in quality if not chronologically. Serious, alert, well-educated, eager, sensitive, charming, he perfectly expressed this new government of mind and spirit which had replaced the government of patronage and crude personal advantage. His career was a career of energetic devotion to principle; his times were times of strenuous effort on behalf of high social goals. His personality was exactly cut to the mold of his career and his times.

If we can say, as I think we can, that before this century the sources of all political idealism was (however remotely) religion, I think we can also say that in our own century the source of all political idealism has been socialism, and, since the Russian Revolution, specifically the socialism of the Soviet Union. I do not mean that whoever has worked for political progress has necessarily been a socialist. I mean only that it has been from socialist theory that political progress has chiefly taken its inspiration, and from the socialist example its practice. On all progressive citizens of this country, the treatment of Russia by the democracies at the time of the Revolution and in the decade which followed had left a large impress of guilt. For here was an actual experiment in—well, not socialism perhaps, but Communism (the difference was to be regarded as one of degree) and look how shamefully we had treated it! Roosevelt's recognition of the Soviet Union was an invitation for all those who felt this guilt to rally around him. And his domestic policies—his bold incursions upon big business, his courageous stand on behalf of labor, his fearless understanding that the modern economy had carried us past the day when laissez-faire could be considered a governmental virtue—signalled an administration unafraid to move toward the socialist source of its ideals. The middle-class Hiss need never have been a Communist to have found in the Roosevelt regime an excellent field for playing out his social guilts: there were thousands like him. Nor need he, anymore than Roosevelt himself, have been a Communist, or even a socialist, to have been in favor of domestic changes which, although moving in the general socialist direction, yet so soundly met the requirements of this stage in our economic evolution that no party which would win or stay in office now dare retreat from them.

It was absurd to think of Roosevelt as a Communist, and it still is. Or even as a socialist. Only those who were opposed to any form of social progress could call Roosevelt a Red. But he did not mind being called a Red—and precisely here lay both his strength and his weakness. It was Roosevelt's great strength that, truly liberal in his political goals, he refused to be intimidated by the bad name by which reactionaries might call him. It was his great weakness that he took the word "Red" only at its cant value, and refused to see the reality of the Red threat and its menace to democracy. This strength and this weakness, both, the liberals who followed him into office shared with him.

I have spoken of the impact of European fascism on the American liberal. But the possibility of fascism was not limited to Europe, it could happen here. In fact, it was already happening here: the reactionaries who labelled every progressive measure of Roosevelt's as the insidious work of Bolshevism were its vanguard. Anyone of firm liberal intention must refuse to be frightened by them, must be only flattered to be thought their enemy. And if, in the interests of progress, one found oneself—as, for instance, Mrs. Roosevelt did so frequently— on the same sides of certain issues with avowed Communists, it was an association to be borne with equanimity, for only in the darkened mind of reaction was Communism a danger. One was inviolable in one's anti-fascist democratic Americanism.

Much has been said, by those who think Hiss innocent, about the patent contradiction between his impeccable public life and the nefarious private activities of which he has been convicted. It has been felt that for him to be guilty as accused he would have had to be a Jekyll-and-Hyde personality, never letting his right hand know what his left was doing. But leave the espionage out of account for the moment, and consider Hiss only as an undercover Communist. If we examine the ideological atmosphere in which he conducted his public life, how much actual contradiction was there between his public and his private commitments? How much intellectual acrobatics did it take for a secret Communist to be in public affairs? Surely not enough to split a personality. Actually, he need only temper his passions, sup-press his ultimate aims and stay with the immediate practical ideal-ism—and he could both think like a Communist and act like a good servant of a liberal America.

And this is, of course, what Hiss's staunch partisans know, though they cannot let themselves be conscious of it. They know not only how thin a line divided their own principles from Hiss's overt prin-ciples, but also how narrow a bridge Hiss had to span between his overt and his hidden beliefs. Could they too have taken the step Hiss took—the step, at least, to the Party, if not the step to espionage? Certainly not. And yet—the emotional-intellectual factors involved in such a choice are mysterious. Who knows? Perhaps there but for the grace of God go themselves. (The anti-Hiss liberal also thinks, "There but for the grace of God go I." But by "there" he means Chambers as well as Hiss. And he refers, usually, not to a mysterious possibility in his emotional and ideological life but to a choice fully confronted.) They defend Hiss to defend their own areas of ideological agreement with Hiss. And they defend him so absolutely, with such emotions of outrage at whoever thinks him guilty, because they dare not contemplate where they themselves might be blown by the uncharted winds of fashionable doctrine. Hiss must be innocent to prove that they are themselves innocent.

The misery which so many nice people feel at the thought that Hiss is guilty is thus not to be derided or taken lightly. The Hiss case represents a capsule of self-knowledge which it is not easy to swallow.

• • •

I have said that if this case is to serve any purpose in our lives there must be salvaged from it a better notion of liberalism. I mean by this two things. The case will have been useful, I think, if it helps us detach the wagon of American liberalism from the star of the Soviet Union and if it gives liberals a sounder insight into the nature of a political idea.

Most American liberals are not Communists. They would not dream of joining the Communist Party. They would be horrified at the possibility of a Communist America. And they severely and sincerely condemn certain aspects of the Soviet regime. But their great point of difference with the anti-Communist liberals is that, whereas the latter fear the Soviet Union and anyone who tolerates it, they measure the degree of their liberalism by the degree of their tolerance of Russia.

Their position is supported by their fear of war. They hope to avert war with Russia by "understanding." They believe that to fear Russia is to place oneself squarely on the side of the war-mongers. This was not their position on Hitler Germany. They did not substitute understanding of Nazism for opposition to Nazism. These are the same people who were most resolute against fascism, but they cannot admit that the socialist revolution has produced an equally virulent totalitarianism. They may acknowledge that the Soviet Union has certain totalitarian features. What they refuse to see is that by definition totalitarianism is nothing if not a totality. Either you have a free vote, or you do not. Either you have the freedom to criticize your government and change it, or you do not. Either you can write and speak and work as you choose, or you cannot—and all such criteria as "free for whom," "free for what," are only rationalizations. When the anti-Communist liberal says you need not be either a war-monger or a reactionary just because war-mongers and reactionaries are on the same side with you on this or that specific issue, they counter with the statement that you need not be a Communist just because you are on the same side with Communists on a specific issue.

And certainly, they are right to this extent: there is no reason to fear being in agreement with Communists on a specific issue, *if* one brings to this agreement as much awareness of a Communist danger as of the reactionary danger. But this is a big "if." For it is the very essence of contemporary liberalism that it thinks so differently about reaction and about Communism.

The liberal who brings to all his associations the clear knowledge that he is opposed to totalitarianism in whatever form—that of the Soviet Union no less than of Hitlerism—has nothing to fear from the motives which may be assigned to him because of his decisions on specific points. Clarity and honesty are all the protection he needs against being tainted. Take, for instance, the official in the State Department who advises a certain line of conduct which happens to coincide with the Russian line. Does he fully realize that the interests of Russia are the interests of expanding totalitarianism? If he does and can yet believe that the line is to the best interests of a democratic America, then let him proceed with a clear conscience.

But the task of persuading the liberal who is not afraid of Communism that he should be afraid of it is a gigantic one, and one which involves changing a climate of opinion and feeling over the whole of our culture. Perhaps, however, it is here that the Hiss case can be helpful, by clarifying for the liberal the historical process of which he and Hiss have been a party, and by impressing upon him a new sense of reality of political ideas.

Politics is power. Every nation is a power nation. This has been so since the beginning of organized social life and will always be so. Political idealism is a direction power may take; it is not a negation of power. The liberal in politics is as directly involved with power as is the reactionary, however much better the uses to which the liberal may wish to put his power. And every political idea, no matter how liberal, relates to power. This is the *real* reality of politics and of political ideas.

Only when the liberal recognizes that his political ideas are ideas which relate to power can he recognize the kind of responsibility he must take for his ideas. "Ideas are weapons" is a slogan of modern American liberalism, but the slogan was raised, not to warn liberals of their fierce responsibility as thinking people, but, rather, to encourage them in what seemed the small improbable hope that they too could be effectual. The liberal has deceived himself that because he is in a minority his ideas have the strength of a slingshot compared to the cannon of reaction. It is a dangerous deception, and has made the liberal irresponsible. The Fuchs case dramatically demonstrates that the idealism of an idea does not necessarily diminish its power.* The

---

* *Klaus Fuchs, a refugee German physicist and Communist Party member, was employed by the United Kingdom atomic energy program during World War II, and was sent to work on the Manhattan Project at Los Alamos. Fuchs was the famous "Atom Spy" who transferred to the Soviet Union, via Harry Gold and Julius and Ethel Rosenberg, virtually everything he knew about atomic weapons.*

idealistic idea of a single individual placed in the right circumstances can be as strong as an atom bomb.

Ideas are not to be separated from the acts to which they might lead; and whether or not, in any particular instance, they do actually lead to acts is irrelevant. They might lead to acts; they often do lead to acts; they must therefore be judged as if they were acts. The Communist idea must be judged as a Communist act. And similarly, the idea of tolerance of Communism must be judged as an act of tolerance of Communism.

The liberal who refuses to separate his liberalism from his tolerance of Communism must ask himself how far he would be prepared to act on this tolerance. Would he be willing to keep someone in high government office who was stealing our documents for transmission to Russia? If not, why not? Just because of his abhorrence of stealing? Very well, then. Would he be willing for a Communist who was not a spy to be in high government office? And if not, why not? What can possibly be wrong with being governed by someone whose political philosophy is tolerable?

Obviously it is only if one regards a Communist as the representative of totalitarianism that one has any ground for questioning his right to hold office in a democracy. If someone represents a tolerable political system, we can have no objection to his presence in government—and no need to prove that he is anything but what he is. We can even have no objection to his functioning in office *as* a Communist, even though this might lead to his legislating *us* into Communism.

This is the responsibility that the liberal must take for his ideas, including his ideas about Communism. This is the outcome any liberal not afraid of Communism must be willing to confront.

Hiss, of course, has been found guilty not only of being a Communist but of being a Communist spy. The difference between the two seems to be to be important only in terms of personal morality and psychology, not in terms of idea. We must keep it in mind that, to the committed Communist, personal morality as we conceive it is bourgeois morality or no morality at all. The only morality to a Communist is revolutionary morality, and according to revolutionary morality, Hiss performed a moral act because he was furthering the revolutionary goal. It is interesting to study why someone like Hiss who was bred by standards of bourgeois morality should have switched to so different a moral code; but such a study has only a coincidental pertinence to his objective acts. What is immediately pertinent to his acts is his ideas. In lying and stealing Hiss took the fullest responsibility for his political ideas. He contemplated where his ideas might lead, and he was nevertheless willing to have these ideas and perform his acts. He really understood the reality of politics.

Which is precisely why so many liberals cannot bear to think Hiss guilty: his guilt confronts them with a reality of politics which is at such odds with their own ideality. But this is also why the Hiss case may be useful—because it can help teach liberals that political ideas are political acts, and acts of political power. The espionage to which Hiss's Communist commitment led him is the awful evidence that ideas are not the innocent little things we think them, that they have a commanding life of their own, that they can look both ideal and legal but turn out to be neither. The Hiss case faces the liberal with the most cogent representation he has yet had of the kind of responsibility he must take for his thoughts.

. . .

As I write the conviction of Hiss has already had one of the unhappy consequences that was predicted for it. The discovery of a Soviet agent in American office was bound to encourage the search for others, and the McCarthy investigations are in progress. Hiss's defenders warned us that his conviction would be a signal for a grand-scale witchhunt for

Communists in government, and one in which innocent liberals would be tarred with the Communist brush. The way McCarthy conducts himself confirms their fear.

Their fear was based, however, upon the belief that Hiss was himself an innocent liberal. If you believe that Hiss was guilty, you must also fear that innocent liberals will be smeared by a McCarthy. But you also acknowledge the fact that had it not been for the un-American Activities Committee Hiss's guilt might never have been uncovered. And you reserve the possibility that a McCarthy, too, may turn up someone who is as guilty as Hiss. What you lament is the tragic confusion in liberal government which leaves the investigation of such important matters to the enemies of liberal government.

The anti-Communist liberal maintains, that is, a very delicate position which neither supports a McCarthy nor automatically defends anyone whom a McCarthy attacks. He decries witchhunts. He demands that there be no public accusations without proper legal evidence. And even where this evidence is presented, he calls as much attention to the political motive of his accuser as of the accused. But he does not make the mistake of believing that just because the wrong people are looking for Soviet agents in the American government, there are none. He does not deceive himself that whoever a McCarthy names is ipso facto an innocent liberal.

He deplores, indeed, the very need to speak of a liberal as either innocent or not innocent. For he knows that were we really as realistic about politics as, in our practical idealism, we like to think we are, there would be no such confusion of innocence and non-innocence among liberals. There never was before the Communist revolution. A liberal was simply a liberal, and it was quite enough to be.

3

ARTHUR KOESTLER

The Complex Issue of the Ex-Communists

NEW YORK TIMES MAGAZINE,
FEBRUARY 19, 1950

THE SECOND TRIAL OF ALGER Hiss happened to coincide with the publication of a book in which several former Communists and Soviet sympathizers, including myself, relate their experiences. This explains the letter from which the following extract is taken. The writer is unknown to me—she is a woman obviously of German origin who now lives in a Latin-American country.

> Reading about Alger Hiss I always think: there but for the grace of God and the Communist party, stand I. I belong to your generation, in age and in spirit. I was one of those who, had the party only asked for, would have spied on God Almighty without the least bit of a bad conscience. It is not my merit that they never did ask me things like that, because the only function I ever held was that of a dumb cashier of party dues and later on I was fortunately only a no-account typist in one of their organizations in Berlin, still later, in Spain the same during the Civil War, in a party office in Barcelona. It was around that time, summer 1937, when I changed my mind about our "Religion" and no doubt, had Alger Hiss gone through this school he would have changed his mind also. But Americans were rather a few years later in finding out, you know the political reasons for that very well, I suppose. It

seems one has to be a European with a left-wing past to understand the Hiss story. . . .

That is where the call for you comes in. Defend Alger Hiss on ground of his motives. I only know of the Hiss case what I have read. . . . Still, the story seems in a way very clear to me and though I believe he did what he is accused of, I see it in the light of his then decent motives. The question would rather be: have the United States really been harmed through him? I cannot believe that. It must be his difficult position and regard for his family that makes him insist on his "innocence" which, in a higher sense, is real. Come to think of it, for the American public the case is really a bit involved, but you could make it clear. Maybe, if you did, you would prevent a suicide. Could not this trial be brought around to the real issue: even if he did steal the documents, what were his motives?

Probably, sometime between now and then, when Alger Hiss changed his mind as so many did who had been Communists in good faith, he was in no position to announce that change. It must have been like this and Whittaker Chambers is the real villain because he didn't keep his mouth shut about things past and done with.

• • •

I have quoted this long extract because I believe that it expresses, in an admittedly exaggerated and overstrung manner, the vague feeling of uneasiness in a considerable section of the European and American public. The outstanding aspect of the trial was that it was not a case of the state or society calling a citizen to account for an alleged crime. It was a public and deadly duel between two individuals—one persecutor, one persecuted. Thus the abstract equation of justice between individual and society became transformed into a personal equation between two men, and the whole picture distorted by the emotional reactions to these two utterly different human types.

As far as personal impressions and the testimonies of high-standing witnesses go, the persecuted Hiss appeared as the prototype of the decent, modest, hard-working, well-spoken, happily married, idealistic American liberal who, even if assumed to be guilty, could not be suspected of having acted for any base reason or for personal gain. His persecutor on the other hand appeared as a man who unblushingly admitted having committed perjury, traveled with forged passports, lived with mistresses under false names and was described by some academic gents as a psychopath. To put the whole matter in a nutshell: from the spectator's point of view the casting of the parts was all wrong—Chambers should have got the part of Hiss and Hiss the part of Chambers.

. . .

But the roles were only apparently miscast. For there is a tragic consistency and deep symbolism in both characters. Without the doubting verdict of the jury, there are many who agree that Hiss's innocence is "in a higher sense real," and that he kept passing those documents to the spy ring happily like a starry-eyed Boy Scout doing his one good deed every day. These people would feel that he is the classic type of well-meaning dupe who becomes addicted to the Soviet myth as if it were a drug and who nevers finds his way back from the lost week-end in Utopia.

Hiss denied to the end and persisted stubbornly on his single track: Chambers confessed, recanted his past and came out on the side of the angels. One would think that this after all decisive fact should tilt the balance of sympathy toward Chambers. Yet my correspondent excuses Hiss' impenitence by his "difficult position" and calls Chambers the "real villain" because "he did not keep his mouth shut about things past." And here again she seems to lend a shrill

voice to a vague public sentiment. For though it is said that one repentant sinner causes more rejoicing in heaven than ten righteous
men, people here on earth not unnaturally prefer the ten righteous
men; and the public spectacle of the repentant sinner causes at best a
feeling of embarrassment, at worst a feeling of repugnance. And here,
I believe, is the core of the whole problem.

. . .

I remember how at a New York cocktail party some time ago a lady
journalist of obvious sincerity attacked me with some vehemence. I
don't remember what exactly she said, but the gist of it was that people
who had once been Communists should shut up or retire to a
monastery or a desert island instead of going 'round "teaching other
people lessons." She spoke with deep conviction, and what she said
obviously reflected a widespread popular feeling: mankind's instinctive horror of the renegade.

This horror probably has its roots in the collective unconscious,
in past loyalties to church, clan or tribe which, even if apparently
buried, remain potent emotional forces. Even those who in principle
agree that there are considerations of a higher order which may force
a man to override his loyalties and who accept the ethical justification
of a given act of renegacy—even those who feel esthetically repelled
by the spectacle of the act itself. In short, people don't mind if you
betray humanity in the name of some particular cause; but if you
betray your club or party, they will turn from you in contempt.

. . .

This leads us to the curious fact that in our society most people are in
the habit of manipulating two mutually exclusive sets of ethical rules
without being conscious of the contradiction between them. The first

is expressed by sayings like "right or wrong, my fatherland," or "if the party demands it, I will spy on God Almighty himself," and by the value set on unconditional loyalty. The second demands that a man become a traitor, renegade, or apostate if the interests of humanity or of peace, justice or freedom demand it.

Some of the war trials of the last years were good examples of the confusion created by the simultaneous application of these contradictory rules of ethical conduct. Even more startling is the example of France, where people were shot, imprisoned or sentenced to "national ignominy" for having loyally obeyed the orders of their own legal Government. I do not wish to plead the case of either the prosecution or the defense: I wish merely to point out that if you feel contempt for Kravchenko or Chambers, then you should feel sympathy for Laval or Schacht;* and vice versa, if you condemn people for having "collaborated" with a totalitarian regime then you must acquit those who have deserted such a regime.

But of the two co-existent and contradictory rules of ethical conduct, the first, which demands unquestioning loyalty to some flag, social body or institution, is much older and deeper embedded in our

---

*Soviet defector Victor Kravchenko wrote a memoir titled I Chose Freedom. Pierre Laval, former premier of the Vichy French government, was executed for collaboration with the Nazis. Dr. Hjalmar Schacht was a German financial expert and politician and the central figure in National Socialist rearmament. Later, Schacht was implicated in the July 1944 plot to kill Hitler and was imprisoned for the remainder of the war. After the International Military Tribunal in Nuremberg acquitted Schacht of all charges, he was tried and sentenced by a denazification court to eight years in a work camp. He was finally released in 1948. Absolved of all accusations related to his activities during the Third Reich, Schacht began a successful second career in 1950 as an economic and financial consultant for developing countries.

unconscious psyche. This may be illustrated by comparing the public's attitude to a Catholic convert on the one hand, to a defrocked priest on the other. Everybody, including hardened atheists, respects the convert; but even atheists are embarrassed or repelled by a defrocked priest taking a girl out to a dance.

Now, in fact, both are renegades who have repudiated their former convictions. But the convert has only deserted the amorphous mass of unbelievers who do not represent a social institution and have no flags, emblems or party cards; whereas the priest has deserted a church with powerful binding symbols. Hence even those who agree on principle with his decision have an uneasy feeling that somehow he shouldn't have done it—or at least if he had to do it he should not take a girl out to a dance, though for everybody else this is a perfectly proper thing to do.

. . .

I think one must accept the fact that Chambers and Kravchenko and the rest of us who have borne allegiance to the "God that Failed" will always be looked upon somewhat like defrocked priests regardless of the differences in each individual's history and motives. It is no use to argue whether this attitude is justified or not. It should be recognized as a psychological fact. And the fact itself would be without much interest if it merely concerned the few individuals in question. In this case, the simplest solution for these would be to follow the lady journalist's advice and satisfy the demands of good taste and discretion by retiring to a monastery or a desert island.

But if Chambers had followed this advice, his repentance would have become meaningless and the public would never have learned certain facts which it was essential for it to learn. And the same is true of Kravchenko and Barmine and Silone and the others. My correspondent asks why they can't "keep their mouth shut about things past and done with"; and people with esthetic sensibilities, repelled by this flow of renunciations, disclosures and ringing mea culpas, ask with a shudder the same question.

. . .

The answer is simply that these things are neither "past" nor "done with." The inner structure of a totalitarian regime and the physiology of its tentacles stretching abroad; the facts about the arctic subcontinent of slavery, about the servitude of satellite Governments and the psychology of the Communist parties of the West—all these data, essential for the ideological and strategical defense of our civilization, could never have been assembled if these men had had the discretion and good taste to keep their mouths shut. For only those who have worked inside the hermetically closed regime know its true character and are in a position to convey a comprehensive picture of it; and in this sense at least it is true that one repentant sinner is a more valuable asset than ten righteous men who have never swerved from the path of democratic virtue.

Obviously the decisive fact about Chambers is that he has performed a service of great social utility. It is equally obvious that not all acts of social utility curry favor with the public or make the man who performs them appear in a favorable light. But it is essential that these two facts, the first of an objective the second of an emotive character, should remain neatly separated; and that the emotional factor should not obscure political judgment or interfere with the discharge of justice.

. . .

It is not to be expected that the public should like the runaway "priest"—even if the "church" from which he has run away happens to be devoted to perverse idolatry. It is not even important that it should believe in the purity or otherwise of his motives to quit. The public is entitled to feel attracted or repelled by him, but it is not entitled to let its bias interfere with its judgment: to talk of betrayal where loyalty would mean persistence in crime: to talk of persecution; to defend an evil regime on the grounds that those who denounce it are no saints. The greatest danger to liberalism today lies in such starry-eyed confusion.

4

GRANVILLE HICKS

Whittaker Chambers's Testament

NEW LEADER, MAY 26, 1952

W HITTAKER CHAMBERS HAS written a momen-
tous book. It has its faults: some sentimentality, some pompousness,
some bitterness. But these faults are part of its greatness as a human
document. There has been no comparable work of self-revelation in
our era, and if it would be rash to call it the equal of St. Augustine's
Confessions or the *Confessions* of Jean Jacques Rousseau, it has passages
of their quality.

About the old controversial question—whether Alger Hiss or
Whittaker Chambers was telling the truth when they delivered their
conflicting evidence before the House Un-American Activities Committee and again in the two trials—there can no longer be any doubt.
In view of Hiss's singular evasiveness, we should have been convinced
by the Committee hearings. I was convinced by the reports of the
first trial. How anyone could fail to be convinced by the books I
cannot imagine.

But, of course, the issue was larger than that. Indeed, as Chambers sees it, this was a struggle between God and the Devil, and the
Devil nearly won. Twice Chambers was close to suicide, and once it
was accident—or, if he insists, Providence—that saved him. It does

seem almost miraculous that he found strength enough to survive his ordeal and then write this book.

It must have been a terrible book to write. I live, as Chambers does, on a farm. I have never farmed it, and I am afraid, looking at these thirty-nine acres, that without a *Time* salary I never could. But I can understand what Chambers feels for his place in Maryland, and I know that he must have been tempted, once the trials were over, to cultivate his garden. That he felt compelled to go on bearing witness is proof of deep seriousness and an unflinching sense of responsibility.

Approximately half the book deals with the hearings and trials, and half with Chambers's life before his break with the Communist party in 1938. Fascinating and important as the latter half is, I was particularly interested in his account of his childhood and youth. He was born into the middle class, of parents who disliked one another and were both dissatisfied with their lot. The way in which his mother brought him up alienated him from his schoolmates, and he became a solitary child, solacing himself, as lonely children so often do, with books. By the time he reached adolescence, he could say to himself: "I am an outcast. My family is outcast. We have no friends, no social ties, no church, no organization that we claim and that claims us, no community."

It is fashionable today to explain Communism in psychological terms, and at least one current investigation into the subject concentrates almost entirely on the individual Communist's relations with parents and siblings. Like any other monistic theory, this kind of explanation can lead to gross absurdities, for Communism has many causes and childhood maladjustments have many consequences. Yet there is some truth here, and Chambers's story is a perfect illustration of it. After graduation from high school, he ran away from home. A few years later, he even more finally cut his family ties by joining the Communist party.

The tensions of that particular family had their effect not only on the life of Whittaker Chambers but also on the life and death of his brother. The brother, too, was almost a classic instance, but of the death wish. He tried to destroy himself in one way and another, and at last succeeded. If Whittaker Chambers did not join him in death, as the brother urged, it was because he had found something to believe in—Communism.

In *Witness,* Chambers has come closer than anyone else to describing the appeal of Communism. He disposes at once of the "widespread notion that men become Communists for reasons of personal gain." He denies that the Marxist dialectic is a major factor. He puts it this way:

> Under pressure of the crisis, his decision to become a Communist seems to be the man who makes it as a choice between a world that is dying and a world that is coming to birth, as an effort to save by political surgery whatever is sound in the foredoomed body of a civilization which nothing less drastic can save—a civilization foredoomed first of all by its reluctance to face the fact that the crisis exists or to face it with the force and clarity necessary to overcome it. Thus, the Communist Party presents itself as the one organization of the will to survive the crisis in a civilization where that will is elsewhere divided, wavering or absent.

No one has said it better than that.

Being a man who would not separate belief and conduct, Chambers, unlike the leftish intellectuals who had first told him about Communism, promptly joined the party. It is often assumed that, once conversion to Communism has taken place, the individual feels that all his problems are solved. That is rarely, if ever, the way it happens, and certainly it did not happen that way with Chambers. "The Communist," he writes, "lives in permanent revolt and anger against the injustice of the world around him. But he will suffer almost any degree of injustice, stupidity and personal outrage from the party." That is largely true, and yet Chambers's career in the party was a stormy one, and finally, during the factionalism of the Lovestoneite struggle, he dropped out of party activities. But his faith persisted, even though it could not liberate him from doubt.

It was during his unofficial leave of absence that Chambers wrote four short stories, which appeared in the *New Masses* in 1931 and 1932 and made a powerful impression on persons like myself who were just beginning to read the magazine and were frequently disconcerted by its contents. The first and most powerful of these stories, "Can You Hear Their Voices?" (originally, "Can You Make Out Their Voices?") was praised by Elistratova, a leading Soviet critic. Her praise, Chambers says, was embarrassing to the American party, since he was not in good standing, but Moscow had spoken and he was asked to become editor of the *New Masses*.

Some time later, J. Peters, a Soviet agent with whom he was working, told Chambers that he had opposed the publication of the stories in Russia. "They are against the party," he asserted. Chambers, after saying that he then thought Peters's views "somewhat narrow," continues:

> I think now that anyone who has the patience to read those four stories will agree that I was wrong, and that Comrade Peters was right. For in retrospect it is easy to see that the stories are scarcely about Communism at all. Communism is the context in which they are told. What they are really about is the spirit of man in four basic commitments—in suffering, under discipline, in defeat, in death. In each, it is not the political situation, but the spirit of man which is triumphant. The success of the stories was due to the fact that for the first time that spirit spoke to American Communists in a context and a language which it was permissible for them to hear. For the same reasons, Peters feared the stories. For he rightly sensed that Communism may never make truce with the spirit of man.

I have just now re-read the stories, and have again been moved by them, though not, of course, in quite the way that I was twenty years ago. Certainly I agree that they are about the spirit of man, but not that they are "scarcely about Communism at all." They are about Communism as an expression, as *the* expression, of the spirit of man, which is exactly what Chambers and I and a great many others believed it to be. Obviously, we were wrong, but I am not sure that we were so absolutely wrong as Chambers now thinks.

Perhaps the history of Communism and the intellectuals in the '30s might have been somewhat different if Chambers had not left the *New Masses* after a couple of months. He went to the magazine, he says, just as the great leftward swing of the intellectuals was beginning. As I recall, he had none of the social graces of certain of the party's apostles to the gentiles; in fact, he was rather harsh with us and even, or so it seemed then, condescending. Yet he was intellectually head and shoulders above the men who did take the starry-eyed converts in tow, and he should have had a considerable influence. It also seems possible that his disillusionment would have begun earlier if he had stayed in that milieu.

He left the *New Masses* to enter the underground. He admits that he felt a "quiet elation" on being chosen for such work, which seemed to him more important and more genuinely revolutionary than editing the *New Masses*. I suspect, moreover, that he had a deep-seated inclination toward conspiratorial activity. (Many people have, as a number of respectable academicians demonstrated in the OSS during the war.) At any rate, though he hesitated, he did not hesitate long.

So well were the underground apparatuses concealed from the eyes of ordinary party members that I had been out of the party for some time before I believed in their existence, and I still read about them with amazement if not with incredulity. If I, knowing what I did, could be skeptical, it is no wonder that a great many intellectuals refused to believe in the possibility of Hiss's guilt. I was never for a moment taken in by the argument that a man of Hiss's background, training, position, etc., etc. could not be a Communist, but I was loath to admit that such a man would engage in petty espionage, and the whole revelation of a Communist conspiracy in high Government circles shocked me. It did not seem possible that these men and women had been willing to place themselves, absolutely and blindly, at the disposal of the Soviet Government, But I know now, and we all know, that it happened, and for this awakening the nation should always be grateful to Whittaker Chambers.

Chambers worked with Soviet espionage apparatuses for a matter of six years, and to most of those associated with him he must have seemed a model of revolutionary faith, but there were many times when his mind was troubled, and in 1936 and 1937 he was acutely disturbed by the purges that were going on in Russia. The actual decision to break with Communism came in a moment of religious revelation, and he began his preparations not merely to escape, but to protect himself and his family against the vengeance he expected. After nearly a year in hiding he got a job as a book reviewer on *Time*, and quickly rose to a senior editorship. At the peak of his success came the summons to testify before the Un-American Activities Committee, and his ordeal began.

Chambers tells the story superbly, but I am concerned here less with the events described than with the interpretation he places upon them. Communism is, of course, a system of absolutes, and that is one of its great sources of appeal. Some persons, on breaking with Communism, break with the whole idea of absolutes; they become pluralists rather than monists, liberals instead of authoritarians. Others turn to some alternative sense of absolutes.

Chambers belongs in the latter category; that is, he now accepts the absolute truth of Christianity, and is a member of the Society of Friends. Furthermore, he still regards Communism as an absolute—but, of course, as an absolute evil. Thus there can be no question for him of blaming the failure of Communism on Stalin.

"The human horror of the Purge," he writes,

was too close for me to grasp clearly its historical meaning. I could not have said then, what I knew shortly afterwards, that as Communists, Stalin and the Stalinists were absolutely justified in making the Purge. From the Communist viewpoint, Stalin could have taken no other course, so long as he believed he was right. The Purge, like the Communist-Nazi pact later on, was the true measure of Stalin as a revolutionary statesman. That was the horror of the Purge—that acting as a Communist, Stalin had acted rightly. In that fact lay the evidence that communism is absolutely evil. It was Communism that was evil, and the more truly a man acted in its spirit and interest, the more certainly he perpetuated evil.

And again:

> The point was not that Stalin is evil, but that Communism is more evil, and that, acting through his person, it found its supremely logical manifestation. The important point was not the character of Stalin, but the character of Communism, which, with an intuitive grasp that was at once the source of his strength and his mandate to power, Stalin was carrying to its inevitable development as the greatest of the fascist forms.

It cannot well be denied that these quotations bespeak an absolutist temperament. Were all the evils of the Stalin regime inevitable from the moment Lenin took power? Chambers quotes Lenin's deathbed remark: "The machine has got out of control." But of General Krivitsky's assertion that Kronstadt was the turning point he says: "The fascist character of Communism was inherent in it from the beginning. Kronstadt changed the fate of millions of Russians. It changed nothing about Communism."* Did the evil begin with the

---

* *Soviet intelligence defector Walter Krivitsky was found dead of a gunshot wound in a Washington hotel. The 1921 Kronstadt Rebellion was an uprising among Soviet sailors in Kronstadt. The sailors, who had supported the Bolsheviks in the Russian Revolution, demanded economic reforms and an end to Bolshevik political domination. The Red Army crushed the rebels.*

formation of the Bolshevik party, then, or with the *Communist Manifesto?* Chambers's answer is even earlier:

> The Communist vision is the vision of man without God. It is the vision of man's mind displacing God as the creative intelligence of the world. It is the vision of man's liberated mind, by the sole force of its rational intelligence, redirecting man's destiny and reorganizing man's life and the world.

Chambers could not be more explicit:

> Hence the Communist Party is quite justified in calling itself the most revolutionary party in history. It has posed in practical form the most revolutionary question in history: God or Man? It has taken the logical next step which three hundred years of rationalism hesitated to take, and said what millions of modern minds think, but do not care or dare to say: If man's mind is the decisive force in the world, what need is there for God? Henceforth man's mind is man's fate.

The roots of Communism, then are in rationalism and liberalism. Nor does Chambers evade the political implications of his position. He speaks of the "miscellaneous socialists, liberals, fellow travelers, unclassified progressives and men of good will" who share the vision but lack the Communist's courage and the Communist's faith. He terms the New Deal "a revolution by bookkeeping and lawmaking."

"In so far as it was successful," he continues,

> the power of politics had replaced the power of business. This is the basic power shift of all the revolutions of our time. The shift *was* the revolu-tion. . . . Whether the revolutionists prefer to call themselves Fabians, who seek power by the inevitability of gradualism, or Bolsheviks, who seek power by the dictatorship of the proletariat, the struggle is for power.

It is no wonder, he insists, that the non-Communists in the New Deal were unaware of how they were being used by the Communists, since there was so little difference between them.

Unquestionably, Communism is an expression of certain tendencies in modern civilization. But so is capitalism. And so, for that matter, is Quakerism, which is one of the essential embodiments of the Protestant spirit. Communism is peculiarly devoted to what Arthur Koestler calls "consequent logic." "If you say A," Alex Trachtenberg used to tell me, quoting Stalin, "you must say B."* But Chambers is also a devotee of consequent logic. Those who have said A, he maintains, are indistinguishable from those who have said B and C or X and Y and Z.

We are engaged in a desperate struggle. Shall we assert that anyone who believes the human mind to be our principal resource is an enemy or at best an untrustworthy ally? If we fear the concentration of power in the hands of business, and wish to balance the power of business with the power of Government, are we to be classed as potential Communists?

Where do we take our stand in the fight against Communism? If Chambers were *completely* logical, he would have to advocate a return to some point in the past, before the earliest beginnings of industrialism, before the rise of science. Arnold Toynbee, though he is unwilling to commit himself on the point, seems to believe that the breakdown of Western civilization occurred early in the sixteenth century. At that point, we might begin our struggle—if we could. But of course, we can't. Our battle has to be waged in the latter half of the twentieth century, in the situation and with the weapons history has given us. And if, as both Toynbee and Chambers point out, victory is not inevitable, neither is defeat.

The present situation is infinitely more complicated than it seems to either the Communists or Whittaker Chambers. That makes our task terribly difficult, but it also gives us hope, for insofar as the situ-

---

* *Alexander Trachtenberg was the former head of International Publishers and a Communist Party leader.*

ation is complex, it is flexible. History has not moved in a straight line from the Reformation to a steam engine to the *Communist Manifesto* to Kronstadt to Yalta. Stalin is not the *heir* of the ages.

Our best hope, consequently, is not to oppose Communist dogma with some other dogma, but to meet rigidity of mind with flexibility of mind. If we are in danger of losing the battle, that is in part because we are in danger of giving up not so much the freedom as the activity of the mind. I have attended anti-Communist meetings that sickened me because they stank with that mindless self-righteousness that I learned to hate in the Communist Party. I have talked to undergraduates about the character and the danger of Communism, only to be asked to give them a program that would do for their generation what Communism seemed to do for mine, and I have realized with despair that I had failed to teach them the one lesson I wanted to teach—that our basic mistake lay in demanding *the* way of salvation.

So I reject Whittaker Chambers's conclusions, but I do not reject Whittaker Chambers. You do not have to agree with a man's ideas to respect and admire him, and I have finished *Witness* with a strong conviction that Mrs. Chambers was not far wrong when, in the courtroom, she called her husband a great man. His greatness is in part intellectual, for the acuteness of his intelligence has been demonstrated again and again, but it is more fundamentally moral. "I did not wish to testify before the House Committee," he writes. "I prayed that, if it were God's will, I might be spared the ordeal." But he did testify, knowing full well all the time just what lay before him.

There are moments in his accounts of the trials when Chambers speaks with bitterness. Remembering his hours on the witness stand, remembering how Lloyd Paul Stryker described him as "a thief, a liar, a blasphemer and a moral leper," remembering all the filth that was heaped upon him, I can only marvel that he writes as temperately as he does. A friend of mine who was covering the trial wrote me at the time: "You would find it agonizing, as I do, to observe Stryker's savagery, to hear the tittering in the court, to listen while the court stenographer reads erotic-proletarian poetry composed by Chambers twenty years ago, to watch while Chambers calmly assents to the vile language used by Stryker in describing his (Chambers's) past." And all this Chambers endured, though he was convinced that he was going to lose.

Chambers's behavior in the courtroom was magnificently courageous, but as a moral achievement it is overshadowed by the writing of this book. He did not write it for the sake of self-justification; he had gone beyond the need for that. He wrote it because he had not fully borne witness. He had to speak out, unhampered by the rules of committees and courts, and say *all* that he knew and believed about Communism, civilization today, and the nature of man.

That Chambers is sometimes mistaken in his interpretation of the motives of other people I can believe. For one thing, it is scarcely conceivable that he should not have been biased by what he had undergone, and, even more important, his views were colored by the dogmas he had adopted. But he has looked into himself more deeply and more truly than any man of our times, except for a handful of great creative writers, and he has set down, without shrinking, what he has seen. Whether the book is, as he believes, a testimony to the grace of God, it is a testimony to the spirit of man.

5

S I D N E Y   H O O K

The Faiths of Whittaker Chambers

N E W   Y O R K   T I M E S   B O O K   R E V I E W ,
M A Y   2 5 ,   1 9 5 2

THE NAME OF THE AUTHOR, the theme of his work, the nature of our times all conspire to make this volume one of the most significant autobiographies of the twentieth century. It is not among the hundred great books. Yet it throws more light on the conspiratorial and religious character of modern communism, on the tangled complex of motives which led men and women of goodwill to immolate themselves on the altars of a fancied historical necessity, than all of the hundred great books of the past combined. The phenomenon of which it treats is historically unique not only in scale but in meaning. It demands understanding, not mere denunciation. The keys to that understanding can be provided only by reflection on our recent historical experience.

A certain perspective, especially freedom from partisanship, is essential if the reader of this book is to do justice to its different facets. Many will already have judged it before they have actually read it. This will be a pity because the book covers much more than the unhappy story of Alger Hiss. It contains interesting vignettes of the Communist movement, a record of religious conversion, the saga of a farm, an account of desperate courage alternating with moods of spiritual dispair—all knit together by the essentially mystical and romantic personality of the author. The literary quality of the writing is impressive. In this respect the serialization did the book a disservice.

. . .

The main theme, however, is the Communist movement, above and under ground, the men and women who served it, and the logic of the commitment which led them into an eager faithlessness not only to their country but to the moral values in which they were nurtured. Here we must sharply distinguish, as unfortunately Mr. Chambers does not, between the facts to which he bears witness and the interpretations he places upon them. Were these interpretations valid, they would have as fateful a bearing upon the prospects for democratic survival as the revelations of the facts concerning Communist conspiracy. It will be necessary therefore to look hard at them.

First, about the facts. The internal evidence of this book is so overwhelmingly detailed and cumulative, it rings with such authenticity, that it is extremely unlikely any reasonable person will remain unconvinced by it. It is not that new facts about Hiss and his fellow conspirators are revealed but that the facts already known are placed in the historic context of Chambers' own development and almost day-to-day activities. To doubt them is tantamount to doubting Chambers' political existence as well as those of his collaborators. The absence of personal rancor against Hiss, the evidence that the author testified "reluctantly and in agony," the explanation of why he did not tell his entire story at once—a quixotic piece of foolishness—add credibility to the account.

As far as the charges that rocked the nation are concerned, this book, even more than the verdict of the trials, may well be called the vindication of Whittaker Chambers. Its pages show that he has long since atoned for his own complicity in conspiratorial work by his suffering at the hands of Hiss' friends whose outrageous smears against his personal life and that of his wife surpassed in virulence anything known in recent American history. It is indeed odd to observe that ritualistic liberals were much less indignant with those who betrayed the faith of their country than they were with the "informers" who revealed the betrayal—an attitude not displayed toward informers or renegades from fascism like Rauschning or Otto Strasser.* The mood of anti anti-communism, as the Hiss case shows, blinds one to political realities and creates an emotional vested interest in concealing the truth.

The facts in this book have a public side vastly more important then the private fortunes of Hiss and Chambers. What they show is that the highest instances of the Government were informed on four separate occasions of Chambers' charges that an important group of American officials in the State Department, Treasury Department, Patent Office and Aberdeen Proving Grounds were functioning as members of a Communist party underground apparatus. One need only read the names and successive positions occupied by this group, among several in operation, to understand that, in the event of hostilities with the Soviet Union, they could easily have functioned with a deadliness comparable to the Foote ring in Switzerland and the Sorge

---

* *Hermann Rauschning was a Nazi politician who was president of the Danzig senate. Rauschning became disillusioned with the Nazis, resigned in 1934, and fled to Switzerland in 1936. He published books warning of the Nazis' true intentions. Otto Strasser was a leader of the "left wing" of the Nazi party. He was expelled from the party by Hitler for opposing Hitler's political and economic views. As racist as his political adversaries, he continued to attack some of Hitler's policies while espousing vicious anti-Semitism in Switzerland, where he lived in exile.*

ring in Japan, both of which made enormous contributions to Stalin's victory.*

. . .

The truly puzzling and still inexplicable thing about these facts is not that the American Government was deceived—American innocence of politics based on a *Weltanschauung* is almost invincible—but that no accredited Government agency was asked to investigate the truth of Chambers charges when he first made them. Had this been done and those whose guilt was subsequently revealed quietly dropped from Government service, and elementary precautions taken against further penetration, the recent history of American political and even cultural life would have been profoundly different. As it is, one of the men in the Chambers ring, identified in 1939 as a Communist conspirator supplying then-secret information from Aberdeen Proving Grounds, kept his post until 1948.

Given these facts and the organized campaign of calumny against him, one can understand the subjective compulsions which have led Chambers to interpret his experiences as he does. This interpretation takes two forms, political and philosophical, both none the less questionable for being widely shared.

Chambers is convinced that it was not by chance that the New Deal served as a host body for Communist infiltration. He argues that despite their differences, the New Dealers and the Communists

---

Alexander Allan Foote was a British spy for the Soviets. Russian Richard Sorge worked in Japan as a Soviet spy. Sorge was able to give Joseph Stalin advance warning about the Anti-Comintern Pact (1936), the German-Japanese Pact (1940), and Japan's attack on Pearl Harbor. His greatest achievement was to inform the Soviet Union of Operation Barbarossa as early as December 1940.

were revolutionary brothers under the skin. The New Dealers sincerely abhorred the Communists but were unable, and then unwilling, to ferret them out because the latter were harder, brighter, vastly more knowing and unscrupulous antagonists of the same general type. Every move to oust Communists was regarded as a move against the Administration, and all a Communist under threat of exposure need do was to cry "Witch hunt!" to rally the innocent New Dealers to deny the facts of Communist penetration. Chambers quotes a close friend, himself a New Dealer, saying to him: "I see why it might not pay the Communists to kill you at this point. But I don't see how the Administration dares to leave you alive."

To say that the New Deal—an eclectic, unorganized, popular reaction to the intolerable evils of an unstabilized capitalism—was a social revolutionary movement is to play with words. The principles of social welfare are indigenously American, and Roosevelt, during the early months of 1933, could have led the country very much farther along these lines than he actually did.

· · ·

Until the Seventh Congress of the Communist International in 1935, Roosevelt in the eyes of the Communists was a Fascist. It was only when the Popular Front strategy and the tactics of the Trojan horse were adopted that the Communists organized their mass infiltrations and began to speak the language of the New Deal. Chambers should know that when it suits their purposes, Communists can speak anybody's language, the language of the Church Fathers as of American's Founding Fathers—and the ignorant or foolish will fall for it all the time.

The only thing that could have kept Communists out of any Administration, New Deal or Old, was the knowledge that communism since Lenin's time was not an open and honestly avowed heresy but an

international conspiracy, centered in the Kremlin, in a state of unde-
clared war against democratic institutions. The corollary would have
been the realization that the Communists were and are prepared to
use any and every means to achieve power, nationally and internation-
ally.

. . .

That this knowledge was absent in almost all Government agencies is
not surprising in view of the fact that both American presidents during
World War II were convinced that England and France would be
greater threats to post-war world peace and freedom than the Soviet
Union. Nor was this knowledge more conspicuously evident in influential circles outside the Government, in universities, for example, in
churches, the press and even business.

Most of Chambers' facts are rendered intelligible by a less sinister
hypothesis than the one he offers. It is that stupidity is sometimes the
greatest of all historical forces. Stupidity explains why Communists
were permitted to infiltrate into the Government. But why were they
retained so long after the data about them were in official hands?
Here Chambers forgets that some of the most vocal opponents of
Communists in Government services seemed more interested in discrediting the Administration and the New Deal than in defending
freedom. The passions of American parochial politics blinded both
sides to the fact that an international civil war was raging in relation to
which prestige, votes, patronage and many issues of domestic policy
were irrelevant. Nor does the author's account do justice to the climate of cloudy opinion which saw in Hitler the sole incarnation of
historical evil in our generation.

Chambers himself places the greatest stress upon the philosophical interpretation of his experiences. The international civil war so
correctly described is regarded not as a struggle between the free soci-

ety and the society of total terror but as the struggle between the Party of God and the Party of Man. The political differences among men are ultimately reducible to differences in theology, between the vision of a world with God and the vision of a world without Him. This in a sense is the thesis of Chambers' autobiography. He offers his life as testimony to its truth. And he writes as a moving and eloquent witness.

. . .

Chambers' story of his life is a minor classic in the history of religious conversions. No one can doubt the sincerity of his hard-won faith, that he has found in it, after much agony, a healing peace and humility. As a quest for personal salvation, it will command the respect of those who cannot share his cosmic hope and whose natural piety takes other forms.

But to make this faith a basis for social salvation is a hazardous enterprise, all the more so because of the desperate lengths to which Chambers carries it. He fervently and repeatedly asserts that the most revolutionary question in history is: God or Man? and that whoever answers "Man" shares the Communist vision whether he is aware of it or not. He recklessly lumps Socialists, progressives, liberals and men of good will together with the Communists. All are bound according to him by the same faith; but only the Communists have the gumption and guts to live by it and pay the price. The others are the unwitting accomplices of communism precisely because they have put their trust in intelligence, not God. Only theists, not humanists, can resist communism, and in the end, save man.

The view that man must worship either God or Stalin faces many formidable theoretical difficulties and has the most mischievous practical consequences. For one thing the disjunction is neither exhaustive nor exclusive. There exists a not inconsiderable body of men who worship both, even without counting those like the Dean of Canterbury and the Patriarch of the Russian Synod, and a still larger body who worship neither. After all, religious faiths have been compatible with the most diverse social principles. Not a single policy about empirical arrangements in human life can be logically derived from transcendental religious premises or from propositions of rational theology.

. . .

Deeply religious men speak with the same divided counsels as non-religious men about the specific problems of war, peace, poverty and foreign policy which must find empirical solutions if communism's false answers are to be rejected. Precisely because, as Chambers admits in an unguarded moment, "religion is not ethics or social reform," it is neither necessary nor sufficient for the discovery of the social programs and political strategy essential to the survival of freedom. Here there is no substitute for creative intelligence.

At one point Chambers invokes against liberalism and humanism, the theology of Barth, Dostoevsky and Kierkegaard without awareness of the irony in these references. The first is a "neutralist" in the current secular struggle; the second, perhaps the greatest dramatist of the human spirit but no friend of a free society; the third taught that between God's purposes in eternity and human purposes in history there is an "infinite qualitative difference." The fact that some of Chambers' fellow-Quakers are appeasers of Stalin while others are valiant fighters in the cause of freedom is enough to establish the irrelevance of his theology to his politics.

Indeed, Chambers has reflected poorly about the facts of his own disillusionment with communism. He writes dramatically of the "screams" of the victims of communism, of the shattering effect of these messages from souls in torment on even hardened Communists.

He is silent about the fact that the truth about the Moscow trials, to whose victims' screams he was originally deaf, was first proclaimed by John Dewey. While Chambers still worked for Stalin's underground, it was *they* who sought to arouse the world to the painful knowledge he is now frantically urging on it. He glosses over the fact that he himself closed his ears to the screams of the victims until his own life was threatened by Stalin's agents, and that in his hour of flight, it was to the party of Man that he turned for aid first of all.

Chambers does not consider the possibility that the opposition of genuine American liberals to the cultural and physical terror of the Kremlin was deeper and more sustained than that of any other group because it was fed by a passion for freedom, and an opposition to all forms of authoritarianism. One would have thought it obvious that Franco, Hitler and Mussolini, and other dictators with religious faith or support, have more in common with Stalin and the Politburo than either group has with the liberals and humanists Chambers condemns.

· · ·

It is unfortunate that Chambers could not have given a wiser and more generous expression to his faith. The logic by which he now classifies liberals and humanists with the Communists is not unlike the logic by which, when a Communist, he classified them as Fascists. Stalinism permits no loyal opposition, for opposition, the lifeblood of democracy, is the enemy in the politics of every totalitarianism. I should hope that Chambers himself would recoil from the implications of his present view that there is no loyal political opposition outside the Faith. When heresy is identified with the enemy, we shall have seen the end of democracy.

Since Chambers is a self-declared mystic and irrationalist, it is pointless to take issue with him on matters he regards as transcending human intelligence. But in the very interest of religious freedom itself, as well as of the effective struggle for democracy, it is necessary to repudiate his contrast between faith in God on the one hand, and intelligence and scientific method on the other, and his further equation of intelligence and scientific method with communism. This is a monstrous piece of dogmatism and a gratuitous gift to communism. It no more follows that faith in intelligence and scientific method must lead to torture and deaths in the cellars of the Lubianka than that faith in God must lead to the Inquisition or the rack and the stake.

. . .

It remains to ask what kind of man is portrayed in this massive book and in the multiplicity of lives he has led. The first and lasting impression is of a man who has suffered much, whose humility is born of a genuine surprise at his own tenacity and survival. These seem to him to be the result of a divine grace, unearned yet partly paid for by a willingness to be a witness to things secular and divine, irrespective of personal consequences. There is also a great honesty in the book, even if it is incomplete about the natural history of his break and conversion. Above all, one is moved by the magnificent courage of this stubborn and sensitive man, who refused to die to please Stalin, who built a new life, threw it away to atone for his past, and found it again. May it inspire others who until now have feared the wolf-pack of the anti anti-Communists to come forward to testify to the truth not only for the sake of their own country but for the sake of their fellow-men everwhere.

On another level, one senses that Chambers has always been a man of feeling, always more interested in salvation of one kind or another than in disciplined thought. The result is an intellectual impatience, a hunger for absolutes, a failure of intelligence concealed in a surge of rapture or in a total commitment to action which requires a

basis in irrational belief to sustain and renew itself. From the mysteries of dialectical materialism to the mysteries of dialectical theology is
no great leap.

The American experience itself is after all the best answer to Chambers. For its secular humanism has developed gradually through grudg-
ing tolerance of religious differences to positive respect for all religious beliefs or disbeliefs. No longer is any man's spiritual freedom
threatened with the doctrinal either-ors of fanatical sectariansm. It is
not unlikely that the same humanistic spirit may be the best defense
on a world scale against the Communist crusade because it can unite
all human beings who, despite their religious differences about first
and last things, value truth, justice, kindness and freedom among men.
For these values are justified both intrinsically and by their consequences, not by their alleged presuppositions.

Chambers' book (a Book of the Month Club choice for June) will
be widely read and deservedly so. That is why it seems to me all the
more necessary to conclude by saying that in the war for human freedom the twice born life of Whittaker Chambers is a tragic casualty.
Instructive to the last about the mortal threat of the Communist movement, for which we should be deeply grateful to him, it does not offer
us an intelligent guide to victory or even survival.

6

IRVING HOWE

God, Man and Stalin

NATION, MAY 24, 1952

T HAT WHITTAKER CHAMBERS told the truth and Alger Hiss did not, seems to me highly probable. Personal tragedy though their confrontation was, it had another, almost abstract quality: the political course of the thirties made it inevitable that, quite apart from this well-groomed man and that unkempt one, there be a clash between two men, one a liberal who was recruited from the idealistic wing of public service, the other a former Communist who repudiated his past and then, as *Witness* testifies, swung to the politics of the far right. If not these two, then two others; if not their shapes and accents, other shapes and accents. And that is why most of the journalistic speculation on their personalities proved so ephemeral: for what did it finally matter whether Hiss was a likable man or Chambers an overwrought one? what did it matter when at stake was the commitment of those popular-front liberals who had persisted in treating Stalinism as an accepted part of "the Left" and why should serious people have puzzled for long over the private motives of Chambers or Hiss when Stalinism itself remained to be studied and analyzed?

Now Chambers has told his story and put down his ideas. *Wit-*

ness is a fascinating grab-bag: autobiography, account of underground work, religious tract, attempt at an explanation of Stalinism. As confession it has an almost classical stature: whatever opinions Chambers may now superimpose on his memory, the narrative itself demands the attention of anyone interested in modern politics. As autobiography, the book is embarrassing: Chambers' memoir of his family seems a needless act of masochism while the portrait of his adult self suggests a man whose total sincerity is uncomplicated by humor, irony, or persuasive humility.

The most remarkable fact about *Witness* is that as a work of ideas it should be so ragged and patchy. In all its 800 pages there is hardly a sustained passage of, say, five thousand words to a serious development of thought; everything breaks down into sermon, reminiscence, self-mortification, and self-justification. Service in the G.P.U. is not, to be sure, the best training for the life of the mind: but there is something in Chambers' flair for intellectual melodrama that seems particular to our time and to the kind of personality always hungry for absolutes of faith. Writes Chambers: "I was not seeking ethics; I was seeking God. My need was to be a practicing Christian in the same sense that I had been a practicing Communist." A little time spent in "seeking ethics" or even a breather from "seeking" anything, might seem to have been in order.

The world, as Chambers sees it, is split between those who acknowledge the primacy of God and those who assert the primary of man; from this fundamental division follows a struggle between morality and murder, with communism merely the final version of the rationalist heresy; and the one hope for the world is a return to Christian virtue, the ethic of mercy. These views Chambers announces with an air of abject righteousness. Indifferent of the caution that the sin of pride takes no more extreme form than a belief in God as one's personal *deus ex machina*, he several times acknowledges a Mover at his elbow and declares the appointment of Thomas Murphy as government prosecutor in the Hiss case to be evidence that "It pleased God to have in readiness a man." From *Witness* an unsympathetic reader might, in fact, conclude that God spent the past several years as a special aide to the House Committee on Un-American Activities.

In reading this book one is non-plussed by the way its polemics violate its declared values. A few illustrations may suggest the quality of Chambers' thought:

Again and again he declares himself interested in presenting the facts. Without questioning his personal story, I must doubt his capacity as a historian and social observer. It is not true that Trotsky "led in person" the Bolshevik troops that suppressed the Krondstadt rebellion. It is not true that "Lenin gave up listening to music because of the emotional havoc it played with him"; the man merely said, if Gorky's report of a casual remark be credited, that music made him want to stroke heads at a time when he felt it necessary to make revolutions. It is not true that "Communists are *invariably* as prurient as gutter urchins." It is an exaggeration to say that in the 1927 faction fight in the United States Communist Party, dirty as it was, each side "prompted scandalous whispering campaigns, in which embezzlement of party money, homosexuality, and stool pigeon were the *preferred* whispers." And it is wild exaggeration to assert that the Communist agents in Washington, dangerous as they were, "If only in prompting the triumph of communism in China, have *decisively* changed the history of Asia, of the United States, and therefore, *of the entire world* (italics mine—I. H.)." Mao, alas, recruited his armies in the valley of Yenan, not the bars of Washington.

Chambers' extreme political turn has dizzied his historical sense. By noting that Alger Hiss was counsel for the Nye committee during the 'thirties, he tries to discredit its exposure of the munitions industry. "The penetration of the United States government by the Communist Party," adds Chambers, "coincided with a mood in the nation which light-heartedly baited the men who manufactured the armaments indispensable to its defense as 'Merchants of Death.'" But surely more was involved: the Nye committee revealed that some arms manufacturers had not hesitated to sell in bulk to Hitler, that their profits had been unconscionably high, that some had pressured both sides in the Chaco to buy their products and thus to prolong the war. The truth of these disclosures does not depend on whether Hiss was counsel for the committee that made them.

Chambers complains bitterly, and with justice, about the smears he has suffered from many Hiss supporters. Unfortunately, he is not himself above the use of similar methods. One of Hiss's attorneys was Harold Rosenwald, about whose face Chambers darkly pronounces: "I had seen dozens much like it in my time." The notion that people can be "placed" politically by the shape of their faces, is both preposterous and, at least in this century, sinister. It may be that Rosenwald does hold the political views Chambers hints at, but this attribution must seem completely shabby when it rests on nothing more than the fact that Rosenwald worked for O. John Rogge in the Attorney General's office and that Rogge "is now the legal representative of the Tito government."

In the course of breaking away from Stalinism, Chambers came to feel that "it is just as evil to kill the Czar and his family . . . as it is to starve two million peasants or slave laborers to death." What, if anything, does this highly charged statement mean? Coming from a pacifist, it would be perfectly clear, for it would suggest that killing is forbidden under any circumstances. We might then hope that to hear as a sequel that "It is just as evil to kill 60,000 civilians in Hiroshima as it was to kill the Czar and his family." But Chambers is not a pacifist, he is willing to "struggle against (communism) by all means, including arms." So the evil of killing the Czar cannot for him be simply that it was a killing, but must be that it was an unjustified killing—which leaves him with the moral enormity: "Several *unjustified* killings are just as evil as two million unjustified killings."

Throughout the book Chambers praises the Christian virtues of humility and meekness. Unfortunately, this credo does not prevent him from declaring "the left-wing intellectuals of almost every feather" to have been Hiss supporters and then from calling them "puffins, shimmers, skuas, and boobies." These delicate designations prompt one to remind Chambers that a good many "left-wing intellectuals" of one or another feather—those who truly deserved to be called "left" and "intellectual"—fought a minority battle against Stalinism at a time when both he and Hiss were at the service of Messrs. Yagoda and Yezhov.*

. . .

What is Stalinism? It is evil, declares Chambers; a proposition neither disputable nor enlightening. Nowhere in his 800 pages does he attempt sustained definition or description, nowhere does he bound the shape of the evil. He seems unconcerned to examine the workings of Russian society, the social rule of the Western Stalinist parties, the relations of the Asian parties to native nationalism. And with good reason. If you believe that the two great camps of the world prepare for battle under the banners, Faith in Man and Faith in God, what is the point of close study and fine distinctions? You need only sound the trumpets.

Almost unwittingly, Chambers moves toward the view that the source of our troubles is the Enlightenment: "The crisis of the Western world exists to the degree in which it is indifferent to God." The French Revolution becomes the villain of history, its progeny every godless society of our time. Chambers accepts, of course, the common, crude identification of Stalin's totalitarianism with Lenin's revolutionary state; the New Deal was a social revolution which crippled

---

* *Genrikh Yagoda and Nikolai Yezhov were chiefs of the Soviet security police.*

"the power of business"; and the motto of "the welfare state" is best expressed by his former associate, Colonel Bykov: "Who pays is boss, and who takes money must also give something." Everyone might thus be lumped together: Voltaire, Jefferson, Lenin, Roosevelt, Hitler, Stalin; not all equally evil; but all, apparently, "indifferent to God. " A man who thinks in such patterns can hardly be expected to notice—or have much reason to care—that Stalinism and fascism, while symmetrical in their political devices, have different historical origins, class structures, political ideologies, and social rationales. Or that the Keynesian measures of the New Deal, far from constituting a revolution, proved a crutch for a stumbling capitalism.

Chambers' approach to history rests, finally, on no social theory at all; it is a return to Manichean demonology. Since for him everything depends on whether one takes God or man to be primary, he can write that "as Communists, Stalin and the Stalinists were absolutely justified in making the Purge. From a Communist point of view, Stalin could have taken no other course. . . . In that fact lay the evidence that communism is absolutely evil. The human horror was not evil, it was the sad consequences of evil." The first two of these sentences are historically false: various Communists opposed the purge and proposed other courses of action, among them the removal of Stalin from power. The last sentence is shocking in its moral callousness. In effect, Chambers is saying that those of us who attack Stalinism for its inhumanity are sentimental, lacking in his austere disdain for what he calls "formless good will." Is it, however, more important to attack Stalin for disbelieving in the primacy of God than for killing millions of men? If the killing is to be regarded as a mere "consequence" of first principles, specific moral criticism of it can only seem superficial. But, in fact, the purges were the result of a decision by men in power, a decision for which they must be held responsible. A society is to be judged less by its philosophical premise about God and man, if it has any, than by its actual treatment of men; "the human horror of the purge" was evil, not merely "sad." What matters is not the devil's metaphysics, but his morals.

Chambers' major insight into the problem of Stalinism—and an acute one—is his insistence that in this era of permanent crisis it provides a faith, a challenge, even an ideal. Feeding on crisis, Stalinism offers a vision. "The vision inspires. The crisis impels. The working-man is chiefly moved by the crisis. The educated man is chiefly moved by the vision." This is an important observation and a necessary corrective to vulgar theories which make of Stalinism mainly an atavistic drive for power. But Chambers, ignoring the fact that the vision of Stalinism is corrupt, treats it is as if it were a revolutionary movement in the Marxist sense. He takes it as a legitimate form of socialism, and pays slight attention to the counter-revolution that occurred in Russia during the very years he was underground.

Is this an academic matter? Not at all: for the essence of Stalinism, in its Russian form, is that it rests on a new kind of bureaucratic ruling class which engaged in "primitive accumulation" by destroying the revolutionary generation and appropriating to itself total economic and political power. Outside of Russia, Stalinism utilizes the socialist tradition of Europe and the nationalist sentiment of Asia for its domestic class needs and international power maneuvers. A unique blend of reactionary and pseudo-revolutionary appeals, Stalinism attracts, in this age of crisis and decay, all those who feel the world must be changed but lack the understanding or energy to change it in a libertarian direction. Dynamic but not progressive, anticapitalist but not socialist, Stalinism causes, in the words of Marx, all the old crap to rise to the top; under its domination, the best impulses of modern man are directed toward the worst consequences. And the problem for the historian is to determine precisely the blend of seemingly contradictory elements that Stalinism comprises.

Chambers himself provides an anecdote which dramatically confirms these remarks. His boss in the underground, Colonel Bykov, was a perfect specimen of the new Stalinist man, the Gletkin type: coarse, obedient, unintellectual, brutal. To Bykov, "the generation that had made the Revolution . . . seemed as alien and preposterous . . . as foreigners. They belonged to another species and he talked about them the way people talk about the beastly or amusing habits of cows and pigs." So disgusting was Bykov that Chambers felt, before introducing him to Hiss, that he would have to apologize for the Russian. Yet, after a brief conversation, Hiss found Bykov "impressive." Why? I would guess that it was the attraction of an extreme bureaucratic personality, of one who instinctively scorned the masses of people for another who had been trained to think of them as objects for benevolent manipulation. If Hiss had possessed a trace of revolutionary or liberal spirit, he would have shuddered at the sight of Bykov, he would have seen on Bykov's hands the blood of Bukharin and Tomsky and thousands upon thousands of others.*

Where will Chambers go? His strength lies in a recognition that we live in an extreme situation; he agrees that "it is necessary to change the world." No longer a radical, scornful of liberals, convinced that "in the struggle against communism the conservative is all but helpless," he accepts, formally, the positions of those reactionaries *manques* who edit the *Freeman*. But only formally; for unlike them, he is drenched with the consciousness of crisis, he has none of their complacence, he continues a disturbed and dissatisfied man, given to extreme gestures

---

Nikolai Ivanovich Bukharin was a Soviet politician and intellectual. He opposed Stalin's proposed collectivization of agriculture in 1928 and lost his Politburo post within a year. Arrested in 1937, Bukharin was tried in March 1938 as part of the Trial of the Twenty-one for conspiring to overthrow the Soviet state. He "confessed" and was shot by the NKVD, the Soviet secret police. Mikhail Tomsky was a member of the Soviet Central Committee. After being informed he was about to be arrested by the NKVD, he committed suicide in 1936.

and ultimate statements. What remains? Only the fact that estranged personality and reactionary opinion form an explosive mixture.

In his final sentence Chambers hints that he believes a third world war both inevitable and necessary. Yet he yearns for some spiritual reformation, a turn to God. What likelihood there is that spiritual or any other desired values would survive in a world-wide atomic war, he does not discuss. Would there, in any case, be much point in reminding him that religious faith has rarely prevented despots from being despotic? That many of our most precious concepts of liberty are the work of skeptics? That Stalinism thrives in pious Rome as in worldly Paris? That it wins supporters in an Orient which had not known a loss of religious faith comparable to that of the West? That if Stalin is an atheist, Franco is a believer? That the priests in Russia pray for Stalin as in Germany they prayed for Hitler?

Very little point, I fear; little more than to have told him during the 'thirties that Stalinism was betraying the German workers to Hitler or by its trials and purges murdering thousands of innocent people. Those who abandon a father below are all too ready for a father above. But this shift of faith does not remove the gnawing problems which, if left unsolved, will drive still more people to Stalinism; it gives the opponents of the totalitarian state no strategy, no program with which to remake the world; it makes our situation appear even more desperate than it already is. For if Chambers is right in believing the major bulwark against Stalin to be faith in God, then it is time for men of conviction and courage to take to the hills.

7

ELMER DAVIS

History in Doublethink

SATURDAY REVIEW, JUNE 28, 1952

HOW LONG WILL THESE ex-Communists and ex-Sympathizers abuse the patience of the vast majority which had sense enough never to be Communists or sympathizers at all? They have a constitutional right, of course, to tell us what we must do to be saved; as they have always done. Twenty years ago they were telling us the direct opposite of what they tell us now; but they were just as sure then as now that they had the sole and sufficient key to salvation, and that those who did not accept it were forever damned. One becomes bored.

The arrogance of the ex-Communists is the most irritating thing about them, but not the most dangerous; and for that arrogance they have, in this country, official countenance. Congressional committees always seem willing to take the word of an ex-Communist against that of a man who never was a Communist. This preference may seem in contradiction to the stringent provisions of the McCarran Internal Security Act against the admission into this country of ex-Communists from abroad; but those provisions are only a phase of the protective tariff. The lucrative home market for exposures and revelations must be protected for domestic industry against the pauper labor of Europe. With this Congressional benediction there is some excuse for the ex-Communists to think they are a superior species.

But they thought that when they were Communists, too; through a hundred-and-eighty-degree turn in their opinions they have clung to this certainty of their superiority to the unsaved—and to the concomitant certainty that their dogmas, whatever they may be, are complete, perfect and infallible. This is the mark of the *anima naturaliter totalitariana*; for I suspect it is not so much that Communism is an ineradicable taint, its after-effects lingering in the system after the patient appears to be completely cured, as that it is people of this habit of mind who are most likely to become Communists. It is no accident that so many ex-Communists have become extreme reactionaries; it is remarkable only that some few of them have escaped into sanity. Aside from these saving few, Communist and ex-Communist are only species of the same genus; and I do not see why we should pay any more attention to them now than we did then.

For it is worth remembering, and worth reminding the young— before the ex-Communists pervert history any further—that not very many people did pay attention to them, even twenty years ago when what was then the American way of life (many people thought it was the only way) had come pretty close to breakdown. Some few thought they had found the answer in Technocracy, a somewhat more numerous few in Communism; but most people preferred to try another of the American ways of life; in the Presidential election of 1932, the Communists got a hundred thousand votes out of forty million. In the "intellectual" world the infection was stronger than elsewhere, yet even this turned out to be no more than a temporary nuisance. It spoiled some potentially good writers, it made considerable noise for a while; but it passed like any other fad, leaving as perhaps its principal legacy the angry writings of ex-Communists turned reactionary, who are still telling us what we must do to be saved. Where is their claim to authority? Not in their record.

. . .

But they seem able to persuade some people who were not there that their aberration was an all but universal aberration. Whittaker Chambers tells us that "from 1930 on a small intellectual army passed over to the Communist party." So it did, and a small army can look like a large army to a man who is in the midst of it; marching in step with his comrades, he might never notice the far larger army on the next road that is headed in the other direction. Alistair Cooke, who was not among us in those days, thought that in Alger Hiss a generation was on trial. That was not true even of his generation of "intellectuals"— not even of young intellectuals who graduated from college, looked around them, and could see no jobs. Some of them fell for Communism; most did not. I suspect that Cooke's friends include some ex-Communists who cannot bring themselves to admit that their error was at all unusual; who must persuade themselves, that if minds of their quality were deluded, all other minds must have been deluded, too.

Deceiving others is not yet too easy; men may write books and editorials and magazine articles, but evidence to the contrary is still available in the libraries. The first essential is to deceive one's self; and that, to the totalitarian mind (whether Communist or ex-Communist), offers little difficulty.

> Control of the past depends above all on the training of the memory. To make sure that all written records agree with the orthodoxy of the moment is merely a mechanical act. But it is also necessary to remember that events happened in the desired manner. And if it is necessary to rearrange one's memories or to tamper with written records, then it is necessary to forget that one has done so.

So wrote Emmanuel Goldstein in "The Theory and Practice of Oligarchical Collectivism" (quoted by George Orwell in *1984*). This, of course, is the well known art of Doublethink; Communists have to learn it, and ex-Communists find it hard to forget. And those of them who have bounced back all the way from one extreme to another find it easier to keep practicing Doublethink because there is one cardinal principle that they have carried with them. Now they admit it is black; but then and now they insist that there is no such thing as gray. If this requires a man to misread history, that is a small matter, so long as it enables him to retain confidence in his own intellectual integrity. And it would be unfair to say that he tries to persuade others to misread history; he remembers that events happened in the desired manner.

These reflections are obviously evoked by the great hullabaloo over *Witness,* and will, I presume, be denounced as part of the "moral lynching" of Whittaker Chambers. Well, on the evidence as known, I think Chambers told the truth about his relations with Hiss; I incline to believe him (with some reservations) about most of the other people involved in subversive activities; and he writes with cogency and authority about the strange and turbid inner world of Whittaker Chambers. But he seems to have understood little of what was going on around him, as is amply proved by his misinterpretations of history cited in the *Saturday Review* by Dr. Schlesinger and Professor Morris (*SR* May 24, 1952). A man who felt that he was returning in 1938 to the same world he had left in 1925, and who seems seriously to have accepted the suggestion that the Roosevelt administration might have him shot, had little awareness of objective reality.

• • •

The reason, of course, is obvious: Communism and the reaction from Communism had been the great fact in Chambers's life; it was inconceivable to him that it was not the great fact, if not in the life of all other individuals, at least in that of the society in which he existed. He quotes, and accepts, Krivitzky's remark that "there are only revolutionists and counter-revolutionists"; which Chambers underlines by adding that "in action there is no middle ground." Yet one of the most protuberant facts of the history of the past twenty years is that there is a middle ground: and that in America and Western Europe the people who hold that middle ground have defeated both extremes. This is a matter of record; but since it doesn't fit in with the divinely handed down interpretation of history it is necessary to remember that events happened in the desired manner, regardless of the facts.

Greater men than Chambers share this habit of mind. I do not suppose that John Dos Passos was ever a Communist; but certainly his sympathies, twenty or thirty years ago, were as near to the red end of the spectrum as they are now to the ultra-violet. At each end, he looked at the world through the appropriately colored glasses; which accounts for his seeing many things so clearly and not seeing many other things at all. He now feels that "we live in a society dedicated to its own destruction. How can it be," he asks, "that in a few short years we have sunk so low?"

The answer is easy: we haven't—except in the opinion of a man who, instead of contrasting 1952 with 1932, merely contrasts his own ideologies of those years.

By coincidence there appeared in print, at about the same time as Dos Passos's melancholy views, a magazine advertisement which shares his opinion and even echoes his words. "We blush for America," says this advertisement; "for to what heights have we risen that we can fall so low?" The particular fall deplored by the advertiser was the repudiation of the terms extorted from General Colson on Koje Island by the kidnappers of General Dodd.* This advertisement is signed by a business establishment, and it is perhaps only another coincidence that its address is right around the corner from Communist headquarters and its argument closely follows the current Communist line about Korea. But the touch of Doublethink is on it; and so it is on Dos Passos's concept of the present state of the nation.

Give Dos Passos credit for courage, however—more than most of the genuine blown-in-the-glass ex-Communists display. "If," he says, "the United States is doomed by forces of history too great for us to overcome, we will at least go down fighting." The people whose side he is on now have been going down fighting for the last twenty years— in 1932, when they predicted that grass would grow in the streets if Roosevelt were elected; in 1936, when the Liberty League demanded liberty for Du Ponts; and ever since. But—though Dos Passos appears not to have noticed it—they didn't go down before the Communists. Chambers and Dos Passos have been at, or near, both ends of the spectrum; at both ends, their thinking was of the same type; and at both ends, Roosevelt licked them. No wonder they detest his memory.

Eleven years ago, when Dos Passos was indulging in a brief interlude of objectivity before going the rest of the way from one extreme to the other, he wrote that "the history of the political notions of American intellectuals during the past twenty years is largely a record

---

* *On May 9, 1952, communists from the Korean War imprisoned on Koje Island seized the U.S. camp commandant, Brigadier General Francis T. Dodd, who had been appointed in February 1952 with orders to "tighten up discipline" at the camp. Brigadier General Charles F. Colson succeeded Dodd as camp commandant, but was replaced four days later by Brigadier General Haydon L. Boatner.*

of how far the fervor of their hopes for a better world could blind them to the realities under their noses." The disappointment of those hopes blinds them still; they admit now that black is black, not white; but they insist that gray is black, too. I can venture those criticisms of Dos Passos, for some of whose gifts I have much admiration, in the confidence that they will not disturb him at all: he has discounted all criticism beforehand. He is pretty sure that "the 'liberals' who control communications in the press and the radio and the schools and the colleges in this country have already crawled under the yoke of the Communist party"; we are not dues-paying members (maybe he thinks we are too parsimonious) but we are the dupes of a sinister hoax. Thus lightly to dismiss all contrary opinion no doubt helps a man to feel comfortable with himself; but I do not think it makes him a very useful guide to the people—a vast majority—who are not blind to the realities under their noses.

. . .

A curious thing about these ex-Communists is that they seem to derive a melancholy satisfaction from the conviction that they are on the losing side. A Chinese, just at present, might be excused for thinking so; but there is no evidence for it in American history, except as rewritten by Doublethink. I suspect the answer is that they are naturally religious, temperamentally inclined to view the world in terms of catastrophe and apocalypse; some day the heavens will be rolled up like a scroll: *dies irae, dies illa, solvit saeclum in favilla*; and they can view this with equanimity, since their personal salvation is secure. But once again, this makes them undependable guides for the vast majority which believes—as the vast majority of Americans has believed throughout our history, and has repeatedly proved—that something can be done about it, even if not so much as could be wished.

And the essential damage that could be done by these totalitarian thinkers—totalitarian no matter which end of the spectrum they may be on—would be to convince other people that there is no use trying to do anything about it; that those who are trying are only crypto-Communists even if they may not know it. A notable example is Chambers's comments on the New Deal revolution; which, as he and Senator Taft agree, is a Socialist revolution in the name of liberalism. It has been amply pointed out that people who call it that do not know what Socialism means; but Chambers does indeed hit its essential point when he calls it "a shift of power from business to Government." It was that, and I happen to believe that was a good idea—always provided that you do not give excessive power to Government; as we have not. (Even Chambers has to acknowledge that it was Government, after all, which convicted Hiss.)

Chambers apparently does not approve of that shift, and thinks we were better off when business had the power. It is the privilege of any citizen to think so; but when he says "it was a struggle for revolutionary power, which in our age is always a struggle for control of the masses," he confuses, or is likely to make his readers confuse, two kinds of revolutions carried out by two different methods. The Roosevelt revolution was the sixth we have had; and like all the others, it stopped before it went too far. There was a revolution in the early days of independence, a counter-revolution in 1787, a counter-counter-revolution in 1800; none of them found it necesary to resort to the guns of a cruiser, the dispersal of an elected assembly by bayonets, or the mechanisms of the police state. We had another partial revolution in Jackson's day; still another, begun by the Congressional elections of 1866 and consummated twenty years later by the Supreme Court's decision that the Fourteenth Amendment protects corporations, transferred power from Government to business. The Roosevelt revolution merely reversed that. Chambers has a right to dislike the reversal, but when he implies that the Roosevelt revolution and Communist revolution differed only in degrees, whoever is deceived thereby is not wise.

All these are matters of record, and will remain so unless—which I do not expect—the Doublethinkers get control of the country and "make sure that all written records agree with the orthodoxy of the moment." Until then, they are more of a nuisance than a menace—as they were in the days when they thought that salvation was to be found in Moscow. They are religious people; as Dr. Schlesinger has pointed out, a man may be religious without feeling certain that he has the complete and unalterable final truth and that those who disagree with him are damned in time and eternity. But these people must feel that. Some of them, finding that final truth is not in Moscow, have sought and found it in Rome; hardier characters have become their own Popes, and are just as sure of their own infallibility as they were in the days when they parroted the resolutions of the Comintern.

. . .

There is another kind of thinking, which some religious people find not inconsonant with their view of the relations between man and God. I described it in these pages twenty years ago and it seems pertinent to quote that description now:

> To admit that there are questions which even our so impressive intelligence is unable to answer, and at the same time not to despair of the ability of the human race to find, eventually, better answers than we can reach as yet—to recognize that there is nothing to do but keep on trying as well as we can, and to be as content as we can with the small gains that in the course of the ages amount to something—that requires some courage and some balance.

That kind of thinking has played a great part in American history, from Benjamin Franklin to John Dewey; and it has worked. But the Communists about whom I was writing then had no use for it, nor have most of them now that they are ex-Communists. There must be a final truth and they must have it; experimental thinking is only sounding brass and tinkling cymbal; and if its successes are written in the record of American history from Jefferson (yes, and Hamilton) through Lincoln down to Franklin Roosevelt, that fact can be obliterated by remembering that events happened in the desired manner—by knowing that press and radio and schools and colleges are all controlled by the Communists and that the Roosevelt administration had its critics shot.

I repeat—one becomes bored.

8

KINGSLEY MARTIN

The Witness

NEW STATESMAN AND NATION,
JULY 1952

INFORMERS ARE USUALLY regarded as a detestable product of the Roman Empire, the Soviet Union and Nazi Germany. Yet they flourish in many countries today, including, strangely enough, the democratic United States. They are of many types, and there are many motives for delation. To have been a Communist, and to have served the Soviet Union and to have turned against it, are, in themselves, passwords to fame and fortune. Announce that you have repented and are prepared to reveal the horrors of Communism, and a swarm of journalists will be on your doorstep in the morning, lucrative invitations will reach you from the glossier magazines, and the F.B.I. will seek your co-operation in rooting out spies and traitors. Your past sins will be forgiven; safe from prison yourself, you may play your part in destroying your old friends. No wonder that thoughtful people tend, on principle, to dismiss the testimony of informers, while the massed public, credulous and hungry for sensation, gloats over revelations which may well contain a measure of truth, but which are almost certainly influenced by the popular demand for *autos da fe*. In such a situation it is indeed difficult to assess the value of any particular testimony. The fact that greed, fear, political partisanship and personal malice are motives for delation does not prove that some informers are not inspired by genuine patriotism, or a desire to atone for disloyalty of which they now repent.

In the seedy ranks of ex-Communist informers, Whittaker Chambers stands in a class by himself. He was a Communist spy who decided, he tells us, in much anguish and conflict of mind, to repudiate his former Communist faith, and to enter wholly into a life dedicated to God and anti-Communism. The public knows him as the man whose evidence convicted Alger Hiss, and the bizarre story of his upbringing, his activities as a spy, his work as one of the chief editors of *Time* magazine, and his long duel with Hiss, has recently been told in a long, effective, and often brilliantly written autobiography entitled *Witness*. Thousands now regard him as a kind of saint; the greater the sin, the more abject and complete the confession, the more holy the penitent. Others point to the less satisfactory aspects of the book; to its often false pathos, its undoubted cunning, to the gaps which a careful reader may notice in the confession. He refers with bitter resentment to suggestions by the supporters of Hiss that he may not always have been mentally stable—a suggestion which should surprise no one in view of the fact that Chambers reveals that he more than once contemplated suicide and at least once attempted it. Indeed he was brought up in a home where, as a child, he found it comforting to take a knife to bed with him, while his mother took an axe. His father and grandfather were drunkards and his grandmother lived in a locked room, sometimes trying to set the house on fire, and at others emerging to attempt murder.

For myself, I find the literary skill of Mr. Chambers more than offset by his sentimentality and self-pity. He tries throughout to present himself as a lonely and persecuted figure who, until near the end of the ordeal of the Hiss trial, was friendless, lacking financial and moral support. Loneliness is a state of mind and I would not question Chambers's claim to courage and independence. But his picture of himself as a lonely and persecuted figure is scarcely consistent with his backing by one of America's greatest publishing houses, whose timely generosity he gratefully acknowledges, or with the fact that the Congressional Committee, which heard his case against Hiss, was, like the F.B.I., delighted to discover so valuable a political ally.

The main importance of Chambers's book is that it attempts to raise the whole issue between himself and Hiss beyond its personal and its immediate political level. Mr. Chambers presents himself as a "witness"; not, he explains, a police witness in a trial, but a witness in the sense of a martyr—one who is prepared to die for a principle. Here, he suggests, is the battle between good and evil: Chambers the witness for Heaven; Hiss appearing for the Lord of Hell. Chambers, as befits a convert to Christianity, is careful often to speak affectionately of his enemy. The discerning reader, however, will notice that he was bitterly jealous of Hiss. Love and hatred contend in every reference to the Hiss household.

Early in the book Chambers tells us that once he was told by his mother to kill a chicken. It was only after the most profound conflict that he became, as he says, the family butcher. "Something in me, the deepest thing that makes me what I am, knows that it is wrong to kill anything. But there is something else—a necessity—which forces me to kill." He killed, he explains, whenever he had to, but always with a sense of guilt. This ambivalence is to be found throughout in his relations with Hiss. The role of informer, of killer, horrifies him. But there was something inside him which compelled him to go through with it. He hates himself, his victim and the society which has conditioned them both.

To satisfy his conscience Chambers is compelled wildly to exaggerate the influence of Hiss and of Communism in the United States. He explains that lack of hope in the future of capitalism may well lead other men, as it led him, into becoming an agent for the Soviet

Union. Indeed, he suggests that this is the logical end for any courageous man who follows reason alone. He then describes Washington
before and during the war as run by Communists and fellow-travelers. This part of the book will be, of course, most useful to
MacCarthyites [*sic*], who will love to read that "all the New Dealers I
had known were Communists or near-Communists." Chambers even
suggests that the triumph of Communism in China was really due to
the help of Washington Communists. He thinks that the concessions
to the Soviet Union at Yalta and San Francisco were due to the presence of Hiss on these occasions.

Men of Chambers's temperament desire a cause to which they
can wholly submit themselves. Any authoritative religion, Communism or another, will serve. Chambers worked with courage and devotion to Stalin. He left the Communist Party, if we may believe him,
for good reasons: because of the cruelty and ruthlessness of the
organisation; because of the absurdities of the purges by which today's
triumphant informers and inquisitors become tomorrow's traitors in
an unending series. Having thrown aside this evil religion, Chambers
substitutes a God who has much in common with Stalin. He tells us,
in a remarkable passage, that Communists are outside the human race.
Although as a Christian he tells us that there is always a hope of
salvation and repentance even for a Communist, he also says that in
the struggle loosed upon mankind by Communists, every man is absolved "from the bonds of common humanity with that breed," and
that it is "a pious act for him to raise his hand in any way against
them." Does a man as astute as Chambers really not see that he is here
again committing the sin of which he now repents? He describes a
man who leaves the Communist Party because in Russia he hears
screams; because of concentration camps; because of intolerance and
brutality. Chambers is not so simple a man that he can think that
Russia has a monopoly of cruelty and diabolism. Spain is a very religious country, but those who listen can hear screams from Madrid,

even though they may be muffled by diplomatic convenience or military necessity.

I wonder, too, whether Chambers happened to read a recent account in *Colliers*—I choose this example because he may buy the magazine at any bookstall—in which a doctor describes the system of torture used against political prisoners—perhaps Communists—by Peron's secret police? The worst enemies of the U.S.S.R. allege nothing more horrible than these revelations of the Catholic Argentine. If Chambers is an honest man, can he really believe that the Church in the world today is a safeguard against oppression, sadism, and the screams of the tortured heard in the night? And as a Quaker who believes that right and wrong are not to be tested by considerations of expediency, I cannot see how Chambers can escape the necessity of pacificism and the repudiation not only of Soviet philosophy, but also of that professed in Christian countries. He argues that the evil of killing is the violence "committed against the soul—the soul of the murderer as well as the murdered," and he quotes a conversation between Lady Astor and Stalin.

> How long are you going to keep on killing people?" Lady Astor would ask Stalin brightly. "As long as it is necessary," he answered, and asked in turn: "How many people were killed in the First World War? You killed that many people for nothing," he had added, "and you blame us for killing a handful for the most promising social experiment in history?

Chambers' comment is, "In terms of the modern mind, which excludes from its reasoning the undemonstrable fact of God, Stalin's answer was unanswerable. It could only be answered by another question: 'And man's soul?'" But what answer is that to Stalin's question?

Only gradually does the reader appreciate the enormity of the thesis which is put forward by Whittaker Chambers. The world is divided into Good and Evil; reason as understood since the Renaissance, leads a man logically step by step through liberalism to Communism, and Communism is the final evil. Against this, the system of the Devil, God fights, and the world will only be saved, even if it be physically destroyed, by the men of God. Thus, all the people we call liberals, and, above all, intellectuals, are enemies of society. They are men less courageous than Hiss, because they stop short of surrender to the Devil and try to improve society by reason and compromise, though this is a society which can, in fact, only be improved by acceptance of the mystical ways of God. There are passages in which Chambers' hatred of intellectuals recalls to mind the famous remark of the Nazi leader who said that every time he heard the word "culture" he felt for his revolver.

In short, Chambers appeals to that disappointed strata of society which hates, as he makes it clear that he hates, all those of established reputation; those who have any claims to authority as a result of privilege; a university training denied to him, or opportunity due to birth or money. Such men drift into Communist or Fascist parties in many countries. At the root of Chambers is hatred and bitter envy of a man like Hiss, once his friend. The jealousy and hatred that well up within him must not be directed consciously against Hiss, but concentrated as Communist hatred is directed, against the established order. Hiss must be a symbol, the representative of evil men, liberals, intellectuals, New Dealers, graduates of the Harvard Law School. These are the unconscious allies of Communism, servants of the Devil. Many of those who fear Communism but have also learnt to hate the existing order will find here aid and comfort. Whittaker Chambers is not any kind of Hitler, but *Witness* has much in common with *Mein Kampf.*

9

R E B E C C A   W E S T

Whittaker Chambers

A T L A N T I C   M O N T H L Y ,   J U N E   1 9 5 2

It IS WORTH WHILE TAKING some trouble to recognize the historical significance of the part played by Whittaker Chambers in the Hiss trial before reading *Witness*. For his own interpretation of it is often mistaken, owing to the defects of his qualities, and the explosive impact of the Hiss case on the spectators has given an illusory impression of uniqueness. But it could hardly have had such power to distress us had it been an isolated event. It was the most recent manifestation of a recurrent threat to society, which recurs because it is the work of mischievous human tendencies which appear to be ineradicable. It was yet another dervish trial.

There could be nothing more inappropriate to a court of law than the presence of a mob of dancing dervishes. But in they rush, and the examination of witnesses can hardly be carried on because of the commotion caused by the invaders, twirling and turning all over the courtroom, and the lawyers' speeches are not to be heard because of their holy howlings. Finally they take over the control of the proceedings. All attempts at deciding the accused person's guilt according to the facts of the case and the principles of law are abandoned. Whether his life is preserved or forfeited depends on which party line triumphs in the tumult. More and more people join the dervishes in their spinning and their screaming, and by the time they have frothed at the mouth and fallen to the ground the courtroom is wrecked. It may well happen that at the end of one of these dervish trials the whole of civilization will be wrecked.

These deplorable events occur only when there is a certain conjunction of circumstances. First of all, there must be a series of events which arouse the suspicion that a crime has been committed, and at the same time are so tangled that it is hard to verify or disprove that suspicion. The alleged crime must be of a certain magnitude and offensiveness, and it must be committed in a community split across by an ideological division. The people who in the first instance allege that the crime took place, and those who deny it, must be facing each other across that gulf. What happens after that, as Whittaker Chambers shows, depends on the character of the protagonists and the power of the community to resist moral infection.

Victorian England showed us artless but ominous specimens of the process. In the seventies Arthur Orton came from Australia and claimed to be Sir Roger Tichborne, who had disappeared twelve years before. During the long series of legal actions which followed, the urban industrialist population campaigned for the claimant, for the reason that the position of the landowners as the governing class seemed to them so arbitrary that they could easily imagine a great family suiting its own convenience by fraudulently disowning an eccentric head. In the eighties the politician Sir Charles Dilke was cited as correspondent by a fellow member of Parliament whose young wife had confessed to committing adultery with him throughout her married life. The confession was comically incredible, but nevertheless was believed, because at that time it was a reasonable supposition that no woman would tell such a story unless it were true, as she would be condemning herself to complete social death. But since Sir Charles was a republican and a champion of labor unions, breakers of political prejudice washed over the case and drowned the man who might have been the greatest statesman of his time.

During the nineties the dervish trial which was to surpass all others in frenzy took place in France. Captain Alfred Dreyfus was accused of espionage in the interests of Germany, and his guilt was asserted and denied by opponents more rancorous than those who had wrangled over Arthur Orton and Sir Charles Dilke, because the ideological issues involved were far graver. By this time the English urban populations which had supported the Tichborne claimant had seen their industrial masters wrest a share in political power from the old landowning classes, and were themselves preparing to demand a further partition for their own benefit. Of Dilke's two causes, republicanism was dead and labor unionism was on the way to triumph. But Dreyfusards and anti-Dreyfusards faced each other across an ideological gulf which still yawns deep and wide.

On one side, there was anti-Semitism, which is a threat against the very constitution of man. In refusing to judge Jewish individuals according to their merits, and in condemning the whole race, it rejects the empirical basis on which art and science are founded. It refuses to allow the exquisite machinery of our nerves to perform their miraculous task of collecting information about what is not ourselves. Against the anti-Semites were ranged the men who would not betray their humanity.

That was the disposition of the contending forces when the trial began. But the dervishes yelled and gyrated, and all was confusion. An abscess of hatred burst on the brain of France. Anti-Semitism was met by anti-Catholicism not less gross, and the whole French Army was condemned because certain French officers had been liars and forgers. Sane people ran about screaming insane propositions. It was even argued seriously that to protect the honor of the French Army it was necessary to pretend that the officers who had lied and forged had not done so, and that Dreyfus, who had committed no act of espionage, had done so, thus leaving the liars and forgers inside the Army and kicking the innocent man out.

There was rioting in French streets and rioting in the French mind. Most serious consequence of all was the common conviction that justice had not been done. Dreyfus was never acquitted by due process of any court of law. He was pardoned by the President of the French Republic in 1900 and six years later was acquitted by the Court of Appeal, which was thereby acting illegally, for it had power to order a retrial, which it refrained from doing because of the inflamed state of public opinion, but had no power to acquit the prisoner. So this result was unsatisfactory to Dreyfusards and anti-Dreyfusards alike, with a deep dissatisfaction. For Western man now needs the assurance that he lives under just laws justly administered, as much as he needs food and drink and shelter. This appetite has been slowly bred in our kind by Judaism and the Roman Empire, the Christian Church and secular culture, and it has now the force of an instinct.

As the Dreyfus case came to an end in France there began in Germany the case of Prince Philipp zu Eulenburg. There the accuser was a Jew, the journalist Maximilian Harden, and he acted as the agent of German liberalism in bringing charges of homosexuality against a Prussian junker who was an intimate friend of the Kaiser and a supporter of his absolutist tendencies. Here again the matter was not settled by due process of a court of law. The prosecution of Prince Philipp was abandoned and a wave of cynical distrust passed over Germany, affecting even the conservative element, which shifted its allegiance to the General Staff of the German Army, since it had always been hostile to Prince Philipp. Thus the First World War was brought a stage nearer.

When it had come and gone, France had to be rebuilt by men and women who had been children during the Dreyfus case, and had grown up in an atmosphere which made them feel distrust of their own community. That distrust has kept them in a state of political chaos ever since, and led to the fall of France in 1940. The Dreyfusards and the anti-Dreyfusards had said many things against each other which were far too brilliant to be forgotten; and at the back of the public mind was a hoarding scrawled with phrases which together composed an indictment against the whole of France, and a sensitive people depressed itself perpetually with self-satire. The Germans are not such lords of language as the French, and the scandal of Prince Philipp left few memorable passages of wit or rhetoric to haunt posterity; and the very existence of the Weimar Republic demonstrated that the struggle between the Hohenzollerns and liberalism had been settled. One might have though that nobody remembered the trial. But as soon as the Nazis came to power their actions showed that somebody had remembered it and was going to develop the dervish trial deliberately as a political weapon.

The Nazis burned down the Reichstag, which was in any case offensive to them as a symbol of representative government. They charged some innocent men with the crime, and did not trouble to make a watertight case against them. That way they could not lose. Their tougher supporters would affect to believe the accused guilty. Their simpler supporters would really believe it. Their simpler opponents would be induced by the trial to believe that Hitler had really been telling the truth when he claimed that there were dangerous revolutionaries about and that he alone could rout them. As for their shrewder opponents, they would see that the accused were innocent, and they would know what to think when van der Lubbe was hanged. They would realize that this government of professional revolutionaries which had seized power against the will of the people meant to use the courts not for the purpose of dispensing justice but for keeping its power. The man would be superhuman who did not move more cautiously after he had learned that piece of news.

The Reichstag trial was a novelty. All other dervish trials had started spontaneously, but this was artificially engendered as a means of making the population abandon resistance to an anti-democratic government. It worked so well that Stalin took it as a model for the purges by which he rooted out all actual and potential opposition, in preparation for the time when he would pursue an unpopular policy of amity with Hitler. This seemed the last metamorphosis of the dervish trial possible in our time, until the Hiss case revealed itself in all its monstrous fantasy.

This was something new and complicated. For it began spontaneously in one country and then was artificially developed on the same site but according to the desires of another country. Even to those of us who were old fashioned enough to reserve judgment on Hiss and Chambers until the courts had brought in their verdict, it was apparent that the case was being exploited for the benefits of the Soviet Union to the detriment of the United States. By the side of the many upright men and women who sincerely believed in the innocence of Alger Hiss and said so for the highest motives, there was ranged another army uninterested in any sort of innocence. Whether Hiss was guilty or not, an extremely able general was fighting a campaign on the terrain of this case, with a double purpose. First, the public was to be persuaded that it was an inherently absurd notion that anybody could be a Soviet spy, that there was a Communist underground, that Soviet Russia had a secret service, that a person reporting a case of Soviet espionage was thereby proving himself a lunatic or an imposter. Second, there was to be created in the United States precisely the same distrust of the law, the contempt for national institutions, the sense of pervading insecurity, which the Dreyfus case created in France. The dervishes who took over this trial howled and gyrated with the precision of the Rockettes; but the amateurs who had joined them frothed at the mouth in the old way. It is doubtful whether it can yet be estimated how much damage has been done to the courtroom.

. . .

It is strange how often *Witness* makes the Hiss case recede into the background and draws the attention to more important matters: to Grandfather Chambers, for example.

That old sinner was a brilliant newspaperman, a blusterer and a drunkard. He used to take his little grandsons on a tour of the Long Island saloons, in everyone of them swilling grandly, as if he were the imperial hog from which the imperial hogshead took its name, weaving and careening on his way home so that the boys had to help him across the road and onto the trolley. But no harm came to the children from these gross outings, no scar was left even on their exceptionally sensitive minds, for he had charity. A stream of warm and unqualified love flowed from him to them, and nothing he could do could harm them. This was not fair. His blustering was not merely violence, it was cruelty. It had withered up his wife and his son, the children's father. But towards the children he felt authentic love, and in his relationship with them he enjoyed the authentic immunity from sin of the saints.

He is only one of the people who were alive when Whittaker Chambers was a child, and now are dead, and are now raised by him from their graves, to walk through his book, in their living flesh, but stamped now with their immortal meaning. This is perhaps the greatest of all surprises disclosed by the Hiss case: that Whittaker Chambers should be capable of writing an autobiography so just and so massive in its resuscitation of the past that it often recalls the name of the master of all autobiographers, Aksakov.* The value of the book

---

* *Sergei Aksakov was a nineteenth-century Russian writer known for his partly fictionalized picture of country life in the days of serfdom* (Family Chronicle). *His* Years of Childhood *vividly describes his joyous youth and is considered one of the finest of Russian literary memoirs.*

does not depend simply on its painfully exceptional material, nor on the sincerity of the author. Whittaker Chambers writes as writers by vocation try to write, and he makes the further discoveries about reality, pushing another half-inch below the surface, which writers hope to make when they write.

He records his unique experience in its uniqueness, without recourse to used and general phrases. His prose rises again to the task of describing the intricate and ambitious misery of the home where he was brought up. It was the scene of a succession of inverted miracles: the empty cup was always filled by an unseen hand with a poisonous draught. The Chamberses were one of those middle-class families which drift into isolation as if they were criminals, though they have nothing so potentially profitable as a crime to their name, and who, since they are isolated, depress themselves still further by believing their fate to be unique. They had so little command over their surroundings that they were scarcely able to live in a house. The plumbing, the unpainted walls, the leaking roof, the dangling shutters, seemed to be given life by their owners' incompetence, and perpetually threatened to get the better to them. The situation was made worse, not better, when Chambers's spirited but plaintive mother determined to make counter-attacks on the hostile masonry and sanitation, and indulged in constructional flights of fancy which Chambers describes in passages suggesting visual forms as acutely illustrative of distress as Piranesi's *Carceri*.

Many of us who, like Chambers, endured rough weather in our childhood can match the instances he gives of adults who found themselves undeterred by any scruple from taunting a child with the poverty of its parents; and we have learned how unwelcome such reminiscences are, and how likely to be greeted with impatient suggestions that they are exaggerated or are the figments of self-pity. But Chambers makes his point, and goes further in offending against the contemporary convention that, though all generations are made of the same stuff, the most recent generation is always in the right in its relations to the preceding one. He states candidly that his parents failed their children again and again, but he admits that they too had been failed by their parents. The mainspring of his father's nature had been broken by *his* father's bullying; and his mother had been let with a broken wing and an excessive disposition to soaring flight by the feckless romantics who had brought her into the world. Moreover, he and his brother had failed their parents. He confesses that they held it against their tormented mother that, because their father would not fulfill the duties of a father, "she was trying to be both father and mother." And by an anecdote concerning the cutting down of a clematis, which is both beautiful and horrible, he proves that his father was a starved man whose need should have pricked his family into finding some way of feeding him.

The double character of that anecdote reveals where Chambers's resistance to fashion leads him. He admits the hideousness of life, writing of the madness of his grandmother and the despair and suicide of his brother as the calamities that they were. "I used to wish that the house would burn down with all its horrors." But he also admits the beauty of life. For he can given an account of a man who is visited by misfortune and include in it the reason why he felt his misfortunes to be a breach of a firm promise made him by the universe. The particular manifestation of beauty which he took as a promise emerges during the book as a finely drawn character: as, indeed, the third protagonist in the Hiss case. It is a character which has appeared in other books, most notably, perhaps, in *Huckleberry Finn*. It is the American countryside.

The forty-year-old cherry trees on the Merrick Road, the aseptic white village houses, the black pyramidal old cypresses standing alone, the green columnar young cypresses growing in groves, the streams slipping over sandy bottoms through the birch and swamp-maple woods, the special stream where all the robins bathed at dawn, the other special stream where the cardinal flower could be found, the fleets of clouds riding over the Long Island salt marshes, the silent invasion of the tides through the cattails, the surf pounding on the beaches—the boy saw in that landscape a fertile tranquility that accused the profitless convulsions of his home life and consoled him for them. We see through his eyes the miraculous quality of the American landscape which touches and astounds all European visitors. The opaque hills and plains give the same sense of purity as the transparent waters of a spring. Henry James, returning after many years of expatriation, recognized this appearance and attributed it to the lack of the stains left by that soiled fabric, history. The land has still that innocent look, save where it is actually covered by buildings. Some corrupting process, at work in all the older continents, seems here to have been suspended.

To Whittaker Chambers the American countryside was not merely earth that had a look of purity. It was a person that made claims that offered help. When he and Alger Hiss visited the derelict farmhouse in Maryland, the two men were not alone. For as the features of a face, as the limbs of a body, were the wisteria that smothered the porch and pushed through the shingles of the roof, the two cedars tall beside the barn, the apple and sour cherry trees in the orchard, the wind that blew along the valley through the unscythed grass. Later when Chambers was about to leave the Party and break with Hiss, he went back to see that farm. The neighborhood retained him. He now owns and works a large and productive farm in those parts, and his account of the sacrifices that he and his family have made to acquire that farm, and the joy they find in working it, reveals that he belongs to a certain well-recognized order of man. He believes that nature is in an aspect of God, and that to grow crops and tend herds is a means of establishing communication with God. He believes that he communicates with God and that God communicates with him. He is, in fact, a Christian mystic of the pantheist school, a spiritual descendant of Eckhart and Boehme and Angelus Silesius.

It is one of the great jokes of history that the dragnet of a Washington committee should have fetched up this man of all men to take part in a dervish trial. For the Moslem dervish is a priest, and so too is the Western dervish of the sort that promotes trials. He is a priest who desires to preserve some institution: to guard the integrity of parliamentary government by extending its basis or restricting it; to retain the monarchy or convert the constitution into a republic; to save the honor of the Army or of the Freemasons; to maintain the unbreached power of Nazi or Bolshevik totalitarianism; to rout all who cast aspersions on the American administrative class; to rout all who impede the operations of the Communist Party. But a mystic distrusts all institutions. No matter whether they are religious or secular, he fears lest the thickness of their walls shall prevent man from hearing when God speaks to him. For that reason he is apt to fall out with the defenders of the most respectable institutions; so he is bound to feel an exalted repugnance when he sees dervishes at work on a trial profaning the truth and casting away the divine gift of reason in order to serve institutional interests. He can make no compromise when he is involved in such a trial. He cannot even make the necessary adjustments. He goes forward on the path dictated by his private revelation, no matter what road the institutionalist engaged in the trial may be following. The resultant collision is bound to be on a sidereal scale, drawing sparks bright as comets.

. . .

Witness demonstrates the strength of the mystic and his use to society. Though he may be discomposed by the howling and gyrating of the dervishes, he leans on his understanding with God. But the book also demonstrates the weakness of the mystic, and explains why the Church has always feared negative dissenters, who fall away from lack of faith, far less than the positive dissenters, who question authority because fullness of faith persuades them that they receive direct instruction from God.

To reach the state of intense perception which makes a mystic, a man must be unselfish but egotistical. He must be supremely interested in finding out the truth concerning the universe, and not at all interested in securing his own well-being in it. But he must cultivate inattention to what others tell him and concentrate on his own experience. This gives his relationships a peculiar character. It is as if he were a telephone subscriber on terms which enabled him to make outgoing calls but prevented him from receiving incoming calls. Whittaker Chambers obviously feels deep love for his wife and his mother. His pantheist turn of mind makes us see them in terms of the countryside: his wife a sheltering hillside which keeps the wind off the pastures, his mother a winding valley where running water and wild woods make one picturesque surprise after another. But few could read of these women without wanting to hurry to them with hot milk and aspirins. Obviously, he has given them great happiness, but they must be very, very tired. There was at work in him something at once less and greater than human nature when he prepared an ingeniously didactic suicide, as morally unassailable as a suicide may be, and yet forgot the burden he would thereby have laid on the family.

Again, he expresses gratitude to the men who stood by him during his ordeal, the newspapermen and the lawyers and the politicians and the friends. But he also describes how he pursued a tortuous policy in his testimony, disclosing this piece of evidence and withholding that, with the intention of keeping true the moral balances of his relationship with Hiss. He felt under an obligation to supply the authorities with information which would enable them to convince a court of law that Hiss had been a Communist, but he also felt under an obligation to shield Hiss from suffering, as far as was possible, so he supplied the authorities with just the amount of information which he thought would be sufficient to convince a court of law, reserving the rest and parting with it only gradually as it became evident that his calculations had been faulty. He obviously had no sense of guilt regarding the unnecessary trouble to which he put his supporters by leaving holes in his case, to say nothing of the jeopardy in which he places the anti-Communist cause, and the encouragement he gave his non-Communist opponents to believe that he was a liar.

There is also support in *Witness* for a still more serious charge against the mystic: that because of his visions he speaks with authority, and that those who listen to him may be misled when he deals with subjects other than those on which he has received divine instruction. Whittaker Chambers compels our respect by his account of his experiences, many of which have been determined by his membership in the Communist Party. It is therefore natural that we should listen to him when he analyzes Communism. But a large part of his analysis is demonstrably untrue, and, indeed, dangerous in its implications.

When he appeared before the grand jury, one of the jurors asked him what it meant to be a Communist, and he told three anecdotes to illustrate typical Communist behavior. He described how Djerjinsky,* when he was a young man in a Tsarist prison in Warsaw, insisted on being given the task of cleaning the latrine, holding that it was the duty of the most developed member of any community to take upon himself the lowliest tasks. He described how Eugene Leviné, the leader of the unsuccessful Bolshevik uprising in 1919, was told by the court-martial which tried him that he was under sentence of death, and answered, "We Communists are always under sentence of death." And he described how Sazonov, a prisoner in a Siberian camp, protested against the flogging of his fellow prisoners by drenching himself with kerosene and setting himself on fire and running about till he was

---

* *Felix Djerjinsky was the founder of the Soviet secret police.*

burned to death. These men illustrate the view which Whittaker Chambers still takes of the Communist Party: that it is a self-sacrificing and courageous body of idealists who fail only because they hold a materialist philosophy and thus reject God and separate man from Him.

Not one of these anecdotes has the slightest relevance to the realities of Communism. As for Djerjinsky, the act of cleaning latrines cannot be held up as an exceptional example of self-sacrifice, for, as members of the armed forces are well aware, there are millions of latrines in the world and nearly all of them get cleaned by someone. But in any case the anecdote overlooks the cardinal point in Communist policy, for Communists are strictly forbidden to do anything to alleviate the material conditions of any person, no matter how unfortunate, except when they can thereby gain credit for the Party and attract recruits. In all other circumstances their duty is to prevent the improvement of material conditions, so that the proletariat will grow in discontent and be more susceptible to revolutionary propaganda.

As for Leviné, when he said, "We Communists are always under sentence of death," he uttered words which are inapplicable to the Communist Party in any part of the globe, and ludicrously inapplicable to Communist Parties in the English-speaking world, unless reference be made to the very real danger that comrades run of being killed by other comrades. If the Rosenbergs go to the electric chair they will be the first Communists in the English-speaking world to suffer the death penalty. Very few Communists have been sent to jail on either side of the Atlantic, except for short sentences. But the victims of Communism number millions, and there are vast areas of the world where the majority of the population can say, "We anti-Communists are always under sentence of death."

As for Sazonov, this is a horrible story, but a very silly one. Even those who in their childhood knew and revered Russian revolutionaries must think it a silly story. It is frivolous in its disregard of the strength of evil. Supposing that a prisoner in a modern totalitarian camp decided to protest against the maltreatment of his fellow prisoners by setting himself on fire, it is probable that the officers of the camp, blunted by contemplation of countless hordes of the starving and suffering, would feel nothing but impatience.

Chambers's generalizations about Communism are not less odd than these particular instances. He asserts that "the widespread notion that men become Communists for material gain" is unfounded, and points to Fuchs as an example of a man to whom the Communist Party could not possibly offer anything that could balance the demands it might make upon him. Many refugees exemplify the working of the Welfare State within a state which the Communist Party organizes in every country for the benefit of its members. When Hitler came to power the machinery for grinding his victims out of Germany very soon fell under Communist control, and it was arranged that as far as possible Communist Germans should be brought to safety while Liberals and Social Democrats and Catholics were left to be destroyed by the Nazis. Stories of such removals are tediously familiar in Europe, where the Communists enjoy an immense advantage for the very reason that, both in the countries they have seized and in the countries they have infiltrated, they offer ambitious men and women bribes, in the form of employment and special privileges and accelerated promotion, which no democratic party could or should offer to its members.

But Chambers not only guarantees that the Communists are not moved by material considerations: he makes on their behalf a staggering claim to priority as idealists. "Communists," he asserts, "are that part of mankind which has recovered the power to live and die—to bear witness—for its faith." Now, the Communist Party certainly uses a little idealistic propaganda for recruiting purposes, a few soft words about poverty and peace. But there is nothing inherently idealistic in Bolshevik Communism, which came into being as a hard-boiled attempt to fill the power vacuum slowly but surely created by the industrial revolution, for the benefit of a middle-class group which saw that their class was in danger of losing its privileges. They proposed to sign a contract with the proletariat, guaranteeing it the monopoly of economic profit in exchange for a monopoly of political power. At the time the idealistic Socialist movements of all Europe opposed the program tooth and nail just because they foresaw that it might inspire a course of action incompatible with idealism; and we Europeans of today feel that we have received sufficient proof that they were right. The British people showed themselves willing to live or die for their faith under the blitz and during the early summer of 1940, when German invasion seemed inevitable. But our Communists were not with us. The Stalin-Hitler Pact still held, and so they were busily working on the side of the Germans and doing what they could to sabotage our defenses; and many of them were visibly relieved to think that if the Germans came they could claim to be their friends. In Berlin, too, a population has been bright with defiance: defiance of a Communist blockade.

Why does Chambers pay these undeserved tributes to a faith he regards as evil? The answer lies in his account of the crucial point in his conversion to that faith. He became, as he puts it, an "irreconcilable" Communist as he stood besides the snow-covered grave of his brother at midnight on New Year's Eve, while the sirens wailed and the fire bells rang, and the crowds in the roadhouses sang and shouted, and a bottle thrown from an automobile crashed on the graveyard wall. He then took a vow to purge the world of the baseness which he conceived to have killed his brother. The purity of Party discipline seemed to him a solvent which would wash away the filth which had choked the boy; and dedication to the single purpose of Communism promised relief from the perils that came of living with no purpose at all. It is to be noted that the three anecdotes he related to the grand jury show men practicing a forgetfulness of self and indifference to pain which is not characteristic of Communist behavior but is part of the technique recommended by all the classic religions to those who wish to develop their consciousness of God.

That moment by the graveside is sacred to Whittaker Chambers because it was the point of departure for a journey which he has found satisfying; and therefore it has never occurred to him that the argument which he was then conducting with himself at that moment was based on false premises. We see why the institution has so often throughout history cried out, in accusation against the mystic: "This man is telling the truth concerning eternity, but he is in error concerning time, and it is in time that we have to do our present duty." There is much in this complaint. But the mystic has often been able to answer: "Because I have sought the truth in eternity I alone have had the strength to tell the truth in time."

. . .

The dispute between the institution and the mystic will go on until the end of the world. But we have one institution which tries to step out of its category and aims at arbitrating in all disputes between opposed individuals and groups: the law. It would be interesting to learn how far the tumult of the Hiss case was due to the lack of laws which might prevent the conversion of normal trials into dervish trials, and how far to the failure to apply such of these laws as exist. Obviously it was unjust to both Hiss and Chambers that the case should have been tried in the press and on the radio and on the platform long before it came into court. This would have been impossible in Britain, because of our strict laws regarding contempt of court which forbid any comment on a case before it is tried and while it is being tried. All responsible British journalists are united in approving these laws. They protect us from advertently or inadvertently prejudicing the course of justice and from being charged with corruption; and their usefulness to the community was proved recently when they prevented the conversion of a trial under the Official Secrets Act into a dervish trial. There is abundant evidence that a number of people were anxious to whitewash a Communist by pretending that he was an independent scientist who wished to hand over information to Soviet Russia because of his admiration for its feats in the war and because he believed that scientific knowledge should be the property of all peoples. Had these people been able to conduct their campaign before the trial, they might have been able to persuade the public that a verdict of guilty must be unjust; but though they have put forward their inaccurate version since the trial, it has been difficult for them to make much headway, since the facts had already been established in court by the prosecution and accepted by the defense.

Mr. Chambers has perhaps the most slender sense of legality that a highly intelligent man could possess. He seems hardly aware of the need to respect the attempts made by the community to reconcile the conflicting rights of its members. He seems, for one thing, to have a blind eye for the idea of contract. This can be seen, oddly enough, in his allusions to his religious affiliations. He says explicitly more than once that he does not accept the Quaker doctrine of nonresistance, yet he is an adherent of the Society of Friends because it is a center of mysticism.

This has its bearing on what is perhaps the strangest incident in the Hiss case: Whittaker Chambers's perjury before the grand jury. Its amazing quality does not warrant the fantastic use of it made by Hiss's supporters, who can hardly be candid when they suggest that Hiss should be considered innocent because the chief witness against him stated on oath that he was innocent and then admitted that he (Hiss) was innocent and then admitted that he was not telling the truth. But it is truly amazing that a man should consent to play a part in the investigation of Hiss's conduct by the law, and then, in order to fulfill what conceived to be his moral duty toward Hiss, should disregard the understanding on which every trial is founded: that witnesses regard the oath they take as binding. This is an act which is explicable only by reference to the egotism of the mystic. In the light of that clue it is troubling and enigmatic. Perhaps the best way of understanding Whittaker Chambers would be to turn back to the records of the Dreyfus case, and try to imagine what it would have been like had the witness who exposed the Army conspiracy been not the straightforward soldier, Colonel Picquart, but Charles Peguy, the Christian poet and philosopher who was Dreyfus's greatest literary defender, and whose relationship with the Roman Catholic Church showed the same inconsistency as Whittaker Chambers's relationship to the Society of Friends. The spectators would often have been greatly perplexed.

10

MARK   DEWOLFE   HOWE

The Misfortune of a Nation

NATION,   MAY   18,   1957

W HEN WHITTAKER CHAMBERS in *Witness* tearfully and joyfully exposed himself, he sought something more than the indecent satisfaction of undressing in public. He believed that if once more he could tell his story to the American people they would appreciate the heroism of his penitence and the immensity of the nation's peril. He evidently built his volume on two assumptions: first, that the jury's verdict foreclosed the issue of veracity as between himself and Mr. Hiss; and, second, that by telling the story of his own shabby life he would add significant perspective to public understanding of the tragic events which led to the conviction of his erstwhile friend.

Alger Hiss has now written an absorbing book which is built upon two very different assumptions. The title he has chosen—*In the Court of Public Opinion*—reveals the purpose which moved him to write his book. But he is not, like Chambers, concerned to establish his heroism and his innocence by telling the story of his life. He seeks to reveal the elements in our legal system and to expose the aspects of our political life which made his conviction possible. Save in the last chapter, where evidence is summarized tending to show the probability that forgery by typewriter was committed, the materials presented by Mr. Hiss are generally familiar to persons who followed the case with reasonably close attention. Those who looked beyond the disputed questions of fact and the central issue of credibility as between Chambers and Hiss were undoubtedly aware of the influence which public emotion, political ambition and malice, and the excesses of the prosecutor had upon the outcome of the case. Nowhere else, however, have these elements by which the due processes of law were distorted been so carefully and persuasively analyzed. Mr. Hiss tells his story, not as the personal tragedy of a man and his family, but as the misfortune of a nation which found, yet did not very much care, that the instruments of government, effective in normal times for the administration of justice, were dangerous and clumsy weapons in a period of national alarm.

. . .

If one believed that the issue in the Hiss case involved nothing more momentous than the decision whether Alger Hiss lied to the federal grand jury it would be easy, perhaps, to say that the petty jury's verdict concludes that issue, or at least that the verdict is sufficiently conclusive to put the nation's conscience at ease. We know, however, that the refutation of Hiss's sworn testimony was largely dependent upon the spongy word of Whittaker Chambers, a sinner who has found more joy in his public confessions than pleasure in his secret vices. If one has any interest in our national taste it is impossible to refrain from asking how American jurors could be persuaded to give credence to such a man as Chambers in preference to such a man as Hiss.

The reason why the grand and petty juries preferred the word of Chambers to that of Hiss was not, I believe, that reliable evidence corroborated his melodramatic story. The forces of persuasion were many and complicated. To say that Mr. Hiss has not discussed and analyzed them all is not to deny the great significance of those which he does analyze. He has, in my judgment, presented a careful and an honest argument to establish his belief that the jury's preference was in large part the result of skilful maneuvering by members of the House Committee on un-American Activities. Resolved to justify their investigations at a time when their continued life was in danger, they saw that the exposure of Alger Hiss might give them a new lease on life. As Mr. Hiss makes abundantly clear, they drifted, partly in malice against the nation's past and partly in hopeful expectations for their own future, into the position of endorsing the patriotism if not the honor of Chambers. Their mounting gratitude for his responsive intelligence and flexible conscience led them to present Chambers to America as a tarnished but repentant hero.

To defend themselves they became the prosecutors of Alger Hiss and they found it advisable to submit the question of his guilt or innocence to the judgment of the people. They used their power, if not their authority, to transform the Committee from an agency of investigation into an instrument of persuasion. By the time the Hiss case came to the federal court for final resolution an eager United States attorney was able to build his case upon foundations of prejudice which the House Committee had firmly laid.

In my opinion there is little doubt that Mr. Hiss has proved his case. He has, in other words, satisfied me that abuses of Congressional power, supplemented by the excessive zeal of the prosecutor, go farther to explain the second jury's verdict than does any presumption that twelve jurors who heard the witnesses accurately measured the conflicting testimony. Mr. Hiss's indictment of the methods by which his conviction was facilitated must disturb those who are anxious to safeguard the integrity of the judicial system and its processes. The lesson that he asks us to learn from his case seems to me to be this: the capacity of courts to administer justice is lagely dependent on the restraint of other agencies of government. A jury's verdict is normally entitled to respect not merely because the formalities of law have been observed, but because the judicial process was chosen by the government and the people as that through which guilt or innocence should be established. When a Congressional committee so conducts its affairs as to suggest that the public at large has primary jurisdiction to hear and decide criminal cases, it commits itself to the subversive enterprise of upsetting the presuppositions of our legal system. Once the decision has been made to bring a case to trial in the court of public opinion it makes relatively little difference whether the prosecuting committee has the bad manners of McCarthy or the more polished skill of Nixon. The bridge to subversion has been crossed. From that moment on, the basis of our confidence in the traditional means of adjudication—trial in a court of law—has been undermined. The federal court before which Alger Hiss was brought to trial was asked to decide a question which the committee had already submitted to a frightened people for their decision. Surely it is not surprising that Alger Hiss should ask us to keep these factors in mind when we ask ourselves whether the jury's decision that he had lied concludes the issue of his guilt.

· · ·

There are sure to be some readers who will be disappointed that Mr. Hiss has not followed the lead of his antagonist and allowed his spirit to run naked and weeping through the streets. One of the ironies in Mr. Hiss's tragedy, perhaps, is the fact that he has never been able or willing to cast aside the stiff reserve of a proud lawyer. If it was inevitable—as perhaps it was in 1948—that the House Committee should succeed in its subversive effort to have the Hiss case tried by the people before it could be heard by the courts, might not the accused have been wiser to meet his attackers more in the open than he did? This is not to suggest that the charges against him were justified or that he committed perjury. It is only to suggest that had he spoken more fully about the evolution of his political beliefs and the changing color of his liberal faith, it would have been more difficult for his prosecutors to persuade the people that he had been guilty of suspicious concealments. Alger Hiss behaved at all times as he would have behaved before a court of law. Perhaps we who consider the committee's effort subversive should honor him for standing in the ancient ways, for behaving more like an outraged lawyer than like an indignant citizen. We cannot help wondering, however, whether he might not have saved himself from disaster by substituting for the familiar defensive tactics suitable in a court of law those distasteful techniques of controversy which are likely to be effective in the court of public opinion.

When Alger Hiss decided to write this book he recognized the court to which the House Committee had assigned jurisdiction. He still defends himself, however, as a lawyer. Those who may have been hoping that Hiss, when it came his turn to appeal to the court of public opinion, would speak with such passion and such fervor that the flame of his indignation would cast light on the darker mysteries of the case will be disappointed in the book. We see again the figure of a proud and thoughtful man. We see, perhaps more clearly than ever before, the shape of forces which made an unjust conviction possible. We are not, however, compelled by new revelations of fact or character to re-assess the elements on which our earlier judgment of Hiss's guilt or innocence was based.

· · ·

To say these things, to indicate that those who hoped for a sensational book will be disappointed, is not to suggest that Mr. Hiss failed to achieve his purpose. He has not sought to prove his innocence, but merely to persuade the American people that the processes of law were distorted by those who brought him to trial. The dignity and integrity of his effort cannot help but strengthen the faith of those who believe him innocent. Perhaps these qualities in the book will also weaken the conviction of some who have believed him guilty. In any case Alger Hiss has made it impossible for those who want to forget the case to justify their forgetfulness by citing its final disposition in the courts. Whether the tribunal of history will accept or reject the jury's verdict we cannot say. It seems clear, however, that it will condemn the action of those who converted an investigating committee of the Congress into a prosecuting agency of the government.

11

D A V I D   C O R T

Of Guilt and Resurrection

NATION,   MARCH   20,   1967

W AS THE DISTINGUISHED Alger Hiss of 1948 actually a marvelously masked Communist agent? Or was his accuser, Whittaker Chambers, a marvelously masked liar? The two characters in the famous "confrontation" interested a San Francisco psychoanalyst, and he spent six years attempting to check out both men on every retrievable detail of their lives.[1] The great design that slowly unfolded was, in sum, the grandest swindle since the Piltdown man. Chambers had been a walking swindle from childhood on; the researcher could find no falsities in the life story of Hiss. Hiss was not Chambers' only victim by the same technique; he was simply his masterpiece.

To review Dr. Zeligs' book as a little exercise in psychiatric techniques, as has been done by others, is a pedantic enormity—something like reviewing *Othello* without Iago. It would be easy to find fault with it as literary psychoanalysis; but it is as a compilation of significant data about Chambers and Hiss that the book is important. The Chambers-Hiss case rested above all on the question of the relative honesty and integrity of the two men involved. Dr. Zeligs' facts are so shocking, so consistent, convincing and well documented as to make the psychiatry a mere distraction. The facts are of urgent interest to the American people, and have political implications of some importance. We are also given an insight into two wildly contrasting and fully drawn human beings in a plot on the edge of melodrama.

I do not blame anyone for refusing to believe that there could be such a person as the "Whittaker Chambers" Zeligs describes; the character is completely improbable. From personal knowledge, I must testify that exactly such a character did exist indeed. I also knew many of the people who believed in him.

Nor is it a count against Dr. Zeligs' work that he does not destroy the whole case against Hiss; what he set out to do was examine Chambers' contribution to it. In doing so, the facts he unearths demolish great portions of the case against Hiss.

Meyer Zeligs starts with Chambers' early life. His parents were two irreligious bourgeois, both socially mobile downward, both artistically pretentious (a big thing before World War I), neither capable of sustaining a good marriage. Out of this situation Chambers evolved his own demure fury.

Zeligs' key thesis is that Whittaker Chambers somehow conspired in his younger (and more attractive) brother's suicide, possibly because of a homosexual, incestuous relationship, and thus inaugurated a life pattern of death, guilt, resurrection. One need not accept this thesis, though it is important to Zeligs. The facts remain. Zeligs is not a prosecutor; the most telling exposures are often dropped into footnotes.

· · ·

According to Chambers, he was born weighing 12 pounds and measuring 14 inches at the shoulders, in Philadelphia on April 1, 1901, in a blizzard (the record shows no precipitation of any kind on that lamentable April Fool's Day). He was christened Jay Vivian Chambers, but this identity did not suit him any more than the actual facts of his birth. He began using invented names such as Charles Adams (at 18), Charles Whittaker (at 19), Whittaker Chambers (19), John Kelly (21), and later Jay David Chambers, David Breen, George Cantwell, Lloyd Cantwell, Carl, George Crosley, David Dwyer, John Land—certainly an incomplete roster.

He had an early compulsion toward atrocity. As class prophet at his class graduation, he predicted that a nice girl would turn prostitute. He exited from Columbia, following publication in the campus bushy-tailed magazine of a sacrilegious playlet placed outside Christ's Sepulchre. He told professors he had syphilis. He somehow maintained a mouthful of appalling teeth, as if asking to be loved *in spite of*. His elusive charm was that of one asking for a blanket pardon, for past, present and future. Most people instinctively refused it.

His lies followed psychic patterns which Zeligs tries to define. Let us limit this bottomless subject only to his relations with Alger Hiss. The items below are distinguished as L (Lie) and F (Fact).

(L) The Hisses visited Chambers at Maxim Lieber's house on the Delaware River. (F) Lieber never saw or heard of the Hisses. (L) Hiss abominated Shakespeare. (F) Mr. and Mrs. Hiss read Shakespeare to each other at night. (L) Hiss had a total contempt for F. D. Roosevelt. (F) Hiss totally loved Roosevelt. (Aside: it was Chambers in both roles of Communist and anti-Communist who loathed Roosevelt.) (L) The Hiss lawyers impertinently called his suicide brother "Dickie." (F) They didn't. Chambers did. (L) Mrs. Hiss was "a birthright Quaker." (F) She was a Presbyterian. (L) Hiss's house was white with green shutters. (F) It was bright yellow with vivid blue shutters. A long time later it was painted as Chambers "remembered" it. (L) Chambers was put up in an upstairs bedroom. (F) There was no upstairs spare bedroom. (L) No piano. (F) Piano. And so on, interminably.

Powerful men and august bodies in this nation received these sleazy lies as significant political truth, at a time when such cobwebs nearly destroyed the American society. For Chambers' enemy was never communism; it was American democracy, you and me. He managed to set America to the task of its own destruction.

The terrible thought is that with Chambers' recipe anybody can ruin anybody else, if he will prepare ahead, and wait. It is of the utmost significance that Chambers did not seek an actual Communist as his prime victim, for there were plenty available. He wanted to bring down the whole structure of democracy. And Hiss had the democratic weaknesses of courtesy and responsibility.

. . .

If Chambers had been a simple madman, there would be no problem. But he was a master mountebank. He quickly picked up the style, tone and jargon of almost any role: conspirator, executive, assassin, poet, littérateur, genius, savior, and might have made an impressive magnate or general or judge, for a short time. For inside the imposture was a hollow man with sound effects. All the people who admired, loved, feared, or even just believed him were pitiably hoaxed. Just to know him was at best an indiscretion.

Chambers personified a rollicking satire on a wide variety of things: great men, philosophy, history, facts, *Time* magazine, politics, propaganda, religion, communism, espionage, power, conservatism, conscience, friendship, etc.

Yet men of affairs, in government, the press, letters, the FBI, believed in him and staked their careers on him—men like William Buckley of the *National Review*, and J. Edgar Hoover. They accepted the cant, the bold front, the false credentials, as the genuine article. Well, it is now time to pick up the stakes.

Richard Nixon owes his career largely to Chambers. A typical Chambers letter to Nixon: "I do not believe for a moment that because you have been cruelly checked in the employment of what is best in you . . . that that check is final. Great character always precludes a sense of comedown."

The late Henry R. Luce was willingly deceived by Chambers for nine years. Chambers wrote Luce: "Your speech is a simple, authentic testimony of the spirit. . . . It is a voice with which I have seldom been privileged to hear you speak, and it moves me deeply. I may not intrude upon it. . . . It proceeds from the spirit, and the mode of the Christian spirit is simplicity. God bless you, Harry. Whittaker." Anyone who could toss off such rarefied sycophancy, couched as hero worship, had to go far. What a pity that Luce bought this from a *farceur.* He deserved better.

Of another kind was Mark Van Doren, for whose infinite kindness to Chambers came a letter after the difficulties of his son Charles, enclosing a note to Charles; "You will never get over this. The world will never leave you alone until you die." Instead of a condolence, a terrible curse, and ungrammatical. Chambers' letters to Van Doren are masterpieces of seemingly profound intellectual narcissism, a quality that English professors tend to confuse with genius.

One Chambers friend who was not deceived was Lionel Trilling, who put into his novel, *The Middle of the Journey,* a Chambers-based character, a paranoiac constantly looking for a "new existence," who finally attacks his best friend. Nevertheless, Trilling was impressed by Chambers.

My disdain of Chambers, at Columbia and then at Time, Inc., was always instinctive, that he was a repellent actor. But I seem to have been nearly alone in that company.

Dr. Zeligs has started something. His book, embodying material beyond the daring of the wildest novelist, will be followed by others. Alger Hiss must certainly be vindicated. The wreckage of other reputations is inevitable. And Chambers, with that cute dimpled chuckle and the sly, friendly gleam, is laughing in the grave at his "friends," the priceless butts who believed in him.

And so at last some day we can shorten the great Roman stricture to "*de mortuis, nil.*"

NOTE

[1] Meyer A. Zeligs, *Friendship and Fraticide: An Analysis of Whittaker Chambers and Alger Hiss.* New York: Viking, 1967.

12

WILLIAM F. BUCKLEY JR.

The End of Whittaker Chambers

ESQUIRE, SEPTEMBER 1962

"WHERE IS RENOIR'S GIRL with the Watering Can?" I asked the attendant at the entrance to the National Gallery. I walked up the flight of stairs, turned left through two galleries, and spotted her near the corner. It was only 12:25 and I had the feeling he would be there at exactly 12:30, the hour we had set. I sat down on the ottoman in the center of the room. I could see through the vaulted opening into the adjacent galleries. I saw him approaching. It could only have been he, or Alfred Hitchcock. Five months had gone by since he had been at my home in Connecticut, but we were never out of touch; almost every Sunday afternoon I would call him, and we would talk, at length, discursively, and laugh together, between the strophes of his melancholy. (And every now and then—rarely, now that he was back at school—I would receive one of those letters.) The Sunday before, he told me he was to be in Washington on the 8th of June.

I was surprised—he loathed Washington, and probably had not been there three times in ten years, although he lived only two hours away. Perhaps, I wondered, one of those infrequent meetings with Nixon—though Nixon was in California now. Perhaps yet one more meeting with the F.B.I. I had told him I would schedule my own business for the same day. He had asked me to keep the evening open, and we agreed to meet for a private lunch. "You've guessed what's up, haven't you?" he said, his face wreathed in smiles. "I haven't the least idea." "John!" he said proudly. We went off talking excitedly. His son would be married that afternoon, and I was to go to the wedding and the reception. "Where shall we eat?" "I don't know," I said—I couldn't, on the spur of the moment, think of the name of a single small restaurant in Washington which might be reasonably proof against Chambers' being recognized—we had had that difficulty so often in New York, when he used to come to *National Review* on Tuesdays and Wednesdays. "I can't think of any place," he said helplessly. "I know!" I interjected. "We must eat at *L'Espionage!*" He smiled.

It wasn't open. We lunched somewhere, and talked and talked for the hour and a half we had. We walked then to the Statler and sat in the corner of the huge lobby. At that moment a reporter I had recently come to know approached me. I rose quickly and stood directly between him and Chambers, whose anxiety for the privacy of his son was intense (the press all but took over at his daughter's wedding seven years before, and the entire family had taken elaborate precautions to keep this wedding out of public view.) The reporter talked on and on, but my taciturn answers finally discouraged him; we shook hands and he left. I turned around. But Chambers was gone.

We met again at seven, in the blistering heat, at the church at Georgetown where a few months earlier John Fitzgerald Kennedy, Jr. had been baptized. Whittaker and his wife Esther, slight and beautiful, with her incomparable warmth; a genial couple, old friends of the Chambers from Baltimore; with his wife and sons, his steadfast friend Ralph de Toledano, who met Chambers during the Hiss trial, wrote *Seeds of Treason*; the bride's parents, a sister of the bride and a friend of the groom. We went from there to a private room at the Statler, where we drank champagne (for the first time in my life, I saw him take a drink) and ate dinner. Whittaker was quiet, but I think he was very happy. I thought back on a letter several years old. *"John's parents live for John, and for little else. In 1952, I sat and reckoned—so many years I must live in order to get John to his majority. It seemed an impossibly long course. Now each day is subtracted from the year that is left. . . . The day I finished the last section of Witness, I took the copy into town and put it in the mail myself. Then I returned to the little house at Medfield, where, for about two years, I had written alone. I sat down at my now needless table and thought that now, perhaps, God would permit me to die. I did not really wish this—much less, I now know than I then supposed. And I could not pray for it because of the children. I thought that I must live until they reached their majority, at least, so that they would be beyond the reach of men in the legal sense. In John's case, this meant some five or six years. It seemed to me an almost unendurable span of time. In the past year I have found myself inwardly smiling because only a few months of that span are left. I have been saying to myself: I am free at last. . . ."*

The bride and groom left. We got up to go. After saying good night all the way around, I drew Whit aside and made him listen to an irreverent story, which shook him with silent laughter. I never knew a man who so enjoyed laughing. I waved my hand at him and went out with the de Toledanos. As we stepped into the elevator I saw him framed by the door, his hand and Esther's clutched together, posing while his son-in-law popped a camera in his face; a grim reminder of all those flashbulbs ten years before. I never saw him again. He died a month later, on July 9, 1961. Free at last.

. . .

I first met Chambers in 1954. An almost total silence had closed in on him. Two years earlier he had published *Witness.* In the months before the book appeared there was a considerable nervous excitement. The book had been postponed several times. Chambers would not let the publishers have it until he was quite through with it. (He told me with vast amusement that a prominent journalist had volunteered to ghost the book for him.) When the preface of *Witness* appeared as a feature in *The Saturday Evening Post*, that issue of the magazine sold a startling half million extra copies on the newsstand. The book came out with a great fury. The bitterness of the Hiss trial had not by any means subsided. For some of the reviewers, Hiss's innocence had once been a fixed rational conviction, then blind faith; now it was rank superstition, and they bent under the force of an overwhelming book. But the man was not grasped by the reviewers, who treated *Witness* as a passion play acted out by archetypes. "I am a heavy man *(Ernst mensch),*" Chambers once wrote me, to apologize for staying two days at my home. There is a sense in which that was true. But he never appreciated, as others did, the gaiety of his nature, the appeal of his mysterious humor, the instant communicability of his overwhelming personal tenderness; his friends—I think especially of James Agee—took endless and articulate pleasure in his company.

Witness was off to a great start. But, surprisingly, it did not continue to sell in keeping with its spectacular send-off. The length of the book was forbidding; and the trial, in any case, was three years old, and the cold sweat had dried. Alger Hiss was in prison, and now the political furor centered about McCarthy. Those who did not know the book, and who were not emotionally committed either to Chambers' guilt or innocence, seemed to shrink even from a vicarious involvement in the controversy, partly because of the dark emanations that came out of Chambers' emotive pen, depressing when reproduced, as was widely done, in bits and snatches, torn from the narrative. "It had been my impression," Hugh Kenner, the author and critic, wrote me recently, "before reading *Witness*, that his mind moved, or wallowed, in a setting of continuous apocalypse from which he derived gloomy satisfactions, of an immobilizing sort. The large scale of *Witness* makes things much clearer. It is surprisingly free from rhetoric, and it makes clear the genuine magnitude of the action which was his life: a Sophoclean tragedy in slow motion, years not hours. I think communism had an appeal for him which he doesn't go into: the appeal of large-scale historic progress, to which to surrender the self. The self awoke and fought its way clear by a superbly individual action (look how his attention comes awake when he is itemizing his essentials for escape: a weapon, a car, etc.) As a Communist he sleepwalked to heavy Dostoyevskian music . . . the constant note was surrender to a process larger than himself; and a heroic quality comes out in the interplay between this essentially musical mode of existence (the terminology is Wyndham Lewis') and his constant awareness of the possibility, the necessity, of equilibrium, choice, the will poised freely amid possibilities. It's in the texture of the *Witness* prose, the narrative line making its way freely through the rhythms, declarations; through the organ-tones of plight."

In 1954 I asked if I might visit him. He had written a long-standing friend, Henry Regnery, the publisher of my book on Senator McCarthy, to praise the book, while making clear his critical differences with McCarthy (". . . *for the Right to tie itself in any way to Senator McCarthy is suicide. Even if he were not what, poor man, he has become, he can't lead anybody because he can't think.*") A few months after the book was published, he was struck down by a heart attack, and it was vaguely known that he spent his days in and out of a sickbed, from which the likelihood was that he would never again emerge physically whole. He managed one piece for *Life* during that period; otherwise he was silent. I had every reason to believe I would be visiting Jeremiah lying alongside a beckoning tomb. The letter telling me I might come began with gratifying vivacity. But the gloom closed in before he had come to the end of the page. "*The score,*" he wrote, "*as the points are checked up, daily and boldly, more and more convinces me that the total situation is hopeless, past repair, organically irremediable. Almost the only position of spiritual dignity left to men, therefore, is a kind of stoic silence, made bearable by the amusement of seeing, hearing and knowing the full historical irony that its victims are blind and deaf to, and disciplined by the act of withholding comment on what we know."* And then, inevitably, because Chambers did not want to curse a stranger with his own profound gloom: *"This may well be more of a posture than a position, and, happily, none of us will be permitted to assume it, or could, without violating our own articulate imperative."*

I found him in bed. The doctor had forbidden him even to raise his head. And yet he was the liveliest man I think I ever met. I could not imagine such good humor from a very sick man, let alone a man possessed by the conviction that night was closing in all over the world, and privately tortured by his continuing fear that the forces aligned against him would contrive to reorder history, impose upon the world the ghastly lie that he had testified falsely against Alger Hiss, and so erase his witness, his expiation for ten years' complicity with communism. (*"If the West cannot use the Hiss Case to its own advantage, the Hiss forces will use the case, against the West; a kind of historical law of opposite and equal reactions seems to be in play."*) We did not, of course, speak of Hiss, nor did we for several months; though later he spoke of him, and of the case, with relaxation and candor. But we must have talked about everything else, and I left later than I should have, hustled anxiously to the door by a wife who knew she was all but powerless to enforce the doctor's rules.

As he began to recover he was, for a while, greatly renewed by a physical and spiritual energy which were dialectically at odds with his organic ill health and his intellectual commitment to the futility of all meliorative action. I talked with him about the magazine I proposed to publish and asked whether he would join the staff. To my overwhelming surprise the answer was Yes—he might do just that. But not, he warned, if the journal was to be a sectarian enterprise, aiming ultimately at a circulation of 5,000. We corresponded through the summer. He was to make up his mind definitively during the fall, after we visited again. I made the mistake in one of my letters of expressing exorbitant hopes for the role the magazine might hope to play in human affairs. He dashed them down in a paragraph unmatched in the literature of supine gloom, even though it finally resisted despair. *"It is idle,"* he rebuked me, *"to talk about preventing the wreck of Western civilization. It is already a wreck from within. That is why we can hope to do little more now than snatch a fingernail of a saint from the rack or a handful of ashes from the faggots, and bury them secretly in a flowerpot against the day, ages hence, when a few men begin again to dare to believe that there was once something else, that something else is thinkable, and need some evidence of what it was, and the fortifying knowledge that there were those who, at the great nightfall, took loving thought to preserve the tokens of hope and truth."*

The tokens of hope and truth were not, he seemed to be saying, to be preserved by a journal of opinion, not by writers or thinkers, but only by activists, and I was to know that he considered a publication—the right kind of publication—not a word, but a deed. Though Chambers was a passionately literary man, always the intellectual, insatiably and relentlessly curious, in the last analysis it was action, not belletrism, that moved him most deeply. He could write, as he did of Arthur Koestler: *"If you re-read* Darkness at Noon *at this late hour you will see how truly it is a book of poetry. I re-read it recently. I came to the part where, after his breakdown, Rubashov is permitted a few minutes of air in the prison yard. Beside him trots the Central Asian peasant who has been jailed because, 'at the pricking of the children,' the peasant and his wife had barricaded themselves in their house and 'unmasked themselves as reactionaries.' Looking sideways at Rubashov in his sly peasant way, he says: 'I do not think they have left much of Your Honor and me.' Then, in the snow of the prison yard and under the machine-gun towers, he remembers how it was when the snow melted in the mountains of Asia, and flowed in torrents. Then they drove the sheep into the hills, rivers of them, 'so many that Your Honor could not count them all.' I cannot go on reading because I can no longer see the words. To think that any man of my time could have written anything so heart-tearingly beautiful, 'wonderful, caus-ing tears.'"*

But in time I began to understand why in 1932 he resigned as editor of the Communist *New Masses*, where he had already earned an international reputation as a writer, to go scurrying abut the streets of Washington, Baltimore and New York, carrying pocketfuls of nega-tives and secret phone numbers and invisible ink.... *"One of the great failures of Witness is that there was no time or place to describe the influ-ences, other than immediate historical influences, that brought me to Com-munism,"* he wrote me. *"I came to communism ... above all under the influence of the Narodniki. It has been deliberately forgotten, but, in those days, Lenin urged us to revere the Narodniki—'those who went with bomb or revolver against this or that individual monster.' Unlike most Western Communists, who became Communists under the influence of the Social Democrats, I remained under the spiritual influence of the Narodniki long after I became a Marxist. In fact, I never threw it out. It has simply blended with that strain in the Christian tradition to which it is akin. It shaped the particular quality of my revolutionary character that made me specially beloved (of course, it is wrong to say such things, but it is true) even among many of the crude, trifling American Communists; so that* [one among them] *could say to a* Time *correspondent with whom she found herself junketing in East Germany after World War II: 'I simply cannot believe that Whittaker Chambers has broken. I could believe it of anybody else, but not of him....' And, of course, it was the revolutionary quality that amused Alger*—mea culpa, mea maxima culpa.

"I remember how Ulrich, my first commander in the Fourth Section, once mentioned Vera Zasulich and added: 'I suppose you never heard that name.' I said: 'Zasulich shot General Trepov for flogging the student, Bogomolsky, in the Paviak prison.' And I remember the excited smile with which he answered (Ulrich was a Left Socialist Revolutionist, not a Com-munist.): 'That is true. But how do you know that?'

"Like Ulrich, I may presume in supposing that the name of

Ragozinikova is unknown to you. But the facts are these. In 1907, the Russian government instituted a policy of systematically beating its political prisoners. One night, a fashionably dressed young woman called at the Central Prison in Petersburg and asked to speak with the commandant, Maximovsky. This was Ragozinikova, who had come to protest the government's policy. Inside the bodice of her dress were sewed thirteen pounds of dynamite and a detonator. When Maximovsky appeared, she shot him with her revolver and killed him. The dynamite was for another purpose. After the murder of Maximovsky, Ragozinikova asked the police to interrogate her at the headquarters of the Okhrana. She meant to blow it up together with herself: she had not known any other way to penetrate it. But she was searched and the dynamite discovered. She was sentenced to be hanged. Awaiting execution, she wrote her family: 'Death itself is nothing. . . . Frightful only is the thought of dying without having achieved what I could have done. . . . How good it is to love people. How much strength one gains from such love.' When she was hanged, Ragozinikova was twenty years old.

"In Witness, *I have told how Sazonov drenched himself with kerosene and burned himself to death as a protest against the mistreatment of others. And I have told what that meant to me at one moment; how, had my comrade, Sazonov, not done that, there would not have been a Hiss case as we know it. This spirit persisted in the Fourth Section as late as 1938.* [Jones] *knows nothing of such people except as a legend. That is why, though* [Jones] *is transfixed with as many arrows as Sebastian, he simply does not understand the* source *of the glance that the Saint bends upon the bowman. I need scarcely underscore the point at which the strain of the revolutionary spirit blends with a Christian élan, or why it was imperative of communism to kill it out.*"

Activism. From the Narodniki to Republicanism, in one defection. During that period, Chambers believed that there was only a single man, among all those who had the slightest chance to succeed Eisenhower at the White House (Eisenhower was down with his heart attack and it was generally assumed he would not run for reelection), who had any idea of what communism was all about. I drove down to Westminster with a common friend to get from him—it was on the eve of the publication of our first issue—his final word. The word was No. There were several reasons why he declined to leave his farm in Westminster and trudge back to New York to resume his professional life (he had all along insisted that if he joined us, he would come regularly to the office, even though we were content to let him peck away at his typewriter in the dark basement of his farmhouse). But the predominant reason was that he would not associate himself with a journal which might oppose Eisenhower's reelection, in the unlikely event he were to run again, or even be indifferent to his prospects for winning; let alone any magazine that might oppose Nixon's nomination in the event Eisenhower withdrew. Chambers the activist reasoned that under the existing circumstances, a vote for Eisenhower was actually a vote for his successor. He puffed away at his pipe.

It was an awesome moment. A climaxing disappointment. It was rendered tolerable by one of those master strokes of irony over which Chambers and I were to laugh convulsively later. My companion was Willi Schlamm, former assistant to Henry Luce, an old friend of Chambers in the hard anti-Communist cell at Time, Inc., and a colleague, from the very beginning, in the *National Review* enterprise. Schlamm is a Viennese, volatile, amusing, the soul of obduracy, and a conversational stem-winder. He had been in on the negotiations with Chambers from the very first, and was modestly certain he could bring his old pal Whit along by the terrible cogency of his arguments. But as we drove down to Maryland from New York, Schlamm got progressively hoarser. Two minutes after we arrived, laryngitis completely closed in. Whittaker was wonderfully attentive—aspirin, tea, lemon, whiskey, bicarbonate, all that sort of thing. But at one point he turned to me, when Willi was out of sight, and gave me a huge, delighted wink.

So he stayed on his farm, and worried. He had a great deal to worry about. There was a pending libel suit against him by a minor actor in *Witness*, and Chambers felt that he had been fighting completely alone. "*Your letter* [stating that his friends were standing by] *did me a lot of good at the right moment. . . . When I go to court with the litigious Mr. X. three days hence, I shall not feel, as until now I have had to feel, that I am just as alone in 1954 as in 1948. It is a somewhat freezing feeling.*"

And Alger Hiss had come out of prison arrantly proclaiming his innocence. "*Alger came out more fiercely that even I had expected. . . . His strength is not what it was. But that it exists at all is stunning. Every time that, in the name of truth, he asserts his innocence, he strikes at truth, utters a slander against me, and compounds his guilt of several orders. . . . It is this which squirts into my morale a little jet of paralyzing poison. . . .*"

His son John was having the normal son's difficulties in college. "*John, like most sensitive youths, is a great nuisance to himself and so many others. He often stirs me to rage. . . . There come moments, even with a beloved son, when we are moved to nod assent to what Carl Brandt once said to me: 'Don't you know that boys at that age are poisonous, simply poisonous?'*"

His broken health, together with a grim financial situation, contributed to a great restlessness. "*I do not even have the capital to farm half-heartedly, and I cannot, as in the past, make good the capital by my own labor power. This inability to work the place is perhaps the greatest burr in my mind at that angle. It torments me since, among other disabilities, I have no talent for being a country gentleman. . . . But we have long been as poor as rats.*"

And then, during that period, he reached the psychological low point of his later years, as he sweated in philosophical bedrock, gathering his thoughts: "*I have been splashing about in my private pool of ice water.*" Again, "*I have ceased to understand why I must go on living.*" Again, "*The year was, for me, a long walk through the valley. No one but me will ever know how close I came to staying in it.*" What was the trouble? "*It had to do with my inability to fix the meaning of the current period of existence in some communicable way. I knew the fault lay in me. So that, all the while I was trying to write, I was simply trying to grow.*"

But he came out of it. "*Between Christmas . . . and New Year, I woke, one dawn, from a dream in which I had been singing (in German, but not aloud, of course) a marching song. In my half-waking state, I continued to sing the song to the end, which goes:* Hell aus der dunklen Vergangenheit/Leuchtet die Zukunft hervor—*Bright, from the darkness of the past/ Beacons the future. From what depths had this song risen, which I had not sung (or heard sung) for decades? But the song was only a signature. What was wonderful, incredible, was the sense of having passed from one dimension into another; a sense of ordered peace, together with an exhilaration ('at last I am free'). I had touched bottom and was rising again to the surface; and, to rise, I had cut loose a drowning weight of extraneous this and that. . . . The dream was, in fact, the turning point of my late years. I take it that such a dream is a recapitulation; it prepares itself, as Camus says of suicide, 'like a work of art, secretly, in the heart' without the artist's being aware of the process.*"

He could write, finally: "*Ehrenburg has just made one of the most memorable utterances of the time: 'If the whole world were to be covered with asphalt, one day a crack would appear in the asphalt; and in that crack, grass would grow.' I offer the lines as the irreducible terms on which the mind can have hope in our age.*"

Eisenhower ran and was re-elected. Nixon was safely vice-president. Six months later Chambers wrote me to say he wanted to sign up with *National Review.* Having made the decision, he was elated. After years of isolation and introspection, he was like a painter who had rediscovered his eyesight. He felt the overwhelming need to practice his art. How many things he wanted to write about, and immediately! Mushrooms, for one thing. Some gentleman, in an act of supreme conceit, had recently published a ten-dollar book of mycology, heaping scorn on one of Chambers' most beloved species of toad-stools. Camus. What a lot of things needed to be said instantly about the *Myth of Sisyphus*. Djilas' *The New Class* was just out and most of the critics had missed the whole point. . . .

I rented a one-engine plane and swooped down on him at Westminster to make our arrangements. For personal reasons I had to make the round trip in one day, and I wanted to act immediately on Chambers' enthusiasm. He met me and we drove in his car to his farm. He told me the last time he had driven to the little grassy strip at Westminster, on which reckless pilots venture occasionally to land, was to greet Henry Luce, who had soared in from Washington to pay him an unexpected visit some months after Hiss's conviction. I remarked that such, obviously, is the traveling style of very important publishers. If he would not acknowledge that common denominator between me and Mr. Luce, I added, then he might recognize this one: such is the style of publishers who employ Whittaker Chambers. He laughed, but told me my manner was grossly imperfected. When Luce arrived, he said as we bounced about on the dusty dirt road in his open jeep, he had waiting for him at the airport a limousine to drive him to Chambers' farm. I made a note for my next landing. . . .

He would not go to New York after all. To do so would be not merely to defy his doctor's orders, which he did regularly almost as a matter of principle, but to defy Esther's wishes, which was something else again. He would work at home. I begged him to desist from what I had denounced as his sin of scrupulosity. During the preceding eighteen months, since the Laryngitis Conference, he had twice volunteered to do a piece for *National Review*. One, I remember, was to be an answer to Dwight Macdonald's unbalanced attack on *National Review* in *Commentary*. He had suggested a deadline of two weeks after we spoke. Ten weeks later he abandoned the project. Meanwhile he had done thirteen drafts. He would not show me any of them.

I was disappointed, but not altogether surprised. I had had a dozen letters from him describing the fate of other letters he had written me. (*"To your gladdening letters, I wrote a close-set, three-and-a-half-page reply, which I have just had the pleasure of setting a match to. . . ."*) At least once he burned a book-length manuscript. (*"I have burned a book half the size of* Witness, *and consider it one of my best deeds. . . ."*) As soon as he regained consciousness after one coronary attack, whose relative ferocity he was sure would end up killing him, he groped his way down to the basement to destroy another great pile of manuscripts.

He wrote on yellow second sheets, by hand, in pencil. Then he would rewrite and rewrite. Then—sometimes—he would type out a third or fourth draft. Then, after a few days, he would often destroy that. "Let us judge whether what you write is publishable." I pleaded: "You have no judgment on such matters. There should be a constitutional amendment forbidding you to destroy anything you write, without the permission of a jury of your superiors, to which I hereby nominate myself." He chuckled. Underproduction would not be his trouble anymore, he said: the way he was feeling he would bury us with copy, and before long I'd be sending him literary tranquilizers. . . .

But, five weeks later, he wrote me to say he must resign: he could not bring himself to submit to us what he had written. I cajoled him, and one day a five-thousand-word manuscript arrived, on "Soviet Strategy in the Middle East." (*"Talk, here in the farmlands"* [it began] *"is chiefly of the heaviest frost of this date in a decade, and what it may have done to stands of late corn. Yet it cannot be said that we are wholly out of touch with the capitals of the mysterious East—Cairo, Damascus, Baghdad, New York. . . ."*)

Two months later, after struggling with the book for eight weeks, he submitted a long review of Ayn Rand's *Atlas Shrugged*. (*"Somebody has called it 'excruciatingly awful.' I find it a remarkably silly book. . . . In any case, the brew is probably without lasting ill effects. But it is not a cure for anything. Nor would we, ordinarily, place much confidence in the diagnosis of a doctor who supposes that the Hippocratic Oath is a kind of curse."*) Miss Rand never forgave me for publishing it. To this day, she will walk theatrically out of any room I enter!

A few months after that he wrote about the farm problem, clearly as an insider. (*"Perhaps* [in the future the socialized farmer] *will not be able, in that regimented time, to find or frame an answer* [to why he lost his freedom]. *Perhaps he will not need to. For perhaps the memory of those men and women* [who fought socialism] *will surprise him simply as with an unfamiliar, but arresting sound—the sound of springheads, long dried up and silent in a fierce drought, suddenly burst out and rushing freely to the sea. It may remind him of a continuity that outlives all lives, fears, perplexities, contrivings, hopes, defeats; so that he is moved to reach down and touch again for strength, as if he were its first discoverer, the changeless thing—the undeluding, undenying earth."*)

And then a piece defending the right of Alger Hiss to travel abroad, while denying that Hiss can be said to have paid his debt to society. (*"The Hiss Case remains a central lesion of our time. That is why, ultimately, I cannot say . . . that Alger Hiss has paid any effective penalty. For precisely he can end the lesion at any moment that he chooses, with half-a-dozen words."*) Chambers knew that his absolute endorsement of the right of anyone to travel would bring criticism from certain quarters on the Right. No matter. (*"Woe to those who grope for reality and any approximate truth that may be generalized from it, in the no-man's land between incensed camps. History and certain personal experiences leave me in little doubt about the fate of such seekers. They are fair game to the snipers of both sides, and it is always open season. But while Mr. Hiss hurries to his plane or ship, and the snipers wait for the man to reach, in his groping, the point where the hairlines cross on their sights, I may still have time to sort the dead cats into tidy piles—those from one camp, here; those from the other, there. As one of my great contemporaries put it: 'Anybody looking for a quiet life has picked the wrong century to be born in.' The remark must be allowed*

*a certain authority, I think since the century clinched the point by mauling
with an ax the brain that framed it.")*

That piece was picked up by The New York *Times*, which also had
run a paragraph calling attention to Chambers' joining the staff of
National Review, a story picked up by AP. He bore the publicity he
got with resignation, though it clearly upset him. If Chambers could
have taken a bath in invisible ink, I have no doubt he'd have done so.
He loathed publicity, even as he loathed gossip. (He passed on a piece
of news to me once which, he admitted, he had got second-hand—
Esther had it over the telephone: *"I think it is true. Or so Esther tells me.
For, at the first tinkle of the bell, I rushed outside to feed the fish in the pond.
Because they do not bark, and do not know the secrets of Washington."*) In
preparing this article I looked in *Who's Who* for Chambers' birth date,
but his name was not listed. I looked in the 1952 edition; no entry
there either. I wrote a furious letter to *Who's Who*—which (I had previously noted) studiedly ignores the existence of all interesting people—
to ask why they discriminate against anyone who isn't a congressman
or a rich dentist. But this time they had me: Chambers had for ten
years refused to complete the biographical questionnaires they had
repeatedly sent him. When the news got out that he had joined *National Review's* staff, he received a telephone call from *Time* Magazine's
Baltimore stringer requesting an interview. Sorry, Chambers said, as
he always did to any member of the press who wanted to see him on
official business. Like *Who's Who*, *Time* refused to take notice of the
affairs of anyone so ungrateful as to refuse to cooperate with its opin-
ion-gatherers *(Who's Who*, after all, could have got all the information
it needed from *Witness*. The *Time* reporter wired the New York office,
snootily declining to pursue a story about so un-cooperative a subject,
and for good measure, sent Chambers a copy of it.

At about that time, I remember, *Newsweek* ran a story under its
regular feature heading "Where Are They Now?" (i.e., the Heroes [or
Villains] of Yesteryear). Chambers, *Newsweek* Periscoped, was still

living in the farmhouse where once he had buried the famous papers in a pumpkin; he had never budged from the farm; and was hard at work on a new book. I wrote to *Newsweek* to say their account was interesting, except that: a) Chambers had moved from the farmhouse in question (during the preceding winter it had almost burned to the ground), and was now living in a little house at the other end of his farm; b) that he was working, and had been for a year, for *National Review*, and came regularly to New York; and c) that he had temporarily abandoned work on the new book. *Newsweek* ran no correction. If *Newsweek* had run an incorrect report on Chambers, clearly it was Chambers' fault. He should have kept *Newsweek* better informed on his movements.

But notwithstanding his desire for privacy and his temperamental dislike for New York *("New York you need to exploit, and I never learned how")* Chambers decided in the Summer of 1958 to come here every fortnight to spend two days in the office, writing editorials and short features for *National Review*. He would arrive on the train from Baltimore at noon and come directly to the editorial lunch, always out of breath, perspiring in his city clothes. He was always glad to see his gentle friend, John Chamberlain, his longtime colleague from Time, Inc. He liked his little cubicle at *National Review* which, five minutes after he entered it, smelled like a pipe-tobacco factory. He puffed away ferociously, grinding out his memorable paragraphs. Everything he wrote had intellectual and stylistic distinction and, above all, the intense emotional quality of the man who, fifteen years before, had said of the Negro spiritual: *"It was the religious voice of a whole religious people—probably the most God-obsessed (and man-despised) since the ancient Hebrews. . . . One simple fact is clear—they were created in direct answer to the Psalmist's question, 'How shall we sing the Lord's song in a strange land?' . . . Grief, like a tuning fork, gave the tone, and the Sorrow Songs were uttered."*

Yet anyone meeting Chambers casually, without preconception, would say of him first that he was a highly amusing and easily amused man. The bottomless gravity seldom suggested itself. He was not merely a man of wit, but also a man of humor, and even a man of fun. Often, in his letters, even through his orotund gloom, the pixie would surface. *("Would that we could live in the world of the fauves, where the planes are disjointed only on canvas, instead of a world where the wild bleats are real and the disjointures threaten to bury us. Or do I really wish that? It would take some nice thinking for, perhaps, toasted Susie is not my ice cream. Perhaps you should make a transparency of* [Gertrude Stein's 'most perfect sentence'] *and hang it as a slogan outside the windows of the* National Review: *'Toasted Susie is Not My Ice Cream.' It might catch you more subscribers than Senator McCarthy at that.")*

On Tuesday nights we worked late, and four or five of us would go out to dinner. By then he was physically exhausted. But he wanted to come with us, and we would eat at some restaurant or other, and he would talk hungrily (and eat hungrily) about everything that interested him, which was literally everything in this world, and not in this world. He talked often around a subject, swooping in to make a quick point, withdrawing, relaxing, laughing, listening—he listened superbly, though even as a listener he was always a potent force. He was fascinated by the method and scope of James Burnham's interests, and the sureness of his analytical mind, though Chambers' own thoughts were so resolutely nonschematic that he tended to shrink from some of Burnham's grandiose constructions, even while admiring the architecture. They made for a wonderful dialectic, Burnham's *sostenutos* and Chambers' enigmatic descants. The next morning, press day, he was at his desk at eight, and we would have a sandwich lunch. At five he was on the train back to Baltimore, where his wife would meet him. And on reaching his farm he would drop on his bed from fatigue. Three months after he began coming to New York, he collapsed from another heart attack.

· · ·

Six months later, in the Summer of 1959, he felt well enough to indulge a dream, more particularly his wife's gentle dream, to visit Europe. She had never been there, and he had been there only once, in 1927, the trip he described so evocatively in *Witness*. We drove them to the airport after a happy day. I noticed worriedly how heavily he perspired and how nervously his heavy thumbs shuffled through the bureaucratic paraphernalia of modern travel, as he dug up, in turn, passports, baggage tags, vaccination certificates, and airplane tickets. His plans were vague, but at the heart of them was a visit to his old friend, Arthur Koestler.

They were at Koestler's eyrie in Austria for a week, an unforgettable week.

Alpbach, where AK lives, is some four hundred meters higher into the hills than Innsbruck. While we were flying from Paris, the worst landslide since 1908 (I am only quoting) had destroyed several miles of the only road up. Nevertheless, we got through, by jeep, on a road just wide enough for a jeep, and not always quite that. On my side, without leaning out at all, I could see straight down several hundred feet. Happily, the Austrian army was at the wheel of the Jeep. K, waiting at the point were our trail emerged, was thinking of the most amusing headlines: 'Whittaker Chambers crashes over Alpine Trail on secret visit to Arthur Koestler. British Intelligence questions surviving writer.' There in Alpbach we spent some days about which I cannot possibly write fully. Perhaps, some moment being right, it will seem proper to try to recover certain moments. Perhaps. Then K had the idea to wire Greta Buber-Neumann: 'Komme schleunigst. Gute weine. Ausserdem, Whitaker C.' 'Come quickest. Good wine. In addition, WC.' In case you do not know, Greta Buber-Neumann is the daughter-in-law of Martin Buber, widow of Heinz Neumann, most dazzling of the German CP leaders (shot without trial), sister-in-law of Willi Muenzenberg (organizer of the Muenzenberg Trust, killed by the NKVD while trying to escape the Gestapo.) Greta herself spent two years as a slave in Karaganda. By then, the Moscow-Berlin Pact had been signed, and the NKVD handed her (and many others) over to the Gestapo on the bridge at Brest-Litovsk. Then she spent five years in German concentration camps, mostly at Ravensbruck. . . . Impossible to tell here this story of her lifetime, which makes the Odyssey, for all its grandeur, somehow childish. . . . So there we sat, and talked, not merely about the daily experiences of our lives. Each of the two men had tried to kill himself and failed; Greta was certainly the most hardy and astonishing of the three. Then we realized that, of our particular breed, the old activists, we are almost the only survivors. . . ."

They went on to Rome *("In Rome, I had to ask Esther for the nitroglycerine. Since then, I've been living on the stuff . . . ,"),* Venice *("I came back to Venice chiefly to rest. If it were not for my children, I should try to spend the rest of my life here. Other cities are greater or less great than something or some other city. Venice is incomparable. It is the only city I have ever loved"),* Berlin *(I feel as though I had some kind of a moral compulsion to go at this time . . . "),* Paris ("You will look up Malraux?" I wrote him—I remembered the gratitude Chambers felt on receiving a hand-written note from Malraux, who had just read *Witness*: "You have not come back from hell with empty hands." *"Malraux is busy,"* Chambers replied. *"If he wants to see me, he will know where to find me"*).

"Europe," he concluded one letter, *"has almost nothing to say to me, and almost nothing to tell me that I cannot learn just about as well from the European press and occasional European tourists in America; or correspondence. . . . Give* [the Europeans] *the means, and these dear friends, that noble Third Force, will cut our bloody throats. As people, they are stronger than we are, and they know it . . . their disdain for us is withering. Give these superior reeds the economic power to see us at eye level, and they will see right over us. . . ."*

Within a few weeks he got sick again, and abruptly they flew back, and again he was in bed.

He wanted to resign from *National Review*. It was partly that his poor health and his unconquerable perfectionism kept him from producing a flow of copy large enough to satisfy his conscience. Partly it was his *Weltanschauung*, which was constantly in motion. Chiefly he resisted *National Review*'s schematic conservatism, even its schematic anti-communism. *"You . . . stand within, or at any rate are elaborating, a political orthodoxy. I stand within no political orthodoxy. . . . I am at heart a counterrevolutionist. You mean to be conservative, and I know no one who seems to me to have a better right to the term. I am not a conservative. Sometimes I have used the term loosely, especially when I was first called on publicly to classify myself. I have since been as circumspect as possible in using the term about myself. I say: I am a man of the Right."* But a formal withdrawal would mean the final institutional wrench. Emotionally he was drawn to us. *"Could I join you,"* he had written as long ago as 1955, on deciding not to join us, *"that might end my loneliness; it might spell hope. It is, in fact, the great temptation. My decision is, therefore, made across the tug of that temptation."* Chambers, the individualist, believed strongly in organizations. He believed, for instance, in the Republican Party. Not the totemic party of *John Brown's Body* as sung by Everett McKinley Dirksen, but the Republican Party as a Going Organization. *"I shall vote the straight Republican ticket for as long as I live,"* he told me. *"You see, I'm an Orgbureau man."* ("I expect," I replied after the 1958 elections, "that you will outlive the Party.") He easily outmatched my pessimism. Already he had written, on the New Year before the elections, *"I saw my first robin this a.m., sitting huddled, fluffed up and chilly on a bare branch, just like, I thought, a Republican candidate in 1958."* And when the returns came in: *"If the Republican Party cannot get some grip of the actual world we live in and from it generalize and actively promote a program that means something to masses of people—why somebody else will. There will be nothing to argue. The voters will simply vote Republicans into singularity. The Republican Party will become like one of those dark little shops which apparently never sell anything. If, for any reason, you go in, you find, at the back, an old man, fingering for his own pleasure some oddments of cloth. Nobody wants to buy them, which is fine because the old man is not really interested in selling. He just likes to hold and to feel. . . ."*

But the day had to come, as I knew it would. *"This is my resignation from NR,"* he wrote sadly toward the end of 1959. *"This is a retype of the beginning of a much longer letter. . . ."*

· · ·

He had made up his mind to do something else. He enrolled at Western Maryland College as an undergraduate. *"Most people incline to laugh. I think they feel that it is such a waste on all sides since I shall not be around long enough to put it to any use of the kind people call 'good.' I've considered that. I do not wish to die an ignoramus. If I can bring it off in terms of health, energy, time, application, then I think the world should let me try. The world is desperately ignorant at the moment when it has most reason to know with some exactitude. . . ."*

Several reasons why he should take this course were instantly clear to me. He had quit *National Review*. He had failed to complete the book that Random House had been expecting for six years. (That book is now being assembled for publication.) He did not want to sit at home, half crippled and denied the life he would, I think, have liked most to lead, the life of a dawn-to-dusk farmer. Chambers was all Puritan about work. Idleness was utterly incomprehensible to him. Even when he was home and without formal obligations, he was unremittingly active, working, reading, writing, beginning at four or five in the morning. At night he often watched television, and then early to bed.

But there was another reason. In Europe, Koestler, whose book *The Sleepwalkers* Chambers had read just before leaving, had said to him sharply: "You cannot understand what is going on in the world unless you understand science deeply." Very well, then, he would learn science. And so the author of *Witness*, former book reviewer and foreign editor for *Time*, author of profound essays on history and theology and politics, of exhaustive articles on the Renaissance and the culture of the Middle Ages, writer of what Dwight Macdonald has called the most emotive political prose of our time, whose voice John Strachey had called, along with those of Orwell, Camus, Koestler and Pasternak, the "strangled cry" of the West in crisis, a sixty-year-old man fluent in French, German, at home in Italian, Spanish and Russian, went back to school.

I remembered suddenly that the hero of *The Sleepwalkers* was Johann Kepler. And I remembered the first question in an examination in physics I struggled with at Yale: "State," it said, in those hortatory accents common to government forms and college examinations, "Kepler's Laws." I hadn't been able to state them, let alone understand them. So Chambers would learn about Kepler. God help us.

He threw himself into his work. Science courses galore. And for relaxation, Greek, Latin and advanced French composition. Every morning he drove to school and sat between the farmers' sons of Western Maryland, taking notes, dissecting frogs, reciting Greek paradigms, working tangled problems in physics. Home, and immediately to the basement to do his homework. Everything else was put aside. He signed up for the summer session, of course, but in the interstice between terms (*"First day of Summer break, and I am wild with liberty. I was still standing, by hanging on to the ropes, when the final bell sounded"*) he drove north to see his daughter, and spent the day with us on a hot afternoon during the summer. How do you get on, my wife asked him, with your fellow undergraduates? "Just fine," he said. "In fact, I have an admirer. A young lady, aged about nineteen, who shares with me the carcasses of small animals, which the two of us proceed, in tandem, to disembowel—the college can't afford one starfish per pupil, let alone one piglet. For months while we worked together she addressed me not a word, and I was afraid my great age had frightened her. But last week, all of a sudden, she broke silence. She said breathlessly: 'Mr. Chambers?' 'Yes,' I answered her anxiously. 'Tell me, what do *you* think of *Itsy Bitsy Teenie Weenie Yellow Polka-dot Bikini'?*" He broke down with laughter. He hadn't, at the critical moment, the least idea that the young lady was talking about a popular song, but he had improvised beautifully until he was able to deduce what on earth it was all about, whereupon he confided to his co-vivisectionist that it happened that this was absolutely, positively, indisputably his very favorite song, over all others he had ever heard. Her gratitude was indescribable. From that moment on they chirped together happily and pooled their knowledge about spleens and livers, kidneys and upper intestines.

I imagine he was a very quiet student, giving his teachers no cause whatsoever for the uneasiness they might have expected to feel in the presence of so august a mind. Only once, that I know of, was he aroused to take issue with one of his teachers.

"An incident from my Greek class, which has left me in ill favor. We came on a Greek line of Diogenes: 'Love of money is the mother-city of all the ills.' Opinions were invited; and when my turn came, I answered with one word: 'Nonsense.' That was too vehement, but there was a reason. Behind me was sitting a Junior, who manages on a scholarship or grant or something of the kind, and whose college life has been made a misery by poverty. . . . All things considered, he is a pretty good student; but his sleepiness makes him an easy professorial butt. In addition, he is not a particularly personable youth. To say in the presence of such a case, 'Love of money is the mother-city of all ills . . .' is why I answered 'Nonsense.' . . . I offered in Greek: 'A lack of money is the root of many ills.' . . . I thought I could speak with some freedom since there can scarcely ever have existed a man in whom love of money is as absolutely absent as in me. I don't even get properly interested in it. Oh, I also offered (while authority was being bandied) St. Thomas Aquinas' 'Money is neither good nor bad in itself: it depends on what is done with it.' But St. Thomas seems not to be in good standing. So, down the generations go the blinded minds, blinkered minds, at any rate. But I wonder what Master Jones, the impoverished Junior, thought about it. I did not ask. He, like the other Greeks who were doing most of the talking, is a pre-divinity student—pre-Flight, as they call it happily here."

During examination weeks he was in a constant state of high boil. He slaved for his grades. And he achieved them, even in the alien field of science: all A's, or A-'s; once, as I remember, a humiliating B+. After the winter, his fatigue was total, overwhelming. *"Weariness, Bill,"* he wrote in the last letter I had from him, shortly before John's wedding, *"—you cannot yet know literally what it means. I wish no time would come when you do know, but the balance of experience is against it. One day, long hence, you will know true weariness and will say: 'That was it.' My own life of late has been full of such realizations."* He learned science, and killed himself. Those were the two things, toward the end, he most wanted to do.

· · ·

"Why on earth doesn't your Father answer the phone?" I asked Ellen in Connecticut on Saturday afternoon, the 8th of July. "Because," she said with a laugh, shyly, "Poppa and the phone company are having a little tiff, and the phone is disconnected. They wanted him to trim one of his favorite trees to take the strain off the telephone line, and he put it off. So . . . they turned off the phone." I wired him: "WHEN YOU COME TO TERMS WITH THE PHONE COMPANY GIVE ME A RING." But he didn't call. The following Tuesday I came back to my office from the weekly editorial lunch—I had thought, as often I did, how sorely we missed him there in the dining room. As I walked into my office I had a call. I took it standing, in front of my desk. It was John Chambers. He gave me the news. A heart attack. The final heart attack. Cremation in total privacy. The news would go to the press later that afternoon. His mother was in the hospital. I mumbled the usual inappropriate things, hung up the telephone, sat down, and wept. *"American men, who weep in droves in movie houses, over the woes of lovestruck shop girls, hold that weeping in men is unmanly* [he wrote me once]. *I have found that most men in whom there was depth of experience, or capacity for compassion, singularly apt to tears. How can it be otherwise? One looks and sees: and it would be a kind of impotence to be incapable of, or to grudge, the comment of tears, even while you struggle against it. I am immune to soap opera. But I cannot listen for any length to the speaking voice of Kirsten Flagstad, for example, without being done in by that magnificence of tone that seems to speak from the center of sorrow, even from the center of the earth."*

For me, and others who knew him, his voice had been and still is like Kirsten Flagstad's, magnificent in tone, speaking to our time from the center of sorrow, from the center of the earth.

13

MURRAY KEMPTON

A Narodnik from Lynbrook

NEW YORK REVIEW OF BOOKS,
JANUARY 29, 1970

Ｔ HESE ARE THE LETTERS Whittaker Chambers wrote to his last and his best—that is, his most respectful—employer.[1] The compliment is less than Mr. Buckley's kindness of nature deserves, since his most conspicuous fellows in the company of Chambers's former employers happen to be Colonel Bykov of the Soviet Secret Police, the late Henry Luce, and John F. X. McGohey, "then United States Attor-ney" for the Southern District of New York. These documents will come as a surprise to those persons who think of Chambers as simple and evil, since they begin in 1954 with a warning to Buckley against Senator Joe McCarthy and approach their end in 1959, with Chambers complaining, like any other sensitive American traveling abroad, about the embarrassments inflicted upon the home country by the Chairman of the Senate Committee on Internal Security and by the Strategic Air Command.

They also provide as much as we can know of Chambers's last endeavor at factional agitation: he seems to have been Vice President Nixon's man on the Board of Editors of *National Review*. This operation was anything but covert: Chambers indeed held back from joining *National Review* at its outset largely because its other editors so distrusted Mr. Nixon for being a centrist. "I am an *org* man," he once wrote Buckley. Mr. Nixon was General Secretary of the last *org* he had; his faith in the Vice President remained a major point of difference with those of his colleagues whose conservative principles were so much superior to those of Mr. Nixon that they had vaulted to the higher level of those of Senator Joe McCarthy.

"Something . . . in your letter," he writes to Willi Schlamm in December, 1954, "leaves the impression that there is an affinity between the *National Review* and a third party movement . . . a third party will be Senator McCarthy and his rally. I shall not be blaming him or them exclusively, if I say that such a move seems to me to be completing by suicide the wreck of the Republican party . . ."

Four years later, when he is abroad, he explains to Buckley:

> The masses must be won by the Republican Left while keeping the Republican Right within the family. Once I hoped that Mr. Nixon could perform this healing bond, holding the Right in line, while a Republican Left formed about him a core. . . . The Republican Party will win the masses, or history will find for it a quiet, uncrowded spot in the potter's field . . ."

. . .

That Mr. Nixon occasionally took counsel with Chambers was no secret; if it had been, Chambers would certainly have broken it, because, if the connection amused Buckley, it also impressed him. Perhaps it was Chambers's loneliness, the experience of having to begin life again so often as a stranger in new surroundings, which explains his need always to carry the aura of an ambassador from some Other Shore: the Hisses, he says, were drawn to him because they thought him a Russian, which, to the extent that the will could conquer an origin in Lynbrook, L.I., he certainly was and remained. His colleagues at *Time* knew that he had been an agent of the G.P.U. so long before the fact became notorious that we have to conclude that he told them early and often. Mr. Nixon was then only the last of those princes and powers of the outer air the suggestion of whose portfolio he bore.

His enjoyment of the mystery which was his alone to understand comes up now and again in these letters as the hint of knowing more than he can say. Some gossip had said that the Vice President did not always speak kindly of President Eisenhower. "But in this area," Chambers wrote, "I must have Mr. Nixon's permission to write (and especially to quote); and if he should feel it better to let the matter die, I am afraid I should have to agree with him." (October 8, 1957)

"There is some very big news in the making, which I am bound not to hint at . . . I think I can and must say this: the first stages of what I refer to have already taken place, and been widely discussed. Only no one sees what is implied. So look, if you are interested, at seemingly minor news of the past fortnight or so. . . . I guess I may say this too: the President's news conference disclosure of an arrangement with No. 2 [Nixon] was not an accident, though the succession was not the big news." (Buckley's explanatory notes make no reference to whatever great event was there portended and subsequently revealed; the chances are that there was none, since the Eisenhower administration was as scrupulous in the avoidance of great events as it was in working up truly interesting secrets.)

Chambers seems to have been troubled early on by worry that Buckley might think he was using his *National Review* essays to reflect Mr. Nixon's mind. "I should expect our (his and my) position to be loosely similar on most issues. Yet I shall never be speaking for him; while I, like him, reach my conclusions independently. Conclusions I reach that may be of any use or of any interest to him, I freely submit. His rejection or concurrence is not my affair." (October, 1957)

Mr. Nixon, he went on to suggest, had consulted with him in 1952 over whether the cause might be better served by supporting General Eisenhower rather than Senator Taft for the Republican nomination. "We disagreed 'sharply' . . . He was judging in political terms and, in those terms, was absolutely right." Mr. Nixon's disregard for Chambers's advice made possible, of course, that happy betrayal of the Republican Right which earned him the vice presidential nomination and constitutes, along with his part in the Hiss-Chambers affair, the only substantial achievements of his career prior to his ascension to the presidency.

. . .

Still, the consultations endured at least into 1960, although the bond between the two seems, like so many of Chambers's other commitments, to have been a domestic affection dressed up as the summons of history: he was always curiously sentimental about persons who from kindness had ruined his career—far from having any need to forgive he seems positively grateful to the old friend who liked him so much that he drafted him into the Communist underground—and Mr. Nixon, more than most other men of affairs, is sentimental about persons who have advanced his. They drifted apart not because Mr. Nixon was distracted by larger matters—he remained indeed most properly solicitous—but because Chambers in the end found that there was very little about Mr. Nixon which could sustain the historical imagination:

"My rule," he finally tells Mr. Buckley, "is never to mention to anyone my contacts with him. I'm going to break it this once, for a reason, but I wish you not to mention what I shall say. Not long ago I had lunch with him. He asked us down one Sunday, and we had a long talk. What was said? Except for two minor points I could not say . . . I suppose the sum of it was: we have really nothing to say to each other. While we talked, I felt crushed by the sense of the awful burden he was inviting in the office he wants . . . If he were a great, vital man, bursting with energy, ideas (however malapropos), sweeping grasp of the crisis, and (even) intolerant convictions, I think I should have felt: Yes, he must have it; he must enact his fate, and ours. I did not have this feeling . . . So I came away with unhappiness for him, for all." (March 10, 1960)

And yet, against all Chambers's habits, how peaceful this last apostasy seems. In the first case, horror, terror, and guilt; in this one, only the moment of inconsequence, when the side of Nothing is left for no side whatsoever. Still, it could be one of Mr. Nixon's better qualities that he makes so small a wrench for those who give up on him and that, in his case, there have always been so few illusions whose destruction might embitter the memory at the moment of parting. The emptiness of the terms of enlistment has at least the use of making peaceful its abandonment.

We have gone on about Chambers's engagement with Mr. Nixon longer than it is worth. But then it has been Chambers's general fate to have struggled to be an historical presence and to end up being treated merely as an historical object, to be offered for notice only when it can be presented as current. By now this object's one remaining topical tag is no more than the accident of its place in the career of a sitting president and its last Witness just one among so many testaments to that president's inadequacy.

. . .

And yet I think Chambers is worth more of our attention—indeed our sympathy—than that. There are, of course, barriers to that attention, let alone that sympathy. Richard Rovere said very early that he did not expect much market for books supporting the official verdict on the Hiss-Chambers case simply because people would rather be told about innocence than about guilt.

Then too there are the distasteful associations of the act for which he is best remembered, not the espionage but the naming of his partner in espionage. The second is a kind of betrayal far worse thought of by private men than the first. Afterwards Chambers's society would seldom extend beyond persons like Mr. Nixon and Buckley, who revered him for his service to his country; yet they brought him no comfort. The harshest words of his enemies could hardly have exceeded the bleakness and the self-contempt of his own picture of himself during the performance of the deed which made him so notorious:

> The informer is different, especially the ex-Communist informer. He risks little. He sits in security and uses his special knowledge to destroy others. He has that special information to give because he knows those others' faces, voices and lives, because he once lived within their confidence, in a shared faith, trusted by them as one of themselves, accepting their friendship, feeling their pleasures and griefs, sitting in their houses, eating at their tables, accepting their kindness, knowing their wives and children. If he had none of these things, he would have no use as an informer.
>
> Because he has that use, the police protect him. He is their creature. When they whistle, he fetches a soiled bone of information . . . He has surrendered his choice. To that extent, though he be free in every other way, the informer is a slave. He is no longer a free man. . . .[2]

These are among the few sorts of feelings it is difficult to imagine any man attesting to insincerely. The gap between Chambers and the persons most outraged by him is that great: they condemn him to the degradation of having lied, while he writhes in the degradation of having told the truth. We can understand his persistence in regretting Buckley's invitations to the occasional evangelical tentshows of the Right. He was a long way from being able to present himself as a Justified Sinner.

. . .

He is cut off from us last of all because, while few of his contemporaries were written about so extensively, almost none has been written about less persuasively. For the last ten years of his life, he engaged no subject without coming back very quickly to himself, and I think he tried to present himself as candidly as he could. But he could not overcome the habit of anointing himself as legate from some Other Shore; he had carried the Mystery too long to put it aside; one's impression of him on stage is of someone perpetually explaining, and still as much a stranger as he was when he appeared. The flood of explanations by others, friendly or hostile, carry no more sense of our being brought closer. Indeed one of the various curiosities of Whittaker Chambers is that the only persuasive picture of him was published in 1947, a year before many Americans had ever heard of him.

Gifford Maxim, the focal figure of Lionel Trilling's *The Middle of the Journey*,[3] is modeled on the Whittaker Chambers whom Trilling knew best, when Chambers was between the Communist Party and *Time*, on the transitory ground of the *Menorah Journal*, and more distinct than he could be under the historical disguises assumed or imposed upon him before or since.

Trilling had known Chambers as a Communist: the memory is both more compelling and purer than it would ever be again, and accords with the moral authority which Chambers tells us he exercised in those days:

> For to Laskell [Trilling's liberal hero], Maxim was never quite alone. Laskell saw him flanked by two great watching figures . . . On one side of Maxim stood the figure of the huge, sad, stern morality of all the suffering and exploited men in the world, all of them without distinction of color or creed. On the other side of Maxim stood the figure of power, noble, fierce, indomitable. Behind Maxim and his two great flanking figures were infinite dim vistas of History, which was not the past but the future.

Laskell's first reaction, when Maxim tells him of his break, is "surprise . . . contempt . . . revulsion . . . It was one thing for a man to abandon his loyalty to the cause he had lived for; it was quite another thing, and far sadder, for him to spread foul and melodramatic stories about it, such terrible stories as were contained in Maxim's silent stare, in his talk of ocean bottoms and pistols behind the ear."

"But, although Maxim might have lost authority, he had not lost his skill." Very soon, although he could not be trusted quite as he had been and the moments of revulsion recurred—"Perhaps only because Maxim spoke them and spoke them often, Laskell felt that never again could anyone say the words tragedy and love"—he retained some of his power to compel belief. For one thing, although those two invisible presences had departed from his side, he seemed otherwise so much what he had been; there was the same "ironic revolutionary eyebrow and the ready, almost maternal, look of solicitude with which he habitually gazed upon human suffering."

It is a while before Laskell can define the difference:

"When you yourself were a member of the Party," he says the last time he is really angry, "you tried to involve us all in your virtue. Now you try to implicate the whole world in your guilt. . . . You have a very fancy kind of mind, Maxim."

That was the single great change; otherwise Maxim, the counter-revolutionary, was surprisingly like Maxim the revolutionary, even to that air of special access to the occult which had been useful to heighten his bearing as a representative of History and which he needed still for his protection as its victim: "He still pretended to his knowledge of hidden motives, but the hidden things he pretended now to see were different from the hidden things he had pretended to see before."

> Maxim had the trick of really good fortune-tellers and palmists of putting things so generally and so dramatically that what was said had to have some sort of relevant meaning, and then if you asked them what they meant, they looked at you with mockery and annoyance, as if you were being willfully stupid, you with your intelligence and sensitivity.

Trilling could, then, recognize the charlatan and still say in 1949, "Whittaker Chambers is a man of honor." It is unlikely that we can ever get a fix on Chambers, but it is certain that we never can if we think there is a contradiction in those two assessments by the same observer. Chambers was not one or the other but both, man of honor and fraud together.

. . .

The habit of the general, dramatic statement which seems somehow relevant persists in these letters. For example, in 1954, Chambers tells Buckley what drew him to Communism, an image which, if its relevance is still not as vivid to him as ever, would hardly seem to have meaning at all:

> In 1907, the Russian government instituted a policy of systematically beating its political prisoners. One night, a fashionably-dressed young woman called at the Central Prison in Petersburg and asked to speak with the commandant, Maximovsky. This was Ragozinikova, who had come to protest the government's policy. . . . When Maximovsky appeared, she shot him with her revolver and killed him. . . . She was sentenced to be hanged. Awaiting execution, she wrote her family "Death itself is nothing. . . . How good it is to love people. How much strength one gains from such love." When she was hanged, Ragozinikova was twenty years old.

Now this is an anecdote which might appear more calculated to unhinge than to strengthen Buckley in his commitment to the defense of established order. Still he seems to have drawn from it the inspiration to go on as he has, it being the nature of anecdotes to have one revelation for me and quite the opposite for thee. Their nature indeed is such that Chambers could take the historical tableaux which had explained to him why he was a Communist and trot them forth intact to explain why he was no longer a Communist. He did add a few more personages, of course, most notably Yurovsky, who shot the Romanovs, and Nechayev, "the nineteenth-century Russian who carried the logic of revolution to its limit, teaching (Lenin among others) . . . that all crimes are justified if they serve the socialist cause." (Curiously enough, after twelve years in the Party, considerable immersion in the legends of nineteenth-century revolutionaries, and a term under commanders who had learned far more from Nechayev than from Ragozinikova, he had never heard of Nechayev until Colonel Bykov mentioned him in 1937, which is rather like serving the Papacy of Alexander VI while focusing all one's attention on The Pastoral Care of Gregory the Great.) But, in essence, the tableaux remain what they were—the attitudes of the Narodniki.

The anecdote as revelation ought then to seem to us a pretty suspicious bit of goods. Still the trick is infectious; trying to understand Chambers, you clutch gratefully at Victor Serge's quarrel with Miguel Almereyda, an old comrade he had begun to suspect of taking German money to arouse the French against the First World War:

> I told him, "You're just an opportunist." . . . He answered, "As far as Paris is concerned you are an ignoramus, my friend. You can purify yourself with Russian novels, but here the revolution needs cash."

Those, of course, are the two points from which one set of revolutionaries has always quarreled with the other. And, if these letters seem to tell us more about Chambers than he was ever able otherwise to tell us, it is because they reveal him accommodating both points within himself; he was able to know himself at once purer and more worldly-wise than the others.

· · ·

Whether the subject was the higher morality or practical affairs, he was a serious, although never malicious, snob. Buckley had established *The*

National Review to shore up the present with various fragments of the ruins of the future; and, ahead of Chambers, he had assembled into his *cadre* William S. Schlamm, who had been wandering since he left the Austrian Communist Party in 1929; Frank Meyer, who had been educational director of the Chicago Communist Party in the Forties; and James Burnham. Chambers's tone about them all seldom descends below affectionate condescension. "Willi [Schlamm] was heaved out of the Communist Party. I broke out. . . . But I have known a dozen minds of the same size and shape as Willi's. He has no surprises whatever for me. . . ." "If the Rep. Party cannot get some grip on the real world . . . [it] will become like one of those dark little shops which apparently never sell anything. If, for any reason, you go in, you find at the back an old man, fingering for his own pleasure some oddments of cloth (weave and design of 1850). . . . You are only slightly surprised to see that the old man is Frank Meyer." "Burnham is a man of honor. . . . He was a Trotskyist, precisely at the moment when Trotskyism was worn to a shadow by reality."

Chambers explains what sets him apart from all such drabs: "Unlike most Western Communists . . . I remained under the spiritual influence of the Narodniki long after I became a Marxist. In fact I never threw it off. I never have."

It is the assurance of purification by reading Russian novels which survives all changes; there is no spite in that assurance but just a degree of hauteur whose equivalent can be remembered only from the evening Malraux went to a working-class quarter to defend DeGaulle against his Socialist opponents and asked: "What do they know of the Left? Were they in Spain?"

· · ·

Yet Chambers is no less snobbish about his superior sense of the practical, being in Buckley's service first the former senior editor of

Time and only after hours the counter-revolutionary. "I am for a magazine ... if its first and steadfast purpose is to succeed.... Another crusade does not interest me at all." In that key, whatever briskness he brought to his last assignment was devoted to the preachment that the first task of a magazine is to reach a market: one's models for style ought not to be mixed up with one's notions of sound public policy. Buckley passes on to him a complaint from Rebecca West about the *New Statesman* and Chambers gives back the cold reply: "If the *New Statesman* is a 'muck heap' I wish General Grant would tell me what whiskey he drinks so I could send the same brand to the other generals." It ought to be odd to find that, having come to rest with a cadre of persons who shared his despair for the West, he should have written pieces for *National Review* rather more casual and less portentous than those he used to compose for *Time* at the dawn of the American Century. But the tone in both cases must have been commanded more by his impulse as a craftsman than by his inspiration as a prophet, his voices having told him that *Time* needed darkening with trombones to be rounded for the market and that *National Review* needed lightening with strings.

Yet he has not changed but simply come to rest; he is still so much the fortune-teller; he remains too mischievous to leave off the intimations of the occult. Even when he is the tipster, he pretends to be the seer:

> I think I am obliged to tell you, if you are interested in a quick turnover, to have a thought to Phila. and Reading Coal Company. It stands at 27 and a fraction.... I have reason to believe that, within the next 12 days, it will make interesting gains.... I know, I know—we old revolutionists are peculiar birds. (January 23, 1957)

He departed after a while having lost hope of being able to teach Buckley but grateful for the affection. He had a history of serving his employers faithfully and being parted from them indifferently.

"Some time after the Hiss Case had formally closed, certain of my effects, including Kafka's Parables," he says, "were sent back to me from Time—somewhat as the effects found in the pockets of a man who has met a fatal accident—his wallet, driver's license, social security stub—are mailed to his relicts."[4]

Thinking of that cold parcel, we have to be glad that Chambers could this once part from an employer who cherished for him an affection and respect which amounted to reverence. Still what Buckley made of him otherwise is hard to say.

. . .

In May, 1959, Chambers made his last effort as Teacher before giving up. Could not the Right, he asked Buckley, begin to "examine and define with a special scrupulousness the civil liberties field." Take the internal Communist peril: ". . . as of now, there seems to me a certain unreality about the Right's general treatment of this subject as if no drastic change had occurred. . . . Why for example should we leave it to liberals to give tongue against the frightening developments in wiretapping? . . . The Right I feel more and more must find its conscience and make it explicit, first of all to the Right."

Ten years later, *National Review* remains as alarmed by the Communists within, as if no change at all had occurred. Buckley has even joined Mr. Nixon as an advisor to his information service. Poor Chambers could not even teach him from genuine experience that Mr. Nixon is someone with whom everyone finds himself left eventually without anything to say. In this small case, as with the large one of Alger Hiss, Chambers's ghost could say: "Scratch across my effort: Canceled." Buckley worshipped and did not listen; the real affection aside, the Chambers of his vision is a saint whose ikon hangs in a Church where his message is never read.

The icon is not recognizable. Neither, to be sure is that mask of the goblin which survives in more general circulation. But perhaps the tricks of Maxim were the most important part of his nature; and so—the thought is not meant cruelly—may have been the masks of Whittaker Chambers. He always, except here, when so plainly what he really wants most is to rest, must have *seemed* to be so much larger than he really *was*. There was always an invisible other presence: He says Hiss thought him a Russian, which added the presence of *Chapayev* and the sailors of Kronstadt; at *Time* there were those sentences about his long nights at the window, adding the presence of the sword over the head. Chambers suggests that Alger Hiss did not understand him. That Buckley did not understand him either is strongly suggested by Buckley's apparent deafness to any intrusion of common sense into the syllabus. Yet Chambers's most intense recollection of his time with the Hisses was of rest and domestic tranquility; and it must have been very like that with Buckley also. We are glad to find him happy here at the last even though it was the curious happiness of the man to find peace of soul and comfort of spirit in The Friend Who Does Not Understand.

NOTES

[1] *Odyssey of a Friend: Whittaker Chambers' Letters to William F. Buckley, Jr., 1954–1961*, ed. William F. Buckley Jr. New York: Putnam, 1969.

[2] *Witness*, p. 454.

[3] *The Viking Press*, 1947, reprinted as *Anchor A-98*, 1956.

[4] *Cold Friday*, p. 209.

14

LIONEL TRILLING

Whittaker Chambers and The Middle of the Journey

NEW YORK REVIEW OF BOOKS, APRIL 17, 1975

T HE IMPENDING REISSUE IN England of *The Middle of the Journey* so many years after it was first published makes an occasion when I might appropriately say a word about the relation which the novel bears to actuality, especially to the problematical kind of actuality we call history. The relation is really quite a simple one but it is sometimes misunderstood.

· · ·

From my first conception of it, my story was committed to history— it was to draw out some of the moral and intellectual implications of the powerful attraction to Communism felt by a considerable part of the American intellectual class during the Thirties and Forties. But although its historical nature and purpose are attested to by the explicit reference it makes to certain of the most momentous events of our epoch, the book I wrote in 1946–1947 and published in 1947 did not depict anyone who was a historical figure. When I have said this, however, I must go on to say that among the characters of my story there is one who had been more consciously derived from actuality than any of the others—into the creation of Gifford Maxim there had gone not only such imagination as I could muster on his behalf but also a considerable amount of recollected observation of a person with whom I had long been acquainted; a salient fact about him was that at one period of his life he had pledged himself to the cause of Communism and had then bitterly repudiated his allegiance. He might therefore be thought of as having moved for a time in the ambiance of history even though he could scarcely be called a historical figure; for that he clearly was not of sufficient consequence. This person was Whittaker Chambers.

But only a few months after my novel was published, Chambers's status in history underwent a sudden and drastic change. The Hiss case broke upon the nation and the world, and Chambers became beyond any doubt a historical figure.

The momentous case had eventuated from an action taken by Chambers almost a decade earlier. In 1939 he had sought out an official of the government—Adolph Berle, then assistant secretary of state—with whom he lodged detailed information about a Communist espionage apparatus to which he himself had belonged as a courier and from which he had defected some years earlier. What led him to make the disclosure at this time was his belief that the Soviet Union would make common cause with Nazi Germany and come to stand in a belligerent relation to the United States.

As a long belated, circuitously reached outcome of this communication, Alger Hiss was intensively investigated and questioned, a procedure which by many was thought bizarre in view of the exceptional esteem in which the suspected man was held—he had been an official in President Roosevelt's administrations since 1933 and a member of the State Department since 1936; he had served as adviser to the president at Yalta, and as temporary secretary general of the United Nations; in 1946 he had been elected president of the Carnegie Endowment for International Peace. The long tale of investigation and confrontation came to an end when a federal grand jury in New York, after having twice summoned Hiss to appear before it, indicted him for perjury. The legal process which followed was prolonged, bitter, and of profound moral, political, and cultural importance. Chambers, who had been the effectual instigator of the case, was the chief witness against the man whom he had once thought of as a valued friend. He was as much on trial as Alger Hiss and his ordeal was perhaps even more severe.

. . .

At the time I wrote *The Middle of the Journey*, Chambers was a successful member of the staff of *Time* and a contributor of signed articles to *Life* and therefore could not be thought of as having a wholly private existence, but he was not significantly present to the consciousness of a great many people. Only to such readers of my novel as had been Chambers's collegemates or his former comrades in the Communist Party or were now his professional colleagues would the personal traits and the political career I had assigned to Gifford Maxim connect him with the actual person from whom these were derived.

In America *The Middle of the Journey* was not warmly received upon its publication or widely read (the English response was more cordial) and some time passed before any connection was publicly made between the obscure novel and the famous trial. No sooner was the connection made than it was exaggerated. To me as the author of the novel there was attributed a knowledge of events behind the case which of course I did not have. All I actually knew that bore upon what the trial disclosed was Whittaker Chambers's personality and the fact that he had joined, and then defected from, a secret branch of the Communist Party. This was scarcely arcane information. Although Chambers and I had been acquainted for a good many years, anyone who had spent a few hours with him might have had as vivid a sense as

I had of his comportment and temperament, for these were out of the common run, most memorable, and he was given to making histrionic demonstration of them. As for his political career, its phase of underground activity, as I shall have occasion to say at greater length, was one of the openest of secrets while it lasted, and, when it came to an end, Chambers believed that the safety of his life depended upon the truth being widely known.

That there was a connection to be drawn between Whittaker Chambers and my Gifford Maxim became more patent as the trial progressed, and this seemed to make it the more credible that my Arthur Croom derived from Alger Hiss; some readers even professed to see a resemblance between Nancy Croom and Mrs. Hiss. If there is indeed any likeness to be discerned between the fictive and the actual couples, it is wholly fortuitous. At no time have I been acquainted with either Alger Hiss or Priscilla Hiss, and at the time I wrote the novel, we did not, to my knowledge, have acquaintances in common. The name of Hiss was unknown to me until some months after my book had appeared.

. . .

It was not without compunction that I had put Whittaker Chambers to the uses of my story. His relation to the Communist Party bore most pertinently upon the situation I wanted to deal with and I felt no constraint upon my availing myself of it, since Chambers, as I have indicated, did not keep it secret but, on the contrary, wished it to be known. But the man himself, with all his idiosyncrasies of personality, was inseparable from his political experience as I conceived it, and in portraying the man himself to the extent I did I was conscious of the wish that nothing I said or represented in my book could be thought by Chambers to impugn or belittle the bitter crisis of conscience I knew him to have undergone. His break with the Communist Party under the circumstances of his particular relation to it had been an act of courage and had entailed much suffering, which, I was inclined to suppose, was not yet at its end.

Such concern as I felt for Chambers's comfort of mind had its roots in principle and not in friendship. Chambers had never been a friend of mine though we had been in college at the same time, which meant that in 1947 we had been acquainted for twenty-three years. I hesitate to say that I disliked him and avoided his company—there was indeed something about him that repelled me, but there was also something that engaged my interest and even my respect. Yet friends we surely were not.

Whether or not Chambers ever read my book I cannot say. At the time of its publication he doubtless learned from reviews, probably also from one of the friends we had in common, that the book referred to him and his experience. And then when the trial of Alger Hiss began, there was the notion, quite widely circulated and certain to reach him, that *The Middle of the Journey* had evidential bearing on the case. In one of the autobiographical essays in his posthumous volume *Cold Friday*, Chambers names me as having been among the friends of his college years, which, as I have said, I was not, and goes on to speak of my having written a novel in which he is represented. He concludes his account of my relation to him by recalling that when "a Hiss investigator" tried to induce me to speak against him in court, I had refused and said, "Whittaker Chambers is a man of honor."

I did indeed use just those words on the occasion to which Chambers refers and can still recall the outburst of contemptuous rage they evoked from the lawyer who had come to call on me to solicit my testimony. I should like to think that my having said that Chambers and I were not friends will lend the force of objectivity to my statement, the substance of which I would still affirm. Whittaker Chambers had been engaged in espionage against his own country; when a change of heart and principle led to his defecting from his apparatus, he had eventually not only confessed his own treason but named the comrades who shared it, including one whom for a time he had cherished as a friend. I hold that when this has been said of him, it is still possible to say that he was a man of honor.

· · ·

Strange as it might seem in view of his eventual prominence in the narrative, Chambers had no part in my first conception and earliest drafts of *The Middle of the Journey*. He came into the story fairly late in its development and wholly unbidden. Until he made his appearance I was not aware that there was any need for him, but when he suddenly turned up and proposed himself to my narrative, I could not fail to see how much to its point he was.

His entrance into the story changed its genre. It had been my intention to write what we learned from Henry James to call a *nouvelle*, which I take to be a fictional narrative longer than a long short story and shorter than a short novel. Works in this genre are likely to be marked by a considerable degree of thematic explicitness—one can usually paraphrase the informing idea of a *nouvelle* without being unforgivably reductive; it needn't be a total betrayal of a *nouvelle* to say what it is "about." Mine was to be about death—about what had happened to the way death is conceived by the enlightened consciousness of the modern age.

The story was to take place in the mid-Thirties and the time in which it is set is crucial to it. Arthur and Nancy Croom are the devoted friends of John Laskell; during his recent grave illness it was they who oversaw his care and they have now arranged for him to recruit his strength in the near vicinity of their country home. Upon his arrival their welcome is of the warmest, yet Laskell can't but be aware that the Crooms become somewhat remote and reserved whenever he speaks of his illness, during which, as they must know, there had been a moment when his condition had been critical. To Laskell the realization of mortality has brought a kind of self-knowledge, which, even though he does not fully comprehend it, he takes to be of some considerable significance, but whenever he makes a diffident attempt to speak of this to his friends, they appear almost to be offended.

He seems to perceive that the Crooms' antagonism to his recent experience and to the interest he takes in it is somehow connected with the rather anxious esteem in which they hold certain of their country neighbors. In these people, who in the language of the progressive liberalism of the time were coming to be called "little people," the Crooms insist on perceiving a quality of simplicity and authenticity which licenses their newly conceived and cherished hope that the future will bring into being a society in which reason and virtue will prevail. In short, the Crooms might be said to pass a *political* judgment upon Laskell for the excessive attention he pays to the fact that he had approached death and hadn't died. If Laskell's preoccupation were looked at closely and objectively, they seem to be saying, might it not be understood as actually an affirmation of death, which is, in practical outcome, a negation of the future and of the hope it holds out for a society of reason and virtue. Was there not a sense in which death might be called reactionary?

This was the *donnée* which I undertook to develop. As I have said, the genre that presented itself as most appropriate to my purpose was the *nouvelle*, which seemed precisely suited to the scope of my given idea, to what I at first saw as the range of its implications. After Chambers made his way into the story, bringing with him so much more than its original theme strictly needed, I had to understand that it could no longer be contained within the graceful limits of the *nouvelle*: it had to be a novel or nothing.

Chambers was the first person I ever knew whose commitment to radical politics was meant to be definitive of his whole moral being, the controlling element of his existence. He made the commitment while he was still in college and it was what accounted for the quite exceptional respect in which he was held by his associates at that time. He entered Columbia in 1920, a freshman rather older than his classmates, for he had spent a year between high school and college as an itinerant worker. He was a solemn youth who professed political views of a retrograde kind and was still firm in a banal religious faith. But by 1923 his principles had so far changed that he wrote a blasphemous play about the Crucifixion, which, when it was published in a student magazine, made a scandal that led to his withdrawal from college. He was subsequently allowed to return, but in the intervening time he had lost all interest in academic life—during a summer tour of Europe he had witnessed the social and economic disarray of the Continent and discovered both the practical potential and the moral heroism of revolutionary activity. Early in 1925 he joined the Communist Party.

Such relation as I had with Chambers began at this time, in 1924–1925, which was my senior year. It is possible that he and I never exchanged a single word at college. Certainly we never conversed. He knew who I was—that is, he connected me with my name—and it may be that the report I was once given of his having liked a poem of mine had actually originated as a message he sent to me. I used to see him in the company of one group of my friends, young men of intimidating brilliance, of whom some remained loyal to him through everything, though others came to hold him in bitterest contempt. I observed him as if from a distance and with considerable irony, yet accorded him the deference which our common friends thought his due.

The moral force that Chambers asserted began with his physical appearance. This seemed calculated to negate youth and all its graces, to deny that they could be of any worth in our world of pain and injustice. He was short of stature and very broad, with heavy arms and massive thighs; his sport was wrestling. In his middle age there was a sizable outcrop of belly and I think this was already in evidence. His eyes were narrow and they preferred to consult the floor rather than an interlocutor's face. His mouth was small and, like his eyes, tended downward, one might think in sullenness, though this was not so. When the mouth opened, it never failed to shock by reason of the dental ruin it disclosed, a devastation of empty sockets and blackened stumps. In later years, when he became respectable, Chambers underwent restorative dentistry, but during his radical time his aggressive toothlessness had been so salient in the image of the man that I did not use it in portraying Gifford Maxim, feeling that to do so would have been to go too far in explicitness of personal reference. This novelistic self-denial wasn't inconsiderable, for that desolated mouth was the perfect insigne of Chambers's moral authority. It annihilated the hygienic American present—only a serf could have such a mouth, or some student in a visored cap who sat in his Moscow garret and thought of nothing save the moment when he would toss the fatal canister into the barouche of the Grand Duke.

Chambers could on occasion speak eloquently and cogently, but he was not much given to speaking—his histrionism, which seemed unremitting, was chiefly that of imperturbability and long silences. Usually his utterances were gnomic, often cryptic. Gentleness was not out of the range of his expression, which might even include a compassionate sweetness of a beguiling kind. But the chief impression he made was of a forbidding drabness.

In addition to his moral authority, Chambers had a very considerable college prestige as a writer. This was deserved. My undergraduate admiration for his talent was recently confirmed when I went back to the poetry and prose he published in a student magazine in 1924–1925. At that time he wrote with an elegant austerity. Later, beginning with his work for the *New Masses*, something went soft and "high" in his tone and I was never again able to read him, either in his radical or in his religiose conservative phase, without a touch of queasiness.

Such account of him as I have given will perhaps have suggested that Whittaker Chambers, with his distinctive and strongly marked traits of mien and conduct, virtually demanded to be coopted as a fictive character. Yet there is nothing that I have so far told about him that explains why, when once he had stepped into the developing conception of my narrative, he turned out to be so particularly useful—so necessary, even essential—to its purpose.

. . .

I have said that he entered my story unbidden and so it seemed to me at the time, although when I bring to mind the moment at which he appeared, I think he must have been responding to an invitation that I had unconsciously offered. He presented himself to me as I was working out that part of the story in which John Laskell, though recovered from his illness, confronts with a quite intense anxiety the relatively short railway journey he must make to visit the Crooms. There was no reason in reality for Laskell to feel as he did, nor could he even have said what he was apprehensive of—his anxiety was of the "unmotivated" kind, what people call neurotic, by which they mean that it need not be given credence either by the person who suffers it or by those who judge the suffering. It was while I was considering how Laskell's state of feeling should be dealt with, what part it might play in the story, that Chambers turned up, peremptorily asserting his relevance to the question. That relevance derived from his having for a good many years now gone about the world in fear. There were those who would have thought—who did think—that his fear was fanciful to the point of absurdity, even of madness, but I believed it to have been reasonable enough, and its reason, as I couldn't fail to see, was splendidly to the point of my story.

What Chambers feared, of course, was that the Communist Party would do away with him. In 1932—so he tells us in *Witness*—after a short tour of duty as the editor of the *New Masses*, he had been drafted by the Party into its secret apparatus. By 1936 he had become disenchanted with the whole theory and ethos of Communism and was casting about for ways of separating himself from it. To break with the Communist Party of America—the overt Party, which published the *Daily Worker* and the *New Masses* and organized committees and circulated petitions—entailed nothing much worse than a period of vilification, but to defect from the underground organization was to put one's life at risk.

To me and to a considerable number of my friends in New York it was not a secret that Chambers had gone underground. We were a group who, for a short time in 1932 and even into 1933, had been in a tenuous relation with the Communist Party through some of its so-called fringe activities. Our relation to the Party deteriorated rapidly after Hitler came to power in early 1933 and soon it was nothing but antagonistic. With this group, some of whose members had, like myself, been at college with him, Chambers was in fairly close contact and he kept in touch with it despite its known hostility to what it now called Stalinism. Two of its members in particular remained his trusted friends despite his involvement in activities which were alien, even hostile, to their own principles.

Although as a member of this group I occasionally saw Chambers and heard that he had gone underground, I formed no clear idea of what he subterraneously did. I understood, of course, that he was in a chain of command that led to Russia, bypassing the American Party.

The foreign connection required that I admit into consciousness the possibility, even the probability, that he was concerned with something called military intelligence, but I did not equate this with espionage—it was as if such a thing hadn't yet been invented.

. . .

Of the several reasons that might be advanced to explain why my curiosity and that of my circle wasn't more explicit and serious in the matter of Chambers's underground assignment, perhaps the most immediate was the way Chambers comported himself on the widely separated occasions when, by accident or design, he came into our ken. His presence was not less portentous than it had ever been and it still had something of its old authority, but if you responded to that, you had at the same time to take into account the comic absurdity which went along with it, the aura of parodic melodrama with which he invested himself, as if, with his darting, covert glances and extravagant precautions, his sudden manifestations out of nowhere in the middle of the night, he were acting the part of a secret agent and wanted to be sure that everyone knew just what he was supposed to be.

But his near approach to becoming a burlesque of the underground revolutionary didn't prevent us from crediting the word, when it came, that Chambers was in danger of his life. We did not doubt that, if Chambers belonged to a "special" Communist unit, his defection would be drastically dealt with, by abduction or assassination. And when it was told to us that he might the more easily be disposed of because he had been out of continuous public view for a considerable time, we at once saw the force of the suggestion. We were instructed in the situation by that member of our circle with whom Chambers had been continuously in touch while making his decision to break with the apparatus. This friend made plain to us the necessity of establishing Chambers in a firm personal identity, an unquestionable social existence which could be attested to. Ultimately this was to be accomplished through a regular routine of life, which included an office which he would go to daily; what was immediately needed was his being seen by a number of people who would testify to his having been alive on a certain date.

To this latter purpose it was arranged that the friend would bring Chambers to a party that many of us planned to attend. It was a Halloween party; the hostess, who had been reared in Mexico, had decorated her house both with the jolly American symbols of All Hallowmas and with Mexican ornaments, which speak of the returning dead in a more literal and grisly way. Years later, when Chambers wished to safeguard the microfilms of the secret documents that had been copied by Hiss, he concealed them in a hollowed-out pumpkin in a field. I have never understood why, when this was reported at the trial, it was thought to be odd behavior which cast doubt upon Chambers's mental stability, for the hiding place was clearly an excellent one. But if a psychological explanation is really needed, it is surely supplied by that acquaintance of Chambers—she had been present at the Halloween party—who traced the unconscious connection between the choice of the hiding place and the jack-o'-lanterns at the party to which Chambers had been taken in order to establish his existence so that he might continue it.

Chambers was brought to the party when it was well advanced. If he had any expectations of being welcomed back from underground to the upper world, he was soon disillusioned. Some of the guests, acknowledging that he was in danger, took the view that fates similar to the one he feared for himself had no doubt been visited upon some of his former comrades through his connivance, which was not to be lightly forgiven. Others, though disenchanted with Communist policy, were not yet willing to believe that the Communist ethic countenanced secrecy and violence. These few judged the information they were given about Chambers's danger to be a libelous fantasy and wanted no contact with the man who propagated it. After several rebuffs, Chambers ceased to offer his hand in greeting and he did not stay at the party beyond the time that was needed to establish that he had been present at it.

. . .

In such thought as I may have given to Chambers over the next years, that Halloween party figured as the culmination and end of his career as a tragic comedian of radical politics. In this, of course, I was mistaken, but his terrible entry upon the historical stage in the Hiss case was not forced upon him until 1948, and through the intervening decade one might suppose that he had permanently forsaken the sordid sublimities of revolutionary politics and settled into the secure anticlimax of bourgeois respectability. In 1939 he had begun his successful association with *Time*. During the years which followed, I met him by chance on a few occasions; he had a hunted, fugitive look—how not?—but he was patently surviving, and as the years went by he achieved a degree of at least economic security and even a professional reputation of sorts with the apocalyptic pieties of his news stories for *Time* and the sodden profundities of his cultural essays for *Life*. Except as these may have made me aware of him, he was scarcely in my purview—until suddenly he thrust himself, in the way I have described, into the story I was trying to tell. I understood him to have come—he, with all his absurdity!—for the purpose of representing the principle of reality.

At this distance in time the mentality of the Communist-oriented intelligentsia of the Thirties and Forties must strain the comprehension even of those who, having observed it at first hand, now look back upon it, let alone of those who learn about it from such historical accounts of it as have been written.[1] That mentality was presided over by an impassioned longing to believe. The ultimate object of this desire couldn't fail to be disarming—what the fellow-traveling intellectuals were impelled to give their credence to was the ready feasibility of contriving a society in which reason and virtue would prevail. A proximate object of their will to believe was less abstract— a large segment of the progressive intellectual class was determined to credit the idea that in one country, Soviet Russia, a decisive step had been taken toward the establishment of just such a society. Among those people of whom this resolute belief was characteristic, any predication about the state of affairs in Russia commanded assent so long as it was of a "positive" nature, so long, that is, as it countenanced the expectation that the Communist Party, having actually instituted the reign of reason and virtue in one nation, would go forward to do likewise throughout the world.

Once the commitment to this belief had been made, no evidence might, or could, bring it into doubt. Whoever ventured to offer such evidence stood self-condemned as deficient in good will. And should it ever happen that reality did succeed in breaching the believer's defenses against it, if ever it became unavoidable to acknowledge that the Communist Party, as it functioned in Russia, did things, or produced conditions, which by ordinary judgment were to be deplored and which could not be accounted for by either the state of experimentation or the state of siege in which the Soviet Union notoriously stood, then it was plain that ordinary judgment was not adequate to the deplored situation, whose moral justification must be revealed by some other agency, commonly "the dialectic."

· · ·

But there came a moment when reality did indeed breach the defenses that had been erected against it, and not even the dialectic itself could contain the terrible assault it made upon faith. In 1939 the Soviet Union made its pact with Nazi Germany. There had previously been circumstances—among them the Comintern's refusal to form a united front with the Social Democrats in Germany, thus allowing Hitler to come to power; the Moscow purge trials; the mounting evidence that vast prison camps did exist in the Soviet Union—which had qualified the moral prestige of Stalinist Communism in one degree or another, yet never decisively. But now to that prestige a mortal blow seemed to have been given. After the Nazi-Soviet pact one might suppose that the Russia of Stalin could never again be the ground on which the hope of the future was based, that never again could it command the loyalty of men of good will.

Yet of course the grievous hurt was assuaged before two years had passed. In 1941 Hitler betrayed his pact with Stalin, the German armies marched against Russia and by this action restored Stalinist Communism to its sacred authority. Radical intellectuals, and those who did not claim that epithet but modestly spoke of themselves as liberal or progressive or even only democratic, would now once again be able to find their moral bearings and fare forward.

Not that things were just as they had been before. It could not be glad confident morning again, not quite. A considerable number of intellectuals who had once been proud to identify themselves by their sympathy with Communism now regarded it with cool reserve. Some even expressed antagonism to it, perhaps less to its theory than to the particularities of its conduct. And those who avowed their intention of rebutting this position did not venture to call themselves by a name any more positive and likely to stir the blood than that of anti-anti-Communists.

Yet that sodden phrase tells us how much authority Stalinist Communism still had for the intellectual class. Anti-anti-Communism was not quite so neutral a position as at first it might seem to have been: it said that although, for the moment at least, one need not be actually *for* Communism, one was morally compromised, turned toward evil and away from good, if one was against it. In the face of everything that might seem to qualify its authority, Communism had become part of the fabric of the political life of many intellectuals.

In the context, *political* is probably the mandatory adjective though it might be wondered whether the Communist-oriented intellectuals of the late Forties did have what is properly to be called a political life. It must sometimes seem that their only political purpose was to express their disgust with politics and make an end of it once and for all, that their whole concern was to do away with those defining elements of politics which are repugnant to reason and virtue, such as mere opinion, contingency, conflicts of interest and clashes of will and the compromises they lead to. Thus it was that the way would be cleared to usher in a social order in which rational authority would prevail. Such an order was what the existence of the Soviet Union promised, and although the promise must now be a tacit one, it was still in force.

· · ·

So far as *The Middle of the Journey* had a polemical end in view, it was that of bringing to light the clandestine negation of the political life which Stalinist Communism had fostered among the intellectuals of the West. This negation was one aspect of an ever more imperious and bitter refusal to consent to the conditioned nature of human existence. In such confrontation of this tendency as my novel proposed to make, Chambers came to its aid with what he knew, from his experience, of the reality which lay behind the luminous words of the great promise.

It was considerably to the advantage of my book that Chambers brought to it, along with reality, a sizable amount of nonsense, of factitiousness of feeling and perception. He had a sensibility which was all too accessible to large solemnities and to the more facile paradoxes of spirituality, and a mind which, though certainly not without force, was but little trained to discrimination and all too easily seduced into equating portentous utterance with truth. If my novel did have a polemical end in view, it still was a novel and not a pamphlet, and I had certain intentions for it as a novel which were served by the decisive presence in it of a character to whom could be applied the phrase I have used of Chambers, a tragic comedian. I had no doubt that my story was a serious one, but I nevertheless wanted it to move on light feet; I was confident that its considerations were momentous, but I wanted them to be represented by an interplay between gravity and levity. The frequency with which Chambers verged on the preposterous, the extent to which that segment of reality which he really did possess was implicated in his half-inauthentic profundities, made him admirably suited to my purpose. If I try to recall what emotions controlled my making of Gifford Maxim out of the traits and qualities of Whittaker Chambers, I would speak first of respect and pity, both a little wry, but also of intellectual and literary exasperation and amusement.

. . .

It was not as a tragic comedian that Chambers ended his days. The development of the Hiss case made it ever less possible to see him in any kind of comic light. The obloquy in which he lived forbade it. He had, of course, known obloquy for a long time, ever since his defection from Communism and the repudiation of the revolutionary position. Even gentle people might treat him with a censorious reserve which could be taken for physical revulsion. Such conduct he had met in part by isolating himself, in part by those histrionic devices which came so easily to him, making him sometimes formidable and sometimes absurd. But the obloquy that fell upon him with the Hiss case went far beyond what he had hitherto borne, and there was no way in which he could meet it, he could only bear it, which he did until he died. The educated, progressive middle class, especially in its upper reaches, rallied to the cause and person of Alger Hiss, confident of his perfect innocence, deeply stirred by the pathos of what they never doubted was the injustice being visited upon him. By this same class Whittaker Chambers was regarded with loathing—the word is not too strong— as one who had resolved, for some perverse reason, to destroy a former friend.[2]

Nor did the outcome of the trial and Hiss's conviction for perjury do anything to alienate the sympathy of the progressive middle class from Hiss or to exculpate Chambers. Indeed, the hostility to Chambers grew the more intense when the case was used by the unprincipled junior senator from Wisconsin, Joseph McCarthy, in his notorious antiradical campaign.

So relentlessly was Chambers hated by people of high moral purpose that the newsletter of his college class, a kind of publication which characteristically is undeviating in its commitment to pious amenity, announced his death in 1961 in an article which surveyed in detail what it represented as his unmitigated villainy.

If anything was needed to assure that Chambers would be held in bitter and contemptuous memory by many people, it was that his destiny should have been linked with that of Richard Nixon. Especially because I write at the moment of Nixon's downfall and disgrace, I must say a word about this connection. The two men came together through the investigation of Hiss which was undertaken by the Committee of the House of Representatives on Un-American Activities; Nixon, a member of the committee, played a decisive part in bringing Hiss to trial. The dislike with which a large segment of the American public came to regard Nixon is often said to have begun as a response to his role in the Hiss case, and probably in the first instance it was he who suffered in esteem from the connection with Chambers. Eventually, however, that situation reversed itself—as the dislike of Nixon grew concomitantly with his prominence, it served to substantiate the odium in which Chambers stood. With the Watergate revelations, the old connection came again to the fore, its opprobrium much harsher than it had ever been, and as discredit overtook the president, partisans of Hiss's innocence were encouraged to revive their old contention that Hiss had been the victim of Chambers and Nixon in conspiracy with each other.

. . .

The tendentious association of the two men does Chambers a grievous injustice. I would make this assertion with rather more confidence in its power to convince if it were not the case that there grew up between Chambers and Nixon a degree of personal relationship and that Chambers had at one period expressed his willingness to hope that Nixon had the potentiality of becoming a great conservative leader. The hope was never a forceful one and it did not long remain in such force as it had—a year before his death Chambers said that he and Nixon "have really nothing to say to each other." The letters in which he speaks of Nixon—they are among those he wrote to William Buckley[3]—are scarcely inspiriting, not only because of the known nature and fate of the man he speculates about but also because it was impossible for Chambers to touch upon politics without falling into a bumble of religiose portentousness. But I think that no one who reads these letters will fail to perceive that the sad and exhausted man who wrote them had nothing in common morally, or, really, politically, with the man he was writing about. In Whittaker Chambers there was much to be faulted, but nothing I know of him has led me to doubt his magnanimous intention.

NOTES

[1] The relation of the class of bourgeois intellectuals to the Communist movement will, I am certain, increasingly engage the attention of social and cultural historians, who can scarcely fail to see it as one of the most curious and significant

phenomena of our epoch. In the existing historiography of the subject, the classical document is *The God That Failed,* edited by Richard Crossman (New York, Harper, 1949; London, Hamish Hamilton, 1950), which consists of the autobiographical narratives of their relation to Communism of six eminent cultural figures, Arthur Koestler, Ignazio Silone, Richard Wright ("The Initiates"), and André Gide, Louis Fischer, Stephen Spender ("Worshippers From Afar"). The American situation is described in a series of volumes called *Communism in American Life,* edited by Clinton Rossiter (various publishers and dates), of which the most interesting are the two volumes by Theodore Draper, *The Roots of American Communism* (New York, Viking, 1957; London, Macmillan, 1957) and American Communism and Soviet Russia (New York, Viking, 1960; London, Macmillan, 1960) and Daniel Aaron's *Writers on the Left* (New York, Harcourt, Brace & World, 1961). The most recent and in some respects the most compendious record of the relation of intellectuals to Communism and the one that takes fullest account of its sadly comic aspects is David Caute's *The Fellow Travellers* (London and New York, Macmillan, 1972).

[2] A psychoanalyst, Dr. Meyer Zeligs, has undertaken to give scientific substantiation to this belief in *Friendship and Fratricide* (New York, Viking, 1967; London, Andre Deutsch, 1967), a voluminous study of the unconscious psychological processes of Chambers and Hiss and of the relations between the two men. In my opinion, no other work does as much as this psychoanalysis in absentia to bring into question the viability of the infant discipline of psychohistory.

[3] See *Odyssey of a Friend: Whittaker Chambers' Letters to William F. Buckley, Jr. 1954-1961,* edited with notes by William F. Buckley, Jr. (New York, Putnam's, 1970).

15

PHILIP   NOBILE

The State of the Art of Alger Hiss

HARPER'S,   APRIL   1976

THE ALGER HISS AFFAIR is tending toward final
judgment. Two forthcoming books purport to settle this perplexing
Cold War Mystery. Both John Chabot Smith's *Alger Hiss: The True
Story* and Allen Weinstein's *Perjury!: The Hiss-Chambers Conflict* reveal
new evidence that promises to upset, if not overturn, long-standing
opinions. Yet Smith and Weinstein argue opposite conclusions. The
resolution of the case will, apparently, be as confounded as its origin.

On December 15, 1948, a federal grand jury sitting in New York
City indicted Alger Hiss for perjury. The charge specified two counts
of false testimony. A bare majority of the jurors asserted that Hiss had
lied when he had denied furnishing copies of confidential State Department documents to Whittaker Chambers in February and Marc h
of 1938, and seeing and conversing with Chambers in the same period. The first trial ended in a hung jury, the second in conviction.
After the appeals were exhausted, the defendant entered Lewisburg
Federal Penitentiary to serve a five-year sentence.

If Hiss had not been such an extraordinary specimen of New
Deal liberalism, his ordeal might have disappeared into history. But
the charisma that transported this handsome Harvard Law graduate

from secretary to Justice Oliver Wendell Holmes, Jr., in 1929, through a series of high government posts in the Thirties and Forties, and culminated in his appointment to the presidency of the Carnegie Endowment for International Peace in 1946, also guaranteed him notoriety after he was branded a Communist agent.

Initially the allegation seemed preposterous. In the summer of 1949, when Whittaker Chambers confessed before the House Un-American Activities Committee that he and Hiss had been comrades in the Communist underground, even the Red-hunting panelists were edgy. For Chambers, a senior editor of *Time,* had no proof. Hiss swore emphatically that he had never laid eyes on Whittaker Chambers and had never joined the Communist party. The public believed him. Chambers was discredited.

But first-term Rep. Richard Nixon, the most junior member of HUAC, had a trick up his sleeve. He arranged a private confrontation of the two adversaries to smoke out the truth. Presented with Chambers in the flesh, Hiss admitted that he had known the man before—but only as a free-lance journalist under the pseudonym of George Crosley. Further hearings chipped away at Hiss's credibility, but Chambers still could not make good on the central issue of party affiliation.

Provoked into a libel suit by Hiss and fearing indictment, Chambers dramatically yielded up a wad of incriminating material—sixty-five pages of typed copies of confidential documents and four slips of paper in Hiss's handwriting—that Hiss had supposedly provided him in 1938 from his office in the trade agreements section of the State Department. Several days later Chambers sprang five rolls of film from a hollowed-out pumpkin on his farm and laid their secret contents to his former friend. Since the telltale copies had been typed on the family machine, a fact the defense did not contest, Hiss had little room to maneuver in court. In his last remarks to the bench before sentencing, the disgraced defendant predicted "that in the future the full facts of how Whittaker Chambers was able to carry out forgery by typewriter will be disclosed."

Despite the verdict and the Supreme Court's refusal to review, reasonable doubt persisted with regard to Hiss's guilt. The case wouldn't shut tight. The bizarre personality of Chambers, the perfervid interest of Richard Nixon, the prosecution's failure to link Hiss to the actual typing of the documents, and the lack of any witness supporting Chambers's party association with Hiss troubled many open minds. Though Hiss was in the left wing of the New Deal, he did not seem the traitorous sort. "Certain it is that the inference that Hiss was 'framed' was strong," wrote Justice William O. Douglas in *Go East, Young Man.*

. . .

"I am a proud man," Hiss declared at the hearings at which he petitioned for reinstatement to the Massachusetts Bar. "I cannot put myself in the position of imagining I had done what I was charged with." After lunching with him in Greenwich Village several months ago, I could hardly imagine it either. Hiss told me the same old story of an unsound informer, forgery by typewriter, ruthless enemies of the New Deal, anti-Communist hysteria, and a poisoned jury. Why would he be peddling this tired line of defense, risking boredom and fresh humiliation, if it weren't true?

"If he was innocent," Alistair Cooke remarked of Hiss's courtroom composure, "this serenity could be only the deep well of security in a character of great strength and purity. In a guilty man, certainly, his detachment would be pathological to the extreme." Even if one grants espionage in the service of a Thirties ally, what kind of monster would compromise his family and friends to save face? "Inside of that smiling face," thundered Hiss's prosecutor in summation, "that heart is black and cancerous." Hiss did not suggest such unmitigated evil at our luncheon. Calm, rational, and strangely unembittered, he elicited sympathy and trust. Surely he could not be one of history's arch-deceivers. Or could he?

Intrigued by Hiss's immutable stand, I conducted an unscientific poll by letter and phone to learn the judgment of his peers. "Based on your knowledge of the Hiss affair," I asked approximately 100 lawyers, journalists, and various intellectuals, "if you had to pronounce Alger Hiss guilty or innocent, what would your verdict be?"

The return approached 50 percent. Several respondents begged off from a direct reply. Norman Mailer, Norman Cousins, *New York Times* columnist Anthony Lewis, and the historian C. Vann Woodward aren't exactly sure. The *Times* Sunday editor Max Frankel reserved his opinion because the poll was "in the service of a subversive idea." And Dean Rusk, a former State Department colleague of the defendant's, cryptically remarked that he doubted "the whole truth became available in the courts—whether from the point of view of the prosecution or the defense."

The new Hiss jury split down the middle. Reasonable men differ on Alger Hiss, and they always will, at least until the solutions of Smith and Weinstein are weighed and measured.

. . .

If the American people understood the real character of Alger Hiss, they would boil him in oil. — Richard Nixon

Hiss's natural constituency, the liberal Left's intelligentsia, deserted him in the Fifties. Arthur Schlesinger, Murray Kempton, Leslie Fiedler, I. F. Stone, Lionel Trilling, Sidney Hook, and Dwight Macdonald long ago allowed for no reasonable doubt. "If Alger Hiss is innocent," Diana Trilling was said to have commented, "I'll commit suicide." And so would her class.

Currently voting for conviction are such strange bedfellows as *For-*

eign Affairs editor William Bundy, columnist Garry Wills, Clare Boothe Luce, journalist John Osborne, William Randolph Hearst, Jr., economist Eliot Janeway and his novelist wife, Elizabeth Janeway, conservative patriarch Russell Kirk, editorialist William Shannon, William Buckley; and, with qualification, author Merle Miller, novelist Laura Z. Hobson, and former diplomat John S. Service.

William Bundy contributed to Hiss's defense fund. As the son-in-law of Dean Acheson, Hiss's former superior at State, and a friend of Donald Hiss, Alger's younger brother, he felt the defendant must have been innocent. A careful study of the trial record and appeal briefs assured him otherwise. Bundy outlined his intriguing theory:

> Mrs. Hiss may have been more active than he, and may actually have handled the transmission—otherwise it seems hard to explain the rather inconsequential character of most of the cables. . . . At the same time, I find it very hard to believe that she could have done this without his knowledge, and the fact that he stuck to a total denial must suggest that he himself was witting, or even perhaps that he remained in some sort of contact with the Soviet apparatus with the idea that he would evolve into an in-place agent.

Some in the "guilty" faction are willing to acquit Hiss on the espionage count. Merle Miller, author of the Truman biography *Plain Speaking,* covered the second trial for *The New Republic.* Astounded by Hiss's apparent evasiveness under cross-examination, he inferred that Hiss was shading the truth about something. "If I had worked at State in the Thirties," Miller said, "I very likely would have been an underground member of the Young Communist League. But it's a big step from bringing booze to a Marxist study group to committing treason." In Miller's opinion, the FBI framed Hiss to foment the Red scare, and Hiss did not come clear on his relationship with Chambers, thereby perjuring himself (on count two) when he denied that he had continued to see Chambers after 1936.

Laura Z. Hobson, author of the 1947 best seller *Gentleman's Agree-*

ment, met Hiss in the early Thirties, when she was married to Thayer Hobson, Priscilla Hiss's first husband. She and Hiss were the go-betweens for their spouses during weekend exchanges of Timmy Hobson, Priscilla and Thayer's only child. She admires Hiss greatly, but feels he may have been a Communist idealist all along. If he did traffic in documents, she observes, they weren't vital to state security. "I can't believe that anybody with as fine a mind as Alger Hiss and who's obviously such a decent human being would ever sell out his country," she said.

. . .

I think if they'd had the goods on Hiss, they'd have produced it, but they didn't. — Harry S. Truman

"It was not invariably, but in general," wrote Whittaker Chambers, "the 'best people' who were for Alger Hiss and who were prepared to go to almost any length to protect and defend him." The ranks have thinned since the Fifties, but many of the "best people" haven't lost their enthusiasm yet. At the Massachusetts Bar hearings, Richard Wait, of the Boston firm of Choate, Hall and Stewart, described the petitioner's moral character as "top hole."

Casting ballots for acquittal are Lillian Hellman, Arthur Miller, Abe Fortas, Nixon's defense lawyer Charles Alan Wright, general secretary of the Communist Party Gus Hall, Marcus Raskin of the Institute for Policy Studies, Yale Law professor Thomas Emerson, historian Bruce Mazlish, and journalists Nat Hentoff, Victor Navasky, and Alexander Cockburn. Robert Sherrill, the veteran Washington muckraker, always despised "finks" like Nixon and Chambers and consequently favored Hiss a priori, as did Carey McWilliams, former editor of *The Nation.*

The Kremlin, must, of course, have the truth about Hiss and Chambers locked in its intelligence vaults. The Moscow line may not be entirely credible, but the party's old U.S. warhorse, Gus Hall, said, when queried, "I can state without reservation that Alger Hiss was never a member of the Communist Party. . . . There has never been the slightest doubt in my mind of Alger Hiss's innocence."

Abe Fortas and Hiss were young New Dealers together. As a former member of the Supreme Court, Fortas felt inhibited about responding to the poll, but his indirection clearly expressed his verdict. "I always had, and still retain," he admitted, "an extremely high opinion of him professionally, as a man of character and integrity, and as a loyal and dedicated American citizen." (I cited Fortas's testimonial to Dean Rusk. Would he at least endorse this description of Hiss despite his hint that the complete story had not been unfolded at the trials? Rusk would not.)

Lillian Hellman remained loyal while others in her crowd fled from Hiss, but she was not uncritical. "I disagreed with the way Mr. Hiss handled his case," Miss Hellman wrote to me, "and I believed then, as I believe now, the rumors that something personal stood in the way of total truth. But a mistake has nothing to do with truth. I believed Mr. Hiss was innocent. Nothing else makes any sense to me."

. . .

Allen Weinstein, historian at Smith and the most hard-nosed researcher of the Hiss affair, summed up its epistemology three years ago when he commented in *The American Scholar* that "although Hiss's *guilt* seems to be still unproved beyond a reasonable doubt, it would be equally difficult, in the light of available evidence, to *prove* him innocent." Times have changed, however.

Weinstein is no longer puzzled. After interviewing sources on all sides, many of whom were unknown to the government and the defense, and traveling as far away as Eastern Europe and Latin America for material, Weinstein has unsnarled the dilemma to his satisfaction.

"On the basis of the evidence so far," he told me, "my account will be compelling to people willing to be persuaded. But I still want to see all the FBI files."

Who's the guilty one? Weinstein prefers to break the details himself, but it is not hard to deduce his conclusion. First, he scoffs at the Gothic horror tales of madness and alcoholism laid to Chambers by the Hiss side. Second, he excludes FBI complicity in a frame-up, which is almost the sine qua non of the defense: "I regard the bureau's involvement as more incompetent than malevolent."

Weinstein purports to have real evidence, not theories, in the form of letters and other documentation: "What I found is more than a powder burn but less than a smoking gun." Although Hiss himself thinks that Weinstein would be more politically comfortable with a hostile verdict, Weinstein broods about the further torment his book may create: "There are moments when I felt like burning a good deal of what I've done, or, as an alternative, writing a novel on the case. . . . Even the most titillating revelations, however true, may be irrelevant."

John Chabot Smith, a former *Herald-Tribune* reporter, studied Hiss intently from the press row at both trials. The conviction disgusted him. "I didn't believe then that Hiss gave Chambers the documents," he says. "But somewhere or other he was holding back or lying about something, and you can't beat a perjury rap by lying on the stand." Hiss rebuffed Smith's first attempt at a biography in 1970 but relented in 1974 after Alden Whitman of *The New York Times* dropped out of a similar project owing to ill health. Smith got along well with his subject and moved into an office provided by Hiss's counsel.

"I was convinced that the missing link had to do with Hiss's personal life," he said, "and only by finding out what it was and making it clear would anyone believe it was Chambers who lied and not Hiss. It is the key—the reason the jury arrived at the wrong verdict." Smith, a genial but discreet man, politely declined to discuss specifics of *Alger*

Hiss: The True Story. He felt his discoveries might appear too sensational outside the fuller context of the book, and would only hint that a public crisis had intruded on a family crisis and that Hiss and his wife had not been equipped to cope with them at once. The defendant's fear of disclosing family secrets, Smith implied, warped his judgment, clammed him up, and created unnecessary suspicion in the jury box. Priscilla worsened matters by appearing less candid than her husband. Smith states that she lied on the stand.

Alistair Cooke speculated in his book *A Generation on Trial* "that if Alger and Priscilla Hiss ever parted, we would surely get the whole truth that so annoyingly evaded us." The couple separated in 1959, and Smith finally prevailed on Hiss to dredge up what he had suppressed long ago—the youthful homosexuality of his stepson Timmy, and his wife's abortion. In 1945, at the age of eighteen, Timothy Hobson was dishonorably discharged from the Navy for homosexual activities. Three years later, Richard Nixon grilled Hiss before HUAC about Timmy's whereabouts. Hiss replied that his stepson was out of touch and available only through his psychiatrist. "You will understand why this is a very difficult subject to talk about because I love my stepson very deeply," he pleaded with Nixon. "Many people take an exaggerated view of what psychiatric assistance means." From this moment on, Smith hypothesizes, Hiss became a reluctant and therefore dubious witness on his own behalf. Since the FBI was digging into Timmy's sexual associations, Hiss surmised that this information could be used against him. Although Timmy offered to refute some of Chambers's testimony at the trials, Hiss would not allow it.

Priscilla was also an emotional burden. She forbade her husband to submit to a sodium pentothal test for fear that her abortion in the Twenties might be revealed, even to his counsel. Her minimal cooperation with the defense inclined more than one of Hiss's lawyers to pin the guilt on her. While Smith disputes any sinister role on Priscilla's part, he does think she affected her husband negatively. "Many things that happened at the Hiss perjury trials," he writes in the biography, "were influenced by Hiss's knowledge of the secret (the abortion) and the way he protected it."

Unfortunately for Hiss, Smith's "key" is made of glass. Although the defendant may have been obsessed by the need to spare his wife and stepson, the effect of his reserve on the jury can never be tested. Smith devotes approximately three pages of his 400-page investigation to these hypotheses. Without any elaboration of the "many things that happened at the Hiss perjury trials," as a result of Hiss's anxiety, the argument is meaningless. Perhaps Priscilla's warnings of a suit after she read the manuscript last summer blunted the author's perceptions. Passages concerning her were extensively edited and her contradictions, large and small, now riddle the text. She and her husband do not even concur on the date she told him of the abortion. She says she told him when they were first married; he says it was ten years later.

Smith's treatment of evidentiary matters is more painstaking. He goes over the stolen documents with the zest of a biblical exegete and suggests that some of the papers were never even delivered to Hiss's office. He also constructs an interesting scenario that accounts for Chambers's stealthy acquisitions, without involving Mr. and Mrs. Hiss. Nevertheless, he cannot demonstrate that Chambers followed it. So his book, though a valuable evocation of the New Deal period and a sometimes inventive piece of detection, is a vastly overreaching work.

· · ·

My own sense of integrity is what's important to me. — Alger Hiss

Alger Hiss is not Alfred Dreyfus. Although issues of espionage, forgery, personal honor, and national security dominated each affair, the analogy does not hold—even if Hiss was wronged. For, unlike Dreyfus, Hiss received a fair trial. He failed to inspire a movement in his defense. And twenty-two years after his release from prison he has yet to exonerate himself.

Despite the general obloquy that followed his perjury conviction in 1950, Alger Hiss never broke. He has remained a Gatsbyesque figure around New York City, charming guests at celebrity parties and gathering converts without even trying. At the same time, he pursued every lead and seized every opportunity to show that he had neither lied or spied. For years, Hiss hoped to get his case back in court, perhaps on a libel count. He came close to suing in England, where libel laws are stricter, and seriously contemplated action against William Manchester for passages in *The Glory and the Dream*. It is his hope that the gradually accumulating FBI papers will disgorge pertinent clues leading to an ultimate reversal of his conviction.

I am aware of evidence damaging to Hiss that was never introduced in court. I am certain Professor Weinstein's historical sleuthing will wound him badly. Yet I would vote Hiss innocent. As Lillian Hellman says, nothing else makes sense.

My argument, perhaps naive and sentimental, turns on psychology. I cannot conceive of a sane person perpetuating a quarter-century of deceit, jeopardizing the welfare of his family and the reputation of his friends, in a doomed attempt to reverse what that person well knows to be the truth.

And Hiss is not crazy. Instead, he is serene. He says he has never done anything in his life that he is ashamed of. If this inner harmony is simply a routine repeated by a deranged player since 1948, then Hiss has deluded me and a large audience of fools.

16

ALFRED KAZIN

Why Hiss Can't Confess

ESQUIRE, MARCH 28, 1978

THIRTY YEARS AGO, a highly unattractive writer at *Time* magazine, Whittaker Chambers, testified before the House Committee on Un-American Activities (which included freshman congressman Richard Nixon) that the brilliant lawyer and former State Department official Alger Hiss, then president of the Carnegie Endowment for International Peace, had been an underground Soviet agent during the New Deal and had sneaked government documents to the Russians through Chambers. Hiss filed suit against Chambers for slander but was himself soon indicted for perjury and eventually spent forty-four months in jail. For thirty years he has maintained his innocence of Chambers' accusations, and he has always had such passionate support in high places that in 1975 he was readmitted to the Massachusetts bar—the first lawyer in the state's history to be readmitted after a major criminal conviction.

Chambers died seventeen years ago. Hiss is seventy-three. Although Nixon from 1948 exploited the Hiss case for all it was worth—even when he was besieged by Watergate he could not stop yammering about how he had helped to nail Hiss—do *you* care if Hiss was an underground Communist during the Thirties? Even if he did pass on some information to the Russians at a time when not Stalin but Hitler-Mussolini-Franco frightened us, and millions of Americans wandered the roads looking for jobs, shelter and some helpful human contact, do Hiss's possible Communist sympathies more than forty years ago matter now? Wasn't the ordeal of Alger Hiss after 1948 just another infliction of anti-Communist hysteria and the cold war? Even if Chambers told the truth, who cares?

I, for one, do care—and so do many others, even Americans born since the Hiss case exploded on our consciousness. If Alger Hiss has been telling the truth for thirty years, as many American liberals believe, then he is a victim of the most outrageous injustice and, in particular, of the fanatical anti-Communism of ex-Communist Whittaker Chambers and of the always unscrupulous Richard Nixon. If he was guilty as charged (eight jurors at his first trial thought so and all twelve did at his second trial—the evidence against him goes far beyond Chambers' "revelations"), what are we to make of a man whose character was defended by the Secretary of State, two Supreme Court justices, two Democratic nominees for the Presidency, some of the most famous newspapers, publicists and writers in the land, but who has held to lie after lie for thirty years?

. . .

If Hiss has been lying all this time, he has surely been sustained not only by his need to reclaim his reputation but by the belief that he symbolizes a "progressive" period to arch-reactionaries and demagogic McCarthyites who have used him for evil political purposes. A European ex-Communist has complained that Hiss's trial never touched on the "real issue: even if he did steal the documents, what were his [decent] motives? Probably . . . when Alger Hiss changed his mind, as had so many who had been Communists in good faith, he was in no position to announce that change. . . . Whittaker Chambers is the real villain because he didn't keep his mouth shut about things past and done with." But Whittaker Chambers, who, unlike Hiss, was given to florid self-dramatization, once wrote to William Buckley that "the Hiss case is a permanent war. . . . I am really not a free agent and scarcely even an individual man. . . . My reactions are a kind of public trust."

If Hiss has been lying all this time, what reason do we have to believe that he *has* "changed his mind as had so many who had been Communists in good faith?" With so much explicit political fanaticism on the part of Chambers and possibly secret fanaticism on the part of Hiss, is the truth important here? There are many, many people to whom the issues are more important than the truth. The Hiss case has been fought over so long and bitterly by opposing political faiths that Allen Weinstein's devastatingly complete and detailed *Perjury: The Hiss-Chambers Case* (Knopf, $15), an impressively unemotional blockbuster of fact, is a revelation of how politicized, partisan and hallucinated most of the pro-Hiss (and even a little of the anti-Hiss) literature has been.

After this book, it is impossible to imagine anything new in the case except an admission by Alger Hiss that he has been lying for thirty years. That would make him a monster to everybody. Hiss came out of genteel poverty in Baltimore and a background of several family suicides to construct a publicly exemplary career that led from Johns Hopkins to Harvard Law to clerking for Justice Oliver Wendell Holmes to famous law firms to the State Department and the Carnegie Endowment. He has always looked so correct, upright, even noble, that it has plainly been impossible for him to undermine himself.

· · ·

But Weinstein shows that Hiss had to lie about so many little things in order to deny any Communist attachment that a pattern was built up, a fictitious life that he has long been forced to believe in himself. Mainly, Hiss must continue to believe himself a political martyr. To repudiate his defense now would be to destroy every claim he has ever made for his reputation, for his personal loyalties, for the Roosevelt Administration itself in peace and war.

Weinstein is a professor of history at Smith who has not allowed his sense of fact to be clouded by pro- or anti-Communist zeal. He began his amazingly thorough research as part of a larger work on the cold war and American society. Believing Hiss falsely accused, he urged that the F.B.I. files be opened and immediately had a file opened on *him* (J. Edgar comes out of the book a narcissistic clown). But Weinstein, under the Freedom of Information Act, eventually obtained over thirty thousand pages of classified F.B.I. files and thousands of pages of additional Justice Department records.

Weinstein is an indefatigably avid researcher with a gift for drawing out people not ordinarily given to confidences about their political past. He gained access to many previously undiscovered, unavailable or unconsulted sources of documentary and oral evidence here and abroad, spoke with over eighty people who had special knowledge of the case or its protagonists—Soviet agents and congressional Red-hunters, spies and former Communists, members of both the Hiss and Chambers families. He interviewed Hiss half a dozen times and over four years clocked more than 125,000 miles of travel. Forty of the people he interviewed had never spoken openly about the case. He even got to five participants in Soviet intelligence during the Thirties.

. . .

The most unexpected confirmation of Chambers' charges came from the records of the Czech and Hungarian secret police. These were studied by a Czech historian, now an émigré in Munich, before the

Russians overthrew the "liberal" Dubcek regime. Hiss had been named as a Soviet agent by other agents. For a man who has maintained for thirty years that he knew Chambers only as a journalist trying to pick up stories about Washington, Hiss certainly left a trail of evidence damaging to himself.

It began in 1948, when he unknowingly confirmed Chambers' previous testimony that Hiss was a bird watcher and had once excitedly spotted the rare prothonotary warbler. Chambers and his wife took over a Hiss apartment rent free; the old Ford that Hiss had peculiarly "donated" to a man he claimed hardly to have known was, on the record, "sold" for twenty-five dollars to a Washington Communist. Chambers said that the C.P. had presented Hiss with a rug in acknowledgment of his services, and Hiss did own the rug. Chambers produced sixty-five typed sheets containing State Department summaries of vital cables dating from January 5 to April 1, 1938 (Hiss swore he never saw or conversed with Chambers after January 1, 1937). All the experts agreed that these pages had been typed on Hiss's Woodstock typewriter, N 230099. The typewriter had been given by the Hisses to their maid, but for over five months Hiss and the maid's family tried to keep the F.B.I. from finding it. When it finally surfaced, Hiss implausibly asserted that either the F.B.I. had built an *exact* replica of his old Woodstock (this turned out to be technically impossible) or that Chambers had sneaked into the Hiss house to type the stuff himself. Even the jury in his first trial (four voted to acquit him) openly laughed when he said, "Until the day I die, I shall wonder how Whittaker Chambers got into my house to use my typewriter."

. . .

Long before the case broke, Hiss had been named as a Soviet agent by French intelligence; his name appeared again when a cipher clerk in the

Soviet embassy in Ottawa defected and described the secret "apparatus" in Canada and the U.S. Gromyko proposed Hiss as first secretary-
general of the U.N. Although former underground Communists in
this country such as literary agent Maxim Lieber detested Chambers
and complained that he was defaming decent people whose "motives"
had been understandable and honorable, Lieber tacitly (to Weinstein)
tied Hiss to his old group. So did Josephine Herbst, the ex-wife of a
prominent Communist writer and underground agent who had fled to
Mexico; so did Julian Wadleigh, Chambers' other source at State. One
particularly damaging detail was Chambers' proof that the Russians
had been given confidential State Department information about
defecting agents and that Hiss had gone out of his way to procure this
information. As late as 1945, Hiss sought access to top O.S.S. secrets
that had nothing to do with his official duties in organizing the U.N.

Despite all this, Hiss was admired and defended (though not always for very long) by Felix Frankfurter, Dean Acheson, the trustees
of the Carnegie Endowment, Adlai Stevenson and many other no-
tables. Hiss had the voluntary services of some of the most prestigious
law firms in the country. President Conant of Harvard wrote the
famous lawyer Grenville Clark: "If Hiss, assuming the falsity of the
allegations against him, can nevertheless be successfully smeared and
ruined, nobody is safe, and great public harm will be done." Even
Chambers described Hiss as charming, gracious, brilliant. Chambers
himself, with his bad teeth, his shambling gait and his record as a
sometime homosexual, was denounced by Hiss's first trial lawyer as a
fiend of immorality, a denier of God. Three famous psychoanalysts
volunteered to defend Alger Hiss by testifying that Chambers was a
psychopath.

Chambers was a melodramatic, self-dramatizing, and he certainly
became the very prototype of the ex-Communist turned professional
anti-Communist. He turned viciously on his old intellectual friends
at Columbia for leading him into "atheistic modernism" and declared

himself an evangelist for the "Christian West." But we know all about Chambers as stinker, messiah, "informer" and "renegade" and pseudothinker. What we do not know about is Alger Hiss. Although *Perjury* is so exhaustive yet low-keyed an account of all the facts that it *should* put the case to rest, Alger Hiss will survive it. Even if nobody else joins him, he will maintain his innocence. He will refuse to confess. He cannot confess. What is most involved in the Hiss case is the historical fact that in the Thirties, Communism did seem to many Americans to be "progressive" and somehow analogous to old American hopes for a better society.

There was an illusion that many people shared—that even many former Communists cannot bear to forget. The illusion was that since they believed so fervently in their dream world of "socialism," Stalin's Russia was, despite all appearances, on the path to democracy. This was backed up by a delusion: Stalin in his fear of Hitler would do anything to work with Western democracy. Yet one of the many shattering facts Weinstein brings out is that long before the 1939 Hitler-Stalin pact, the Gestapo and the Russian K.G.B. were already working together in this country. This was another reason why Communists like Chambers "broke" in 1938. Soviet intelligence agents who betrayed the slightest doubts about the Stalin regime were being called "home" to be purged. Chambers was one of these. Instead, he remained here, to make history. A further proof of how well he knew Hiss is that he went to Hiss and begged him to defect. And if Hiss did not break in 1938, when he was relatively safe, how could he break in 1948? 1978?

. . .

I once had several talks with Alger Hiss and was struck by the rigidity and resourcefulness of his character, by the number of well-known Communists he seemed to be in touch with—and his passionate public patriotism. As law clerk to Justice Holmes, Hiss wrote the famous section of Holmes' will leaving his estate to the United States. Imagine, after something like that, Hiss ever admitting that he had been, however insignificantly, a transmitter of documents. Documents? Typewriters? Fiddlesticks! Alger Hiss will go to his grave honestly believing that he is a better American than you or I.

17

Chambers' Music and Alger Hiss

AMERICAN SPECTATOR, JUNE 1979

T HE HEADLINE READ, HISS ASSEMBLING CASE FOR RETRIAL, VINDICATION. The story was big and bylined ("By Mark Bowden, Staff Reporter"). It had a socko one-sentence lead:

> Alger Hiss may be on the verge of the longest awaited, best deserved last laugh in American history.

It went on:

> His brilliant diplomatic and legal career was ruined more than 25 years ago with perjury convictions and a cloud of cloak and dagger communism. Today the native Baltimorean believes he will have a new trial by spring.

So what else is new? This was new: As you'd guess from its native-son angle, the story appeared, yes in a Baltimore paper: but not in the Baltimore paper that comes to mind. It ran on page one of the October 25, 1976 Baltimore *News-American*: the *Hearst* paper.

The *Sun*, yes, the Baltimore *Sun* will wobble all around the ideological compass. But when the true-blue unproofread *News-American* fixes its gaze on a convicted perjurer whom only the statute of limitations shielded from an indictment for pro-Communist espionage, and perceives him on the verge of the "best deserved last laugh in American history," then the sun in the sky, you'd be inclined to say, has taken to rising in the northwest. As it regularly does, when the press and Alger Hiss are in critical proximity.

Mark Bowden, Staff Reporter, questioned nothing that Alger told him.

> "Those microfilms didn't amount to anything," he explained. "You know what was on them? One was blank. The others were films of pages inside a common U.S. Navy manual that had been available for years on public library shelves. After Nixon had his day with them before the cameras, they were never introduced as evidence during the trial. They weren't evidence of anything.
>
> "But the microfilms worked against me. It didn't matter what was on them. Microfilm is spooky. It sounds like spy stuff, with cameras stuck in belt buckles and watches. The microfilm made Americans think I was a spy, and, I think, ultimately influenced the grand jury and the trial jury."

Yes, yes, there was a lightstruck microfilm roll. And there were two rolls of Navy documents, some of them unclassified (but not from "a common manual"), in which no one ever claimed Alger Hiss had a hand; so naturally "they were never introduced as evidence during the trial."

What Hiss didn't mention to Mr. Bowden was the existence of two more strips of microfilm that did get introduced at the trial. They contained, among other things, State Department documents with Alger Hiss's initials, and how Whittaker Chambers could have obtained them for photographing, if not from Alger Hiss, has been a theme for much improvisation which Mr. Bowden was kindly spared.

A crack "Staff Reporter," which means he writes down what people say to him, Mr. Bowden in the best traditions of the free press wrote down what Mr. Hiss told him, and was not even made wary when Hiss flaunted his expertise at playing journalists—"If you want a good topical angle for a story you might be interested in knowing..."That gambit should have set off inner alarms but didn't.

No, the readers of the *News-American* were allowed to suppose that brilliant Baltimorean Hiss was framed by squalid non-Baltimorean Nixon (Boo). In the long (32-inch) story Nixon is named eight times. Whittaker Chambers ("the confessed spy-ring courier") twice. "Just think of all the people Nixon ruined,'" Alger Hiss exhorts, and Bowden dutifully paraphrases: "He believes Nixon prejudiced the nation against him 'for purely opportunistic reasons.'" Very possibly. But the Hiss nemesis, as reporter Bowden never got around to considering, was Whittaker Chambers, not Nixon: the implacable testimony of Chambers, those damning documents. Nixon in 1976 was merely a better blue herring even than he is now.

The clipping, admittedly, is no longer current. I linger on it because it's stuck in my mind for three years, so admirably does it epitomize the skills by which Alger Hiss has contrived to gain credibility as the American Dreyfus: pilloried, railroaded to Lewisburg for 44 months, latterly toiling as a (for gosh sakes) stationery salesman—*are* there stationery salesmen?—while he expects vindication momentarily. One of his techniques is to keep a heavy thumb on the Nixon button. Another is to feed reporters information he can feel sure they won't check. This is easy because when he went to jail in 1951 today's most vigorous reporters were unborn or toddling. It was easier still before April 1978 since when whoever wants to can check out the facts in a single heavily-documented book, Allen Weinstein's *Perjury*.

Never mind that though belief in a-new-trial-by-spring was reported by the *News-American* in 1976, spring '77 didn't after all come up daisies, nor did spring '78 or spring '79; nor will, we may safely predict, spring '80 or '81 or '82 (by which time Alger Hiss will be an octogenarian). A new trial is not the point. The point is the gullibility of the world's Mark Bowdens, who get the word to some 200,000 readers per story that Alger Hiss was Framed.

Sometimes you will hear that he was framed by Chambers, "a self-confessed perjurer." This is quaint, because Chambers' only substantiated perjury occurred early in the case. He was still shielding Hiss from the worst, and *denied* under oath that Hiss was guilty of espionage! So if Chambers was a perjurer that day, Hiss was a spy. But never mind. Hiss is the American Boy, and the case against him is tainted. He keeps denying everything, doesn't he?

Whittaker Chambers understood why. "Alger Hiss," he wrote to William F. Buckley, Jr., late in 1954, "is one of the greatest assets that the Communist Party could possess. What is vindication for him? It is the moment when one of the most respectable old ladies (gentlemen) in Hartford (Conn.) says to another of the most respectable old ladies (gentlemen): "Really, I don't see how Alger Hiss could brazen it out that way unless he were really innocent.' Multiply Hartford by every other American community. For the CP, that is victory . . . And all that Alger Hiss has to do for this victory is persist in his denials."[1]

Chambers, as everyone knows, had been a member of the Communist underground, circa 1932–1938. On August 3, 1948, he let it be known that Alger Hiss, previously a State Department luminary and by then President of the Carnegie Endowment for International Peace, had been one also. Fifty-five days later Alger Hiss sued for slander. Another nine weeks, and Chambers had produced typed copies of papers, and microfilms of more papers, purloined from the State Department late in the 1930s. He had squirreled them away, he said, while planning his dangerous break with the Party. He said furthermore that he had them, and had passed similar things to the Russians, thanks to his source at State: Alger Hiss. On December 15, 1948, a grand jury indicted Alger Hiss on two counts of perjury: having spoken falsely, first in denying that he had passed those papers to Chambers in February-March 1938, second in denying that he "did in fact see and converse with the said Mr. Chambers" in the months in question at all. On July 7, 1949, a hung jury was dismissed. On January 21, 1950, a second jury found Alger Hiss guilty on both counts. He was sentenced to five years and served 44 months.

So ran the bare scenario, and to cinema-guided tastes it has everything wrong with it. Would *you* let Peter Lorre bring down Robert Redford? Alger Hiss was a graduate of Johns Hopkins ('26) and of Harvard Law ('29), moreover had clerked for Oliver Wendell Holmes, Jr., whereas Chambers dropped out of Columbia and had bad teeth: not matters for the ladies (gentlemen) of Hartford to overlook. Chambers' credibility, by 1948, had little going for it. He was a *Time* hack. Before that he had been by his own admission a CP functionary: not a gallant Communist either, like an English poet, nor a tart screw-you Communist like you know, whatshername, nor even a devoted faceless spearcarrier, but the wrong sort of Communist, with a taste for theatrics, pseudonyms, History, microfilms even; and in the newsreels (remember newsreels?) he had little shifty eyes; and he had reneged on the Party too, and how could you trust him after that? One respects people who stick by their convictions; yes, even when the arsenic of their convictions is destined for your soup.

The Communist Party too had its concern for images. The late Louis Zukofsky, as sharp a skeptical intelligence as I've ever known, was a Chambers classmate; his elegy for Whittaker's brother Ricky (dead by suicide, 1926) bespeaks affection:

> *At eventide, cool hour*
> Your dead mouth singing,
>
> Ricky,
>
> Automobiles speed
> Past the cemetery,

No meter turns.
Sleep,

With an open gas range
Beneath for a pillow. . . .[2]

It's a cold transcension of the many turgid poems Chambers wrote on the same theme. And Zukofsky enjoyed telling how Chambers (about 1926?) recruited him for the Party. To the all-important meeting Zukofsky went, tie in place and by custom trousers neatly creased, and Ma Bloor herself rejected him because he looked insuperably bourgeois ("And my father pressed pants all his life!").

Then a student of no special prospects, Zukofsky was indeed an implausible passer-out of pamphlets. Chambers, though, pudgy, in slacks and open-necked shirt, was a different proposition; he had been accepted on sight. Ma Bloor's son Harold Ware organized the Washington underground in which Chambers was to meet Alger Hiss, and for Hiss, who by Chambers' account went direct to the underground without passing through the open Party, pressed pants and fedora was no disqualification at all: in fact indispensable cover. They still help render implausible the suggestion that he was ever anything as scruffy as a spy: perhaps, at most a member of a left-wing Study Group.

For in that disorienting decade, 1925–1935, when everybody on the hard Left seemed to go by a false name—Chambers at various times was "Bob," "Charles Adams," "David Breen," "Lloyd Cantwell," "Arthur Dwyer," "Hugh Jones," "Karl," "John Kelly," "Harold Phillips," "Charles Whittaker," perhaps "George Crosley"—in that time of roles and show trials, the very mainspring of Party activity was the proposition that things are never as they seem. Communism is almost exclusively concerned with images (though its guns and bombs are real and go off). The Capitalist System survives because people believe the official theory of its workings; let them once discard Adam Smith's cover story, though, and it will collapse. All evaluations, all alliances, are provisional, instrumental; there was a Hitler-Stalin pact before the Hitler-Stalin war.

Amid public realities which according to his creed are wholly unreal, the Communist is always on stage. If in the open Party, he is impersonating one of the prescribed ways of being a Communist: a theoretician, a strike-leader, a marcher, a Friend of the Soviet Union, a shrewd son of toil. If in the underground, he is impersonating a lawyer, a newspaperman, a screenwriter, an English professor—trades in which he is fully credentialed; we may even say that he *is* what he impersonates, that the Communism with which he burns is the off-hours role. This is bottomless. And the Hiss-Chambers case resembles an Ames Box, carefully arranged so that if you look through the peephole you see normal things—a parlor, a Ford car, a typewriter, the bourgeois bric-a-brac of a Washington lawyer in the 1930s, and two dolls, one decent, upright, one shifty, vengeful. It is only when the lid is taken off the box that you can see the scatter of elements out of which that illusion was contrived, their wrenched perspective a tax to the perceptions, their variousness a burden to the memory, their disarray an affront to normal experience, which, whether in arranging cues into 3-D space or threading a story line through happenings, is guided by economy and by experience with the usual.

The mere evidence which compelled the second jury to believe Chambers rather than Hiss dismays by its miscellaneousness, its profuseness, its frequent triviality. Making it cohere was the prosecuting attorney's job, and in *Perjury* Allen Weinstein achieves an even more conclusive coherence, chiefly because he's dug up so much more that we need no longer suspect a controlled selection.

The logic is ultimately simple: It depends on connecting Alger Hiss with those documents Chambers produced. These included (1) ten microfilmed pages which Hiss had handled (he initialled them) and to which Chambers' other source at State, a man named Wadleigh, would not have had access; (2) typed copies of State Department messages, to the extent of 65 pages, the typing of which matched the output of a Woodstock, serial #N230099, which the Hisses had owned and used in the 1930s.

So *prima facie*, the most probable link between State and Chambers is Hiss. But life is not always linear, and if you're encumbered by few enough facts it's easy to doodle alternative topologies. There were two typewriters, one skillfully faked. Alger and Priscilla had parted with the Woodstock before the State papers were copied (and when was that?). Chambers (or someone) snuck into their house and used the machine, or spirited it away and used it. . . . Making a tight prosecution case meant nailing down hundreds of such wearisome details. Conducting a defense meant making the details difficult to establish (it was all ten years ago), meanwhile developing a motive for a monstrous troublemaking Chambers.

Tracing it all has taken Allen Weinstein, a crisp and economical writer, some 325,000 words, including whole pages summarizing tergiversations about typewriters. It was that kind of case. (His researches show, by the way, what was never evident from the public record, that while the FBI and defense gumshoes were both hunting the Woodstock Alger Hiss and his brother Donald knew where it was and lied persistently.)

Having read *Perjury* through twice I can see no reason to dissent from Sidney Hook's verdict, that thanks to Weinstein's expert labors the guilt of Alger Hiss "can no longer be contested on any reasonable grounds."[3]

There are only two ways to discount Weinstein. One is to decline to read him, for fear of having a symbolic allegiance disturbed; Hook remarks that "there is no arguing with symbolic allegiances." The other is to pick nits in the manner of the *Nation,* hoping simple folk will conclude that Weinstein falsified, elided, tampered, or that for all his digging he didn't dig deep enough. (Or perhaps he's an FBI stooge?)

To summarize, Hiss was not framed by Nixon, whose role in the case was ambiguous throughout. (When the "pumpkin papers" burst upon the scene he was a safe distance away, in Panama, just in case there was a backfire.) He was certainly not framed by the FBI, whose director, every time we catch him dictating a memo, sounds like a Commissioner of the Keystone Kops (when he first heard that Weinstein was interested in the case—in 1969—his immediate response was to open a file on Weinstein!). He didn't go to prison on the word of Whittaker Chambers. He was entrapped by numerous and carefully established and inexorable facts.

Which being said, we may safely regret that *Perjury* isn't' perfect. Allen Weinstein is not Dostoyevsky, and when his narrative is over we may feel that we know everything except who the protagonists *were*.

That the Hiss of this intricate narrative should remain schematic, as contrived as an Agatha Christie least-likely-suspect, a jointed paper doll we've watched gesticulate, is unsurprising; the scenario after all establishes that Alger Hiss has been perjuring himself for 31 years and living a lie for at least 45. If there's a real Alger Hiss down under that cope of fanatical self-discipline, it's safe to guess that the Alger Hiss who files briefs and grants interviews lost touch with himself long ago.

Whittaker Chambers is more interesting and more puzzling, and though his own long confessional narrative, *Witness*, offered to bare all as long ago as 1952, tracts of the merely factual remain pointlessly mysterious.

Take the question of the Russian language. At about 16, he tells us in *Witness* (p. 146), he memorized from a book, at his mother's urging, "two or three thousand Russian words," but remained innocent of any grammar. At age 31 (*Witness*, pp. 301–2) he was still, he says, incapable of reading anything in secret Russian messages save the salutation, *Dorogoi Droog*—Dear Friend. Nor (*Witness*, p. 306) could he follow a Russian conversation. At age 58, the Hiss case long behind him, he enrolled in the University of Western Maryland College ("I do not wish to die an ignoramus")[4] in part to study elementary Russian.

Dr. Weinstein tells all this differently, saying "occasionally he even feigned ignorance of Russian, a language in which he was fluent" (p. 116). Weinstein certifies the fluency on the word of unspecified "close friends" (p. 602), and even informs us (p. 602) of the present whereabouts of "the introductory Russian primer used by Chambers to learn the language early in the 1930s." He doesn't mention the 1959 classes in Maryland.

Who were the "close friends," we may wonder; rather, what were their standards of fluency? (To an ignoramus you could sound fluent in French if you merely said rapidly, *"Avec la plume de ma tante, la chat etait assis sur la natte."*) More: since Weinstein has read (and cites) *Odyssey of a Friend,* what does he make of its disclosure of those Russian classes at a rural Maryland college, two years before Chambers' death? Was Chambers really never good at Russian at all, though he picked up other languages easily? Was the lifelong player of roles assuming yet another role, the world-weary man become as a little child, humbly attending classes with adolescents? Was he perhaps going through the motions of opsimathic study to establish (contrary to fact) that in his Party days he'd been ignorant of Communism's mother tongue? If so, why on earth?

Why, for that matter, did he always deny having been in Russia, where he and his wife Esther went on fraudulent passports in early 1933? Postcards in their handwriting with Moscow cancellations survive (*Perjury,* pp.115–16, 602). He was presumably there for top-level indoctrination. Yet the pages of *Witness* which conduct us so circumstantially through the preparation of a secret agent are silent on this trip, and on p. 352 Chambers even remarks flatly, "I have never been in Russia." Why? Was he minimizing Esther's complicity in his secret life?

Though Weinstein is aware of these and other contradictions, he does nothing with them beyond noting their existence. For which we bless him; we've had in this case and others enough psychohistory, something normally confected out of an Identi-Kit on the model of Freud's analysis of Moses. They nag, though they nag at me not because I sniff sinister ramifications, but because their existence makes the latter-day Chambers who's projected in *Witness* and in the letters to Buckley—the weary sojourner in an ultimate Siberia of the psyche, a Last Man whose last luxury is bleak and utter candor—appear to be but one more fabrication, a last role in the long sequence of roles that began as early as 1919, when Jay Vivian Chambers began to use his mother Laha Whittaker's family name. "Whittaker Chambers" was merely the most enduring of his aliases.

> My brother lies in the cold earth,
> A cold rain is overhead.
> My brother lies in the cold earth,
> A sheet of ice is over his head.
>
> The cold earth holds him round;
> A sheet of ice is over his face.
> My brother has no more
> The cold rain to face.

That was "written in the Sand Hill graveyard," he tells us, "the first winter of my brother's death."[5] The second quatrain would be doggerel had it not the first to modulate away from. By rhythm and repetition, a 25-year-old is exorcising a corpse he nearly feels is alive. By rhythm and repetition, in sentences of mounting complexity, he exorcises all his adult life what he calls rather often History. (There are pages in *Witness* on which the word "history" occur a dozen times.)

"History hit us with a freight train," is a phrase from his last letter to Buckley.

Readers have not been wanting who detected a false, a passé, note in Chambers rhetoric. Conor Cruise O'Brien observed Chambers writing in *Cold Friday* that the depth of the special Russian feeling for Byzantium was "perhaps suggested by the fact that Tsargrad alone, among the names of foreign cities, is declined through all nine inflections of the Russian noun." O'Brien leaps: The Russian noun has only *six* inflections, and the mistake is revealing. For "the pressure to distort is a rhetorical pressure. 'All nine of the inflections of the Russian noun' gives just the reverberation Chambers needed at this point in his boomy incantation."

O'Brien leaped too fast, and William Buckley roasted him on a slow pit: there are indeed nine forms of the noun Tsargrad.[6] Still, O'Brien in his shallowness was on to something: Chambers' need to resolve his cadences, in a prose less propelled by the wish to impart information than by the need to give it shape. To turn terrible actualities into music was an insistent pressure, an hourly need. That, we may speculate, was what Communist theory did for him: It shaped actualities of want and warfare into a dissonant music you could dance to. It was a long, agonizing, increasingly dangerous dance, and by 1938 the harsh music had lost all enchantment. In 1949, between the two Hiss trials, a newsman asked him, "What do you think you are doing?"

"At his question I turned to look out at the mists that were rising from the bottom below the house, filling the valley. I answered slowly: "I am a man who, reluctantly, grudgingly, step by step, is destroying himself that his country and the faith by which it lives may continue to exist.'" (*Witness,* P. 715).

With a sharp ear for cadences you can catch overtones of the Gettysburg Address. In breaking with Communism, he had defined a new role and formulated its rhythm. That, if I gauge him aright, was central: a rhythm: one that could accommodate his shorter themes, overarch his longer ones, and permit what he cherished, the harmonization of his mishaps and History. Man, the symbol-using creature, makes shift to make himself at home in the world by the way he talks about it and in no other way; moreover, the most efficacious stratum of language, the one that effects the orienting adjustments between his experience and his sense of himself, is not semantic but rhythmic. Everyone's habits with language have a characterizing cadence, what we recognize when we recognize a "style." Its gestures mime his sense of how the world goes, how *he* goes.

Chambers' taste, especially in paragraph ending, was for the resolve cadence, to an extent perverse in the twentieth century. (His way of signalling an irony is to leave them unresolved.) A rhythm surrendered to is a self-definition. There were facts, presumably, such as knowledge of Russian, which the rhythm would not accommodate. The principle at work here is mysterious but demonstrable; it is related to the fact that every poet's rhythm excludes certain images. Hence, in the edifice of written words Chambers constructed so carefully, those odd little blurs and lapses. He possibly could not have explained to himself why they were necessary. They don't affect the substance of his testimony.

Alger lives yet, to a rhythm of his own. It is the rhythm of the sewing-machine, busily piecing and stitching; the parts glinting, the motor humming, the needle hopping, the pieces of material lapped and fed: no thread in the bobbin, none in the needle.

NOTES

[1] *Odyssey of a Friend: Whittaker Chambers' Letters to William F. Buckley Jr., 1954-1961*, pp. 87-88.

[2] Louis Zukofsky, *"A"*, p. 9 (written 1928).

[3] Sidney Hook, "The Case of Alger Hiss," *Encounter*, August 1978, p. 55.

[4] *Odyssey of a Friend*, p. 260.

[5] Epigraph to Chapter 2 of *Witness* (p. 89).

[6] William F. Buckley, *The Jewelers Eye*, pp. 203-210. A polemic to study for its pacing.

18

J O H N   B .   J U D I S

The Two Faces of Whittaker Chambers

N E W   R E P U B L I C ,   A P R I L   1 6 ,   1 9 8 4

If God exists a man cannot be a Communist, which begins with the rejection of God. But if God does not exist, it follows that Communism or some suitable variant of it, is right.

— Whittaker Chambers, "A Direct Glance"

In this fiction, everything, everybody is either all good or all bad, without any of those intermediate shades which, in life, complicate reality and perplex the eyes that seeks to probe it truly.

—Whittaker Chambers, review of Ayn Rand's *Atlas Shrugged*

W HITTAKER CHAMBERS, who died in 1961, still enjoys a vigorous life in the political mind of America. His notoriety has largely been limited to the question of whether he was telling the truth in 1948 when he claimed that, as a Soviet agent in Washington during the 1930s, he was given classified documents by State Department official Alger Hiss. While supporters of America's role in the cold war have tended to believe Hiss was guilty, critics of America's role have tended to believe—against documentation that could fill a small library—that Chambers, out of psychopathic spite or political enmity, framed Hiss.

But Chambers's importance to American political history did not end when Hiss was finally pronounced guilty in January 1950. Chambers spent the next two years on his farm in rural Maryland, writing his autobiography, *Witness,* and the remainder of his life working with a new generation of American right-wingers trying to develop an American conservative movement. Chambers's contribution to that movement was immense. It is of more than passing contemporary interest.

Ronald Reagan was repaying a very old political debt last month when he named Chambers to receive the Medal of Freedom, the nation's highest civilian award. Chambers's autobiography had a deep effect on Reagan who was, in 1952, moving away from New Deal liberalism and toward Goldwater conservatism. Chambers was the only conservative quoted or even cited by Reagan in his 1965 autobiography, *Where's the Rest of Me?* And since taking office in 1981, Reagan has paid tribute to Chambers in at least one speech every year. Most recently, in his address on February 6 at Eureka College, Reagan credited Chambers with beginning "the counterrevolution of the intellectuals." "Chambers's story," Reagan said, "represents a generation's disenchantment with statism and its return to eternal truths and fundamental values."

In his speeches, Reagan has praised Chambers for his theological and apocalyptic understanding of the struggle against communism. Speaking in March 1983 before the Conservative Political Action Conference in Washington, the President credited Chambers with understanding that "the crisis of the Western world exists to the degree in which the West is indifferent to God, the degree to which it collaborates in communism's attempt to make man stand alone without God." Speaking before the same gathering in February 1982, Reagan quoted at length Chambers's warning that "within the next decades will be decided for generations whether . . . civilization as we know it is to be completely destroyed or completely changed."

There was another side, however, to Chambers's conservatism. While Chambers epitomized the absolutist and the extremist, whether as a Soviet spy or as the anti-Communist of *Witness,* he was also a man of considerable political and intellectual sophistication. As a Communist, he had spent nearly fifteen years trying to understand how a movement on the margins of society could capture the mainstream. By the time he became a conservative, he had already learned from Lenin that a fledgling movement must hew a careful path between opportunism and sectarianism if it is to succeed. Chambers was well aware of the pitfalls of the soapbox and the third party, but few of his comrades on the political right were.

Chambers was also a man of prodigious learning, who had taught himself to read and speak Russian, German and Spanish and, according to some accounts, Hungarian and Chinese as well. While he could be doctrinaire in his political views, he had the intellectual's penchant for understanding, rather than simply dismissing, the avant-garde, from existentialism to Allen Ginsberg and Britain's Angry Young Men.

Chambers also appreciated the historical paradoxes of trying to develop a conservative politics in a nation that had never had an *ancien régime.* For the last decade of his life, as an editor and contributor to *National Review,* the most important conservative publication of its day, and as a close friend of William F. Buckley Jr., its founder, Chambers waged a quiet struggle to make conservatives more realistic about their politics.

Along with Max Eastman and James Burnham, who also ended up writing for *National Review,* Chambers belonged to a particular generation of Americans who came of age in the 1920s rather than the 1930s. They came to the left as radical individualists and bohemian intellectuals, through an interest in the arts and philosophy rather than through the experience of exploitation or poverty or political organization. Their individualism colored and finally subverted their commitment to communism—and in some cases, to the left itself.

But Chambers was more eccentric and alienated than Eastman or Burnham. While they were excelling at Harvard and Princeton, Chambers was getting bounced from Columbia as a sophomore for publishing a blasphemous play in the school's literary magazine. While they achieved public acclaim quickly, Chambers chose to labor in the nether world of the Communist underground.

Brought up in a troubled, bohemian family ill at ease in middle-class Lynbrook, Long Island (his father temporarily left the family for a homosexual lover, his younger brother committed suicide), Chambers was plagued by doubt and guilt, reinforced by sporadic secret homosexual adventures. Chambers's anguish probably made him more receptive, whether as a Communist or an anti-Communist, to overly simple melodramatic world systems. It also lent passion to his writing. Chambers's tendency to denigrate and then overestimate his role in life, however, may have freed him from the average American's obsession with income and status, and permitted him to devote his life to the reckless pursuit of ideas.

In 1932, after a brief career as a writer and editor on *The Daily Worker* and *The New Masses,* Chambers became a Soviet secret agent, serving as a courier and organizing a network of pro-Soviet or Communist officials in the Roosevelt Administration. It was in this capacity, according to Chambers, that he worked with Alger Hiss. Chambers quit the Communist Party and his work as a spy in 1938. He had become somewhat disillusioned with the Soviet Union, but he also feared for his life. Having been accused by a political opponent of being a "Trotskyite," Chambers had been summoned back to Moscow in 1937. He stalled; and when one of his associates disappeared and another was arrested in Moscow, he decided to make a break.

After a year on the run, Chambers resurfaced and was hired by *Time* as a book reviewer. By the early 1940s, Chambers's political views and manner of life had swung full circle. Once a revolutionary Communist, he was now a counterrevolutionary anti-Communist, for whom even the New Deal was anathema. He adopted the Republicanism of his parents and grandparents, and the Quaker faith of his paternal grandmother.

At *Time,* Chambers became part of a group of writers and editors, including future *National Review* editors Willi Schlamm and John Chamberlain, who held out doggedly for an anti-Soviet foreign policy during the period of wartime cooperation with the Soviet Union. In the early 1940s, Chambers's writing and his view of the Soviet Union caught the eye of Henry Luce, who elevated him to foreign news editor in 1943. Two years later, faced with a staff revolt against Chambers's editing, Luce had to shift him to special projects, where his long features for *Life* and *Time* still had considerable impact. But Chambers's career at *Time* was cut short by an intrusion from his past.

In August 1948, Chambers was invited, almost as an afterthought, to testify before the House Un-American Activities Committee (HUAC). By naming Hiss, however, Chambers captured the day's headlines. Uncomfortable in his role as an informer, he spent the next two years trying to establish Hiss's guilt before HUAC, grand juries, the F.B.I., and two court trials. Finally, in January 1950, a jury found Hiss guilty of having lied to HUAC when he denied passing documents and copies of documents to Chambers.

Chambers's public revelation that he had been a Soviet spy ended his career at *Time.* Even after Hiss was found guilty, Luce never re-hired him. Chambers retired to his farm to write *Witness.* It was in places a ponderous and pretentious book, marred by its author's in-flated estimate of his own virtue and importance. As a whole, how-ever, *Witness* succeeded in conveying not only its subject's agitated mental state, but also the peculiar ambience of both the communist underground and the postwar domestic cold war. *Witness* was part of a tradition of Christian confessional literature and part of an entirely modern postwar genre that blended together journalism, autobiogra-phy, and political commentary.

When *Witness* appeared in 1952 it briefly made the best-seller lists, but its tone and length—eight hundred pages—proved too much for most readers. There was one group of readers, however, that found it both inspiring and enlightening: young right-wing intellectuals who were groping during the early 1950s for a way of developing a new conservative intellectual and political movement.

In the late 1940s and early 1950s there was, strictly speaking, no conservative movement in America. There were individuals and orga-nizations identified with the right wing, from Gerald L. K. Smith to Ohio Senator Robert Taft, but they often had nothing in common except estrangement from the New Deal and American globalism. In intellectual circles, there was more common ground, but not quite a unifying focus, from traditionalists like Russell Kirk and laissez-faire individualists like Frank Chodorov to former leftists turned anti-Com-munist like Burnham. Chambers helped to give these groups a focus through the apocalyptic anticommunism of *Witness.*

Chambers, whose break with communism coincided with a reli-gious awakening (a voice had said to him, "If you will fight for free-dom all will be well with you"), saw the struggle between Western civilization (or "the free world") and communism as a struggle be-tween "two rival faiths," between good and evil. Communism was the Antichrist, and the cold war was Armageddon. But communism was not simply the social system developed in the Soviet Union. According to Chambers, what distinguished communism was the Communist's belief that human beings could achieve "order, abundance, security, peace" through politics—through a "purpose or plan"—without resort to God. Communism posed "the most revolutionary question in history: God or Man?" It answered: "Man."

In this sense, modern liberalism, socialism, and social democracy, which also aim to eliminate "age-old senseless suffering" with "a purpose or a plan," were mere variants of communism. Chambers described socialism as "Communism with the class removed." While the "focus of concentrated evil" in the world was the communism embodied in the Soviet Union, the evil essence of communism could be found unfocused in Roosevelt's New Deal or in the British Labour party's program for the nationalization of industry.

Thus, Chambers synthesized the preoccupations of the right. Communism was not merely undesirable; it was evil. And it was present not merely in Moscow, but in Washington disguised in the form of economic planning, or Keynesianism. In a passage that Reagan quoted in his own memoir, Chambers wrote:

> When I took up my little sling and aimed at Communism, I also hit at something else. What I hit was the force of that great Socialist revolution which in the name of *liberalism*, spasmodically, incompletely, somewhat formlessly, but always in the same direction, has been inching its icecap over the nation for two decades.

Chambers's anti-Communist theology was based, however, on two nontheological assumptions. First, Chambers's view of communism was still shaped by his own experience in the party. While Chambers no longer believed that communism was a desirable social system, he continued to accept Stalinism and official Marxist-Leninist ideology as a theory of history and an explanation of Soviet behavior. Chambers interpreted Soviet actions in the light of Soviet ideology, rather than subjecting its ideology to the test of its actions. Thus Chambers ignored the extent to which Soviet communism bore little resemblance to the Marxist paradigm, but was instead a hybrid of Czarist authoritarianism and Marx's nightmare of the state as collective capitalist. Similarly, Chambers ignored the extent to which Soviet foreign policy was dictated by nationalism, Great Power imperialism (another relic of Russia's past), and the experiences of two world wars, rather than by proletarian internationalism. Instead of following the Soviet Line, Chambers saw the Soviet Union as an entirely new kind of nation whose role was to create a World Revolution after its own image.

Secondly, Chambers's view of liberalism was shaped both by the wishful thinking of some Communists during the post-1935 Popular Front period, who saw the New Deal not as capitalist reform, but as the groundwork for socialism, and by the warnings of Frederich Von Hayek's influential 1946 book, *The Road to Serfdom*. Hayek warned that "mixed economies" like those of Britain or the United States risked evolving into economies like those of the Soviet Union or Nazi Germany, with their accompanying political forms. Hayek posed to the Western democracies a stark choice between individualism and collectivism, a category in which the New Deal was lumped together with Stalinism and Nazism. Chambers translated this into "God or Man?"

Chambers's views were, of course, not accepted by everyone who came to be called a conservative. Max Eastman, for instance, found no use for Chambers's theology. But Chambers showed the most active new conservatives how a militant anticommunism could become the basis for the new movement.

In the decade after *Witness*, a new conservative intellectual and political movement did spring up. In 1953, Russell Kirk published his *The Conservative Mind*, which gave the new movement its name. In 1955, William Buckley, with the assistance of Willi Schlamm,

James Burnham, and others, founded *National Review*. By the early 1960s, a conservative faction had formed within the Republican Party that in 1964 would help nominate Arizona Senator Barry Goldwater for the Presidency.

Chambers cast a watchful and sometimes supportive eye toward these proceedings. When Kirk's book appeared, he used his influence at *Time* to secure it a featured review. In 1954 he began a close friendship and correspondence with Buckley that culminated in his joining *National Review*'s editorial board from 1957 to 1959. But Chambers kept his distance from the conservative movement that he had helped to inspire. He was held down from full participation in any movement by successive heart attacks, the last of which killed him. But he also could not fully reconcile himself to the new movement. In one respect, Chambers's problem was internal: he did not know how to apply the worldview he developed in *Witness* to the political issues of the 1950s. But his problem was also with the movement itself. He found himself continually at odds with its position on issues and candidates.

On the most abstract level, Chambers found himself wondering what it meant to be a conservative in a country like America, whose basic ideas reflected the liberal Enlightenment. Chambers concluded that the only solution was to compromise, or, as he put it, "to maneuver." He wrote his friend Duncan Taylor-Norton in 1954:

> Or course, it is the duty of the intellectuals of the West to preach reaction, and to keep pointing out why the Enlightenment and its fruits were a wrong turning in man's history. But it was a turning, and, within its terms, we must maneuver at the point where to maneuver is to live.

When Buckley and Willi Schlamm approached Chambers in 1954 to become an editor of *National Review*, he was forced to confront the dilemma on a more specific basis. Programmatically, Buckley and Schlamm stood for the revocation of the New Deal and the welfare state; politically, they opposed the Eisenhower Administration and Eisenhower's Vice President Richard Nixon, whom Chambers had met and grown to admire in the Hiss case. In a series of letters, Chambers argued that their position was "reactionary" rather than "conservative." Chambers's conservative politics drew upon his version of Marxist dialectics and upon the example of British Conservative Party leader Benjamin Disraeli, Lord Beaconsfield, who convinced the Tories in 1867 to take the leadership in extending the suffrage. "I remain a dialectician," Chambers wrote Buckley and Schlamm,

> and history tells me that the rock-core of the Conservative Position, or any fragment of it, can be held realistically only if conservatism will accommodate itself to the needs and hopes for the masses. . . . That is, of course, the Beaconsfield position.

In saying that he was still a dialectician, Chambers meant that he still believed that social and political change was determined by events outside the control or prescription of any individual—by the inevitable advance of technology under capitalism and by the evolving needs and sentiments of the majority of the people. The role of conservatives, Chambers argues, was not to try to block or revoke those changes, which was futile, but to shape them according to conservative ideals and principles.

Chambers tried to explain this point to Buckley and Schlamm with the example of government price supports for agriculture, which Chambers called "rural socialism." Such supports, Chambers contended, were the inevitable outcomes of new agricultural technology, which produced a new abundance that would drive farmers' prices down to almost zero. The farmers had no choice but to demand price supports, the government no choice but to grant them. "The machine has made the economy socialistic," Chambers wrote. "The government has only enacted one aspect of the fact into law." A conservatism that opposed price supports, Chambers warned, would have to advise farmers to smash their machines, "but a conservatism that would say that is not a political force or even a twitch: it has become a literary whimsy."

In one of his memorable passages, Chambers summed up for Buckley and Schlamm what the conservative position entailed:

> Escapism is laudable, perhaps the only truly honorable course for humane men—but only for them. Those who remain in the world, if they will not surrender on its terms, must maneuver within its limits. That is what conservatives must decide: how much to give in order to survive at all; how much to give in order not to give up basic principles. And of course that results in a dance along a precipice. Many will drop over, and, always, the cliff dancers will hear the screaming curses of those who fall, or be numbered by the sullen silence of those, nobler souls perhaps, who will not join the dance.

After Eisenhower and Nixon's reelection, Chambers agreed to join the *National Review* editorial board. He resigned, however, in 1959, partly for reasons of health, partly because he wanted to go back to college (Chambers spent the last two years of his life at Western Maryland State College studying science and classical Greek, among other things), but also partly because he again found himself at odds with *National Review*'s conservatism.

In 1959 some of *National Review*'s editors were gearing up to oppose Richard Nixon's election in 1960. *National Review* was also leading a nationwide campaign to protest Soviet Premier Nikita Khrushchev's visit to the United States at the invitation of Eisenhower. Chambers protested that the magazine's inability to distinguish Khrushchev from Stalin ("He is no monster . . . in the sense that Stalin *was* a monster," Chambers wrote Buckley). More generally, Chambers argued that the magazine's opposition to any discussion with the Soviet Union amounted to a declaration of war, which Americans were simply not willing to accept. The conservatives were again defying the dialectic. With a touch of irony, Chambers wrote Buckley:

The logic of *National Review*'s policy . . . is war. If gentlemen hold that war is necessary, I, for one, wish they should say so simply. . . . It is not an easy position; it should take courage to set it forth at all. But it would be an intelligible position, and popular, I am told, with SAC (the Strategic Air Command), though I doubt that it would be so with wider circles.

Chambers also found himself at odds with the conservatives' choice of heroes, and with what he regarded as the movement's lack of commitment to freedom. As Buckley learned when he asked Chambers to write a blurb for his 1954 book, *McCarthy and His Enemies,* Chambers despised McCarthy and didn't want to have anything to do with him. Chambers was convinced, he presciently wrote Buckley's publisher in February 1954, that McCarthy's "flair for the sensational, his inaccuracies and distortions, his tendency to sacrifice the greater objective for the momentary effect (would) lead him and us into trouble."

In April 1959 Chambers astounded many conservatives by arguing in *National Review* that Hiss, who had been released from jail, should not be denied a passport. Chambers believed that the defense of civil liberties should be an essential part of the conservative position. Commenting on conservatives' opposition to a passport for Hiss, Chambers wrote Buckley:

> Liberals, by default, preempt the human and intellectually sound positions, when it is precisely the Liberals who, in the name of freedom, are inviting the total State. I think the Right is playing into their hands, and that the time has come for those who claim that general position for themselves to examine and define with a special scrupulousness the civil liberties field.

By the late 1950s, Chambers was no longer calling himself a "conservative," but a "man of the right." He set forth some of his reasons in a letter to Buckley in December 1958. Temperamentally, Chambers, the old individualist, felt himself at odds with the trend toward political and religious orthodoxy that he found among conservatives. "The temptation to orthodoxy is often strong, never more than in an age like this one, especially in a personal situation like mine," Chambers wrote Buckley. "But it is not a temptation to which I have found it possible to yield."

But Chambers also came back to the more general problem of American conservatism:

> I am a man of the Right because I mean to uphold capitalism in its American version. But I claim that capitalism is not, and by its essential nature cannot conceivably be, conservative. This is particularly true of capitalism in the United States, which knew no Middle Age; which was born, in so far as it was ideological, of the Enlightenment. . . . Capitalism, whenever it seeks to become conservative in any quarter, at once settles into mere reaction. . . . Hence the sense of unreality and pessimism on the Right, running off into all manner of crackpotism.

Chambers was not, of course, repudiating the conservative movement, the way he repudiated the Communist Party when he broke with it and the left in the late 1930s. He continued to identify with the broader right, even as he became exasperated with the politics of the new conservative movement. And he remained close to Buckley and Burnham to the end of his life. But the strains that were emerging were not merely tactical. And they affected Chambers's own ultimate assumptions.

The problem with the conservative movement that Chambers sensed in the late 1950s was also a problem with Chambers's own worldview as put forth in *Witness*. The conservative movement's most sectarian and crackpot tendencies were consistent with the position that Chambers had propounded in *Witness*. If communism was the "focus of concentrated evil" in the world, why should an American Administration invite one of its Satanic representatives to visit its shores? If liberalism was really socialism, which was really "Communism with its claws removed," why should conservatives have accepted

Social Security or government price controls for agriculture? If an evil, and not merely undesirable, policy is the issue, what room is there for compromise or maneuver?

The problem can be restated in this way: Disraeli, Chambers's model, revived the Tory Party in Britain not simply by teaching it compromise, but by challenging its antiquated social ideal, which conceived of government as the province of the Crown and landed estates. Similarly, Chambers sought to teach American conservatives the art of political compromise. In *Witness*, however, he provided them with an ideal that brooked no compromise.

Chambers never resolved this contradiction. His published writings of the 1950s, the most impressive of which is his 1957 panning of Ayn Rand's *Atlas Shrugged*, and his letters to Buckley, were published posthumously in *Odyssey of a Friend*. They betray a man impatient with political absolutes. But his unpublished writings, collected posthumously in *Cold Friday*, largely reiterate, with considerably less grace, the apocalyptical themes of *Witness*.

During the 1950s, American conservatives did not have to worry about the contradictions in Chambers's thinking. Their politics, from the John Birch Society's paranoid anticommunism to the more cosmopolitan anti-Eisenhower polemics of *National Review*, derives from *Witness* rather than from Chambers's reflections on Disraeli or Lenin. But in the 1960s, as conservatives began taking over the Republican Party, they found themselves faced with Chambers's dilemma: "how much to give in order to survive at all; how much to give in order not to give up basic principles."

Goldwater's landslide defeat in 1964 forced the more thoughtful conservatives to reassess their political strategy. In an October 1964 speech to members of New York's Conservative Party, William Buckley restated in his own terms Chambers's call for a realistic conservative politics:

A conservative is simultaneously concerned with two things, the first being the shape of the visionary or paradigmatic society towards which we should labor; the second, the speech with which it is thinkable to advanced towards that ideal society; and the foreknowledge that any advance upon it is necessarily asymptotic, that is, that we cannot hope for ideological home runs and definitive victories; not at least, until the successful completion of the work of the Society for the Abolition of Original Sin.

But neither Buckley nor the other conservatives who adopted a more realistic politics after 1964 abandoned Chambers's original anti-Communist worldview. Like Chambers, they tried to reconcile an otherworldly demarcation of politics into good and evil forces with the worldly imperatives of winning office. As a result, they did not find themselves creating a strategy with which they could attain their goals of a world without evil, but a rationalization for proceeding as if it were possible to do so. Within the conservative movement, this has created a curious dynamic. Conservatives have recognized the necessity of taking the Beaconsfield path at the same time as they have denounced every step in that direction as base opportunism.

No American politician has experienced this dilemma more acutely than Ronald Reagan. Reagan's annual references to Chambers's *Witness* in his speeches to conservative and evangelical audiences have not been only for their benefit, but for his. Reagan has continued to evoke Chambers, and the worldview of *Witness* has permeated his speeches over the years. For instance, Reagan's charge that the Soviet Union is a "focus of evil" is simply an echo of Chambers's own charge that communism is the "focus of concentrated evil." But Reagan also demonstrated a clear grasp of the Beaconsfield position, ever since his brilliant campaign for governor in 1966.

Reagan did not, however, have to face the full consequences of Chambers's contradictory legacy until he became President. As governor, Reagan placated conservatives by pointing out the limitations of a state official's office. But as President, Reagan has acquired the instruments of national and world power. What he has lacked is the popular mandate to use them as the conservatives of the 1950s might have wanted him to use them. Reagan's first term has dramatized the internal contradictions of conservative politics.

Within the Reagan Administration, the principal conflicts have revolved precisely around these contradictions. Should the President accede to arms control agreements and propose new ones that ratify military parity between the United States and the Soviet Union? Should he allow American firms to assist the Soviet Union indirectly in building a pipeline to Western Europe? Should the President ally the United States with a lesser Communist nation on the expedient grounds that it promises to help against the more powerful Communist nation? Should the President approve of measures that enlarge the state's reach into the economy and society?

Questions like these have plagued previous Administrations, but they have been resolvable. When the Nixon Administration declared its opening to China, it also altered its and the nation's view of world communism. But the Reagan Administration cannot escape either Chambers's nightmare of Communist evil nor the exigencies of contemporary geopolitics. It is caught between them.

The Reagan Administration's repeated ventures along the Beaconsfield path—for instance, its continued adherence to SALT II, its deflection of the Social Security issue onto a bipartisan commission, and its acceptance of a minor jobs bill and tax increases during the recent recession—have deeply and predictably angered the nation's conservatives. But these conservatives have refused to understand the dilemma they face. They have blamed the Administration's policies they dislike on "White House pragmatists" and have argued that Reagan's staff allow "Reagan to be Reagan." Such formulations ignore Reagan's consistent record as a campaigner and a governor and a President. Reagan does share the conservatives' worldview, but he is also committed to the politics of maneuver. Reagan has been Reagan. He has honored both the Chambers of *Witness* and the Chambers who advocated a "dance along the precipice."

On March 26, when Reagan awarded Chambers the Medal of Freedom, conservatives would have done well to recall that it was not George Bush, nor James Baker, but Whittaker Chambers, ruminating in the basement study of his farm, who condemned America's conservatives to wander between theology and pragmatism, between dreams of redemption and the intractable complexities of politics and diplomacy.

19

ERIC M. BREINDEL

Alger Hiss: A Glimpse Behind the Mask

COMMENTARY, NOVEMBER 1988

D EVOTEES OF THE HISS CASE have long hoped—and thought it conceivable—that Alger Hiss would one day share his version of that historic episode with the American people. Hence the eagerness with which many awaited his autobiography, which has now finally appeared under the title, *Recollections of a Life*.

Hiss, previously a high State Department official, a member of the U.S. delegation at Yalta, and secretary general of the founding conference of the United Nations, was president of the Carnegie Endowment for International Peace in 1948 when he was accused of having been a secret Communist during the 1930's. His accuser was Whittaker Chambers, a senior editor at *Time* magazine and a self-confessed former member of the American Communist underground.

Hiss denied the charge—which had been made under immunity before the House Committee on Un-American Activities (HUAC)—and sued for slander when Chambers repeated the allegations on a national radio program. But Chambers soon upped the ante, charging Hiss not just with membership in a secret cell, but with having regularly passed on classified State Department documents for delivery to the Soviets.

A grand jury was convened. Chambers produced microfilm of documents he said Hiss had given him, as well as handwritten summaries of cables, which Hiss acknowledged were in his own handwriting. The statute of limitations on espionage having expired, Hiss was indicted for perjury, the slander suit was rendered moot, and Hiss was tried, convicted, and sentenced to prison.

It was not necessary to disbelieve the story told by Chambers— first at the perjury trials and then in *Witness,* his autobiography— to hope Hiss would some day offer his own version of the case. Indeed, Chambers's description of a Communist underground in New Deal Washington—an underground that sought both to deliver secret information to the Soviets and to place clandestine Communists in high places—has always been hard to disbelieve. Virtually every time a relevant FBI document has been declassified, and every time a new witness has emerged, a new part of Chambers's original story has been reconfirmed, and his overall credibility strengthened.

Nevertheless, Chambers was able to report only his version. And there were many who thought that Hiss, without confessing to espionage, might eventually decide to volunteer additional information, if only to respond to questions that even his supporters viewed as unanswered—if only to leave, for history's sake, a fuller version of the events that defined his life than *In the Court of Public Opinion,* the dry and unenlightening treatment of the trials he produced after his release from prison in 1954.

. . .

The questions that even Hiss's supporters hoped an autobiographical account by him might answer are many and varied. For even though Hiss's absolute innocence has over the years become a matter of received wisdom on the liberal-Left, many in the Hiss camp in 1948—

including key members of his legal team—were convinced that he was holding something back.

For example, a good number of Hiss's supporters deemed utterly incredible his claim not to have remembered Chambers until the much-celebrated personal confrontation orchestrated by Congressman Richard M. Nixon. During that confrontation, Hiss found it necessary to inspect Chambers's teeth before identifying him as "George Crosley"—a man to whom, by his own testimony, Hiss had given a car, the use of an apartment, a valuable rug, an introduction to a family physician, and much, much more.

No wonder, then, that even Charles Dollard, the president of the Carnegie Corporation—who was close enough to Hiss to have accompanied him to the HUAC-staged confrontation with Chambers—later told Hiss's attorneys that he "does not believe Alger stole the documents, but he also does not believe Alger has told all he knew about his relations with Chambers." And that was directly after the initial Hiss-Chambers confrontation, when the case was still very young and when hardly any evidence documenting the ties between the two men had as yet been introduced. Dollard's view, moreover, was shared by a great number of Hiss associates, including William Marbury, Hiss's lawyer in the slander suit, and Edward McLean, who organized the defense team after Hiss was indicted for perjury.

Even a recent study decidedly sympathetic to Hiss—*A Tissue of Lies: Nixon versus Hiss*—argues that Hiss lied about the nature of his relationship with Chambers. The authors, Morton Levitt and Michael Levitt, do not believe that Hiss was guilty of espionage. But they—like Marbury and McLean, and like Hiss's State Department mentor Francis B. Sayre—see ample evidence of a connection with Chambers far more intimate than Hiss has ever been willing to acknowledge.

There were many theories in the Hiss camp as to what he was holding back and why. Some observers looked beyond the mysterious Hiss-Chambers relationship for answers, and concluded that Hiss was shielding his wife, Priscilla (who died in 1986). Marbury and McLean apparently leaned toward this view, which turned on the premise that Priscilla was the "real" Communist. Hiss's friend and counselor, Secretary of State Dean Acheson, also apparently suspected Priscilla.

There were, to be sure, some Hiss supporters who—while recognizing that Hiss was concealing the nature and extent of his ties to Chambers—refused to believe that either Alger *or* Priscilla had ever had anything to do with Communism and/or espionage. For this group, the most popular theory at the time of the case was that Hiss was hiding a homosexual relationship with his accuser. This relationship, it was thought, might have enabled Chambers—somehow—to "frame" Hiss.

Also popular was the theory that Alger Hiss's stepson, Timothy Hobson, who had been discharged from the Navy as a homosexual shortly before the Hiss-Chambers controversy broke, had in some way been involved with Chambers during the 1930's. Hobson, it should be noted, would have been twelve years old at the time of these alleged contacts, and a relationship between the boy and Chambers still would not explain how Chambers had secured classified State Department documents. Yet for those unwilling, as a matter of principle, to credit Chambers's tale of Communism and espionage, even the most improbable scenarios were attractive.

In any event, it was on this question—the nature of Hiss's relationship with Chambers—that many Hiss supporters, as well as others interested in the case, hoped Alger Hiss would one day elaborate. In *Recollections of a Life*, however, Hiss offers nothing at all new about his ties to Chambers. Instead, to account for Chambers's motive in seeking to destroy him, Hiss embraces the theory—which he first advanced in an interview with the historian C. Vann Woodward in 1959—that Chambers was a homosexual *spurned*.

This notion, too, was popular in the Hiss camp during and immediately after the trials. A sort of cousin to the idea that the two men actually had a homosexual relationship, the "spurned homosexual" theory was a favorite of two other Hiss lawyers, Harold Rosenwald and Lloyd Paul Stryker. Yet even while embracing this theory, Hiss today continues to insist that he does not remember Chambers making homosexual advances toward him. This creates an obvious problem: if the intimacy existed only in Chambers's mind, the theory does not really explain anything—not how Chambers came to know Hiss so well; not how he got his hands on the documents; nothing.

It is a fact—and one which was known to government authorities, and to the Hiss defense team, at the time of the trials—that Chambers struggled with homosexuality during the 1930's. Chambers's homosexual history has also been documented in Allen Weinstein's *Perjury,* the major scholarly study of the case. Yet if Hiss was no more than the object of Chambers's unfulfilled desires, the theory does little for Hiss's effort to demonstrate his innocence. All it does is besmirch Chambers's reputation. It is, in other words, a classic exercise in "gay-baiting."

· · ·

If *Recollections of a Life* fails to shed new light on the Hiss-Chambers relationship, what of the other questions on which both supporters and opponents hoped Alger Hiss might some day elaborate: first and foremost, politics?

When did Hiss turn toward the hard Left? If he was a party-line Communist during the 1930's, did he ever break with Communism? What was Hiss's political orientation at the time of the trials? Has it changed since then? If so, how?

There have always been observers who accepted that Hiss was a leftist during the 1930's, even a secret Communist, but who rejected the notion that he had ever been a spy. It was as a secret Communist, according to this reading, that Hiss came to know Chambers; and it was Hiss's unwillingness to be candid about his political past in the cold-war climate of 1948 that led to his downfall.

During the period in which Hiss admits he knew Chambers, the latter was a Communist courier, organizer, and political "commissar." This is beyond dispute. From the private correspondence (discovered by Allen Weinstein) of the writer Josephine Herbst to the public testimony of former Communists like Lee Pressman and Nathaniel Weyl, evidence that Chambers told the truth about his work for Moscow has long been overwhelming. Even Hiss's lawyers, in the course of their pre-trial research, came to the conclusion that Chambers had indeed been an underground Communist during the '30s in Washington.

Nor was Chambers the only secret Communist among Alger Hiss's friends and acquaintances at the time. There was Pressman, as well as Nathan Witt, Noel Field, Henry Collins, and many others. Hiss has maintained that he never discussed the subject of Communism with these men, all of whom eventually ceased to conceal their Communist sympathies. This claim by Hiss is even less credible than the story he told about his acquaintance with "George Crosley."

Its absurdity is underscored by an insightful passage in a recently published study of the New Deal, *Dealers and Dreamers,* by the late Joseph P. Lash. In that passage, Lash describes the reluctance of underground Communists at the National Labor Relations Board to obey the party's directive that they remain clandestine and politically inconspicuous:

> He (cell leader Victor Perlo) instructed the cells' members to be "extremely inconspicuous" in regard to their political beliefs and to stay away from the mass organizations. The undergrounders did not like that. They wanted to be active. They had become Communists out of a belief that the party fought harder than any other group for a better world, and now, as Communists, they were asked to be less active than ever.

Needless to say, the "undergrounders" did comply. But if they could not take part in mass rallies, the least the secret Communists inside the government could do was discuss the issues that mattered to them in private conversations with like-minded friends.

Some of these men—Lee Pressman and Nathan Witt, for example—had been Hiss's friends since Harvard Law School. Henry Collins and Hiss went back even further, all the way to boyhood and summer camp. Yet Hiss asks us to believe that he never even *discussed* the subject of Communism with any of them. In other words, he never—then or later—asked his lifelong friend Henry Collins why Collins had left government service to head up the pro-Soviet American-Russian Institute. And Hiss purports never to have asked Noel Field why Field left the State Department to live in Europe, where he worked for the League of Nations and became an open Communist.

By 1948, this entire group—all those named by Chambers, save for Hiss—were "out of the closet" and functioning openly within the ambit of the Communist party. A few—John Abt and Victor Perlo, for example—do so to this day. There are some on the Left—Noel Field's brother, Hermann Field, for one—who have argued Hiss went too far during his legal ordeal in dissociating himself from the political idealism of the New Deal era. A book by Hiss in the autumn of his life—he is eighty-four years old and nearly blind—might have been an opportunity for him to unburden himself about the ties he felt he had to hide in 1948. But this is not the book.

・・・

About Hiss's politics in the years subsequent to 1938—which is when Chambers broke with Communism (and, of necessity, with Hiss)—we know next to nothing. We do not know whether Hiss remained committed to Communism, or—if he did—for how long.

At the time of the trials, there were quasi-sympathizers of Hiss like former Assistant Secretary of State Adolf A. Berle, Jr. who believed Hiss's problems stemmed largely from an effort to cover up a brief, youthful flirtation with radical politics. In Berle's words, "Frankly, I still don't know whether this is the boy that got in deep and then pulled clear, or what goes on here."

Or was Hiss still a Communist when he went to Yalta with FDR in 1945? If so, this would explain Andrei Gromyko's surprising willingness to let an American (Hiss) serve as secretary general of the UN founding conference in San Francisco.

A tantalizing piece published in the *Daily Worker,* the Communist-party newspaper, during the 1948 HUAC hearing suggests that Hiss, at least by then, had left the Communist orbit: "Here is a young man who, whatever one may think about his present enthusiasm for . . . the cold war, performed a highly useful service for his country during the New Deal and particularly during the war." The implication here is plain: he used to be one of us (perhaps even during the war), but is no longer. This, if true, leaves the question of when Hiss—to use Adolf Berle's construction—"pulled clear."

One passage in one newspaper article does not, to be sure, constitute proof. And it may be that Hiss never really did leave the fold, that the anti-Communist posture he struck while under investigation was a disingenuous pose, and nothing more. Certainly the Hiss defense, as Allen Weinstein has demonstrated, received significant clandestine assistance from Communist circles during the trials, including access to *Daily Worker* corporate records. (Chambers had once worked for the paper.)

After his release from prison in 1954, Hiss seemed to move leftward in a gradual way, picking up steam—not surprisingly—during the 1960's, as the political climate changed. He grew comfortable in the Old Left circles to which he had long professed no connection. But he asserted publicly that these were *new* links, that he—like many others—had merely been radicalized by Nixon and Vietnam.

Today, he no longer bothers to hide his contacts with party members, past or present. Hiss's current lawyers come from the world of the National Lawyers Guild and the National Emergency Committee on Civil Liberties (an offshoot of the ACLU, formed in the early 1950's by those who felt the parent group was not doing enough on behalf of Communists under investigation), and many of them were involved in representing Communists during the 1950's. They are a rather different lot from the Debevoise and Plimpton, Covington & Burling battery that handled Hiss's affairs in 1948.

But even with respect to his politics during the grim post-jail years, *Recollections of a Life* is a disappointment. There is no attempt to explain the radicalization Hiss purportedly underwent during the 50's and 60's, any more than there is an effort by Hiss, early on, to flesh out his version of the manifestly mysterious relationship with Chambers.

. . .

It is all the more surprising, then, that *Recollections of a Life* does manage to shed some new light on the character and world view of Alger Hiss.

Not with respect to the case itself: only a small part of the book is devoted to the events of 1948, and in these sections, Hiss relies heavily on the reader's ignorance of the actual facts. To cite only one of many examples: in discussing the handwritten documents produced by Chambers, Hiss refers to them as "four small scratchpad sheets of my penciled notes, which I used in briefing my superior, Francis Sayre, about selected cables." Hiss fails to mention that the "notes" were, for all practical purposes, verbatim transcripts of cables. Nor does he point out that Sayre, in 1948, professed no recollection of the briefing system Hiss describes, and no recollection of the issues treated in the cables.

What is new in these pages is Hiss's willingness, for the first time, to offer a glimpse at his view of the history of the 20th century. At isolated moments, while treating historical matters, including events in which he took part, Hiss seems to drop his guard—to say what he really thinks.

Thus, in a chapter entitled "Stalin, the Enigmatic Host at Yalta," Hiss argues that the Soviet dictator demonstrated not just "surprising geniality as (a) host," but also a "conciliatory attitude as (a) negotiator." According to Hiss, no one today remembers that "we, the Americans . . . (made) all the requests" at Yalta, and that "except for Poland, our requests were finally granted on our own terms."

His never tells us what he thinks happened with regard to Poland, and he does acknowledge that Stalin made demands of his own at the conference. But these, Hiss says, came only after we pressed Moscow to enter the war against Japan: "The initiative had been ours—we had urgently asked him to come to our aid." Nor does Hiss detail the "concessions" Stalin thereupon asked for and got.

No other American participant at Yalta has offered so sympathetic an assessment of Stalin's role. Conversely, in a similar vein, Hiss sees the cold war in general as a consequence of American belligerence: "Roosevelt's death and the less conciliatory foreign policy of the Truman administration did change the historic mix at a crucial moment."

Another fascinating glimpse into the real Alger Hiss comes toward the end of the book. There, in a discussion that fairly reeks of disingenuousness, Hiss examines his own failure to produce the history of the New Deal he had long hoped to write. In the course of trying to produce this would-be magnum opus, Hiss ran into a "major problem." He realized that the New Deal had not been a complete success:

> We New Dealers knew that we had not cured the Depression in the
> sense that our reforms would prevent its return; our efforts did not

ensure a fuller life for all Americans. it was not our reforms but the coming of World War II that really cut back unemployment. . . . The realities of history diminished my enthusiasm (for the project) . . .

The view that only a war economy can save a capitalist society from what Hiss calls "alternating glut and scarcity" is the ABC of Marxism-Leninism. And there is also something "Marxist" about the very fact of dropping an academic undertaking because it refuses to confirm a preconceived thesis. Once again, it would seem, we have— if only briefly—Hiss without the mask.

. . .

On the personal front, *Recollections of a Life* offers us the familiar, even-tempered Alger Hiss, a man devoid of any sense of outrage, even while claiming that a miscarriage of justice destroyed his life. This very trait—Hiss's failure to act like a man who has been wronged—has helped persuade some observers over the years that he must, indeed, have been guilty as charged. One acquaintance—who spoke to Hiss by telephone the morning after Chambers first testified—later wrote that Hiss sounded like someone who had "prepared himself for years for the moment when the story would break." The acquaintance was a man who had reason to know such things: Michael Straight. It would emerge many years later that Straight, one-time owner of the *New Republic* and an FDR speechwriter, had himself been recruited for secret work by the Soviets.

In *Recollections of a Life,* we find Hiss discussing his new, post-prison career as a stationery salesman much as he might have described his appointment, say, to the post of Secretary of State: "I enjoyed the work, with its technical challenges and the variety of men and women I met in the offices. . . . My experience . . . at Lewisburg stood me in good stead in coping with the great number of standard stationery items." (Hiss had worked in the storerooms while in the federal penitentiary at Lewisburg.) He reports with pride that a stationery-industry official, commenting on his sales efforts, said he "had not seen the city covered so thoroughly since the Great Depression." And Hiss insists that while working in his new field, he always held to principle:

> I didn't take my customers to lunch or give them whiskey and flowers at Christmas. Notwithstanding my unorthodoxy in these matters, I developed a loyal list of friendly customers. Before long I was able to achieve some success in my life as a salesman.

In his personal aspect, clearly, Alger Hiss is stiff, dogged, unemotional—and very tough. So tough, indeed, that it becomes easier and easier to understand how, in spite of everything, he stood his ground, held to his absurd story, and never cracked—not in court; not in jail; not while unemployed; and not during his gray days as a stationery salesman (before he became a late 60's campus hero).

But is he still a Communist? It is impossible to know for certain, but my own guess is that he never left the party, and that at every turn in his life he served the cause as best he could. In the Roosevelt administration, this meant passing documents. From 1948 on, it meant posing as an "American Dreyfus." Now it means he must stand fast, which is exactly what he does in this book.

20

S A M   T A N E N H A U S

Whittaker Chambers, Man of Letters

N E W   C R I T E R I O N ,   A P R I L   1 9 9 0

W ITHIN THE SPACE OF A generation—that is, since
1964, when *Cold Friday* was published to tepid reviews—Whittaker
Chambers has been all but forgotten as a writer. Those conversant with
the Alger Hiss case know, of course, that from the 1920s through the
1950s Chambers was frequently—at times steadily—in print. But his
most enduring utterance seems to be the testimony he gave before the
House Committee on Un-American Activities in 1948. Scholars of
the Cold War seldom look beyond it to the ample personal record he
left behind in his poetry, fiction, and journalism; few bother even with
Witness, Cold Friday and *Odyssey of a Friend.*[1] The work is there. It just
doesn't seem important. Charitable verdicts usually go no further than
Sidney Hook's late judgment, recorded in his autobiography *Out of
Step* (1987), that had Chambers "escaped involvement in politics, he
probably would have blossomed into a poet of stature." This view—of
Chambers as writer manqué—neatly fits the demonology of the Hiss
case. But is it accurate?

It is indeed the case that Chambers abandoned a burgeoning literary career in 1932, when he slipped into the mousehole of the Communist underground and began a six-year term of espionage. It is also

the case that not long after he resurfaced, in 1938, he joined the staff of *Time*—where he attained considerable influence as a writer and editor—and that, once the Hiss case ended, in 1950, he resumed his literary efforts, which he continued until his death in 1961. The problem is not, then, one of diligence. Is it one of talent? But he met with success as a poet, made a reputation as a translator, enjoyed instant celebrity as a short-story writer, and produced, in *Witness*, "one of the most significant autobiographies of the twentieth century" (said Hook) and a confession of "almost classical stature" (said Irving Howe). Nor, finally, was the problem one of seriousness. Chambers assayed grand issues and his sensibility was keyed to the moral crises of his era. Indeed, one could reasonably argue that he was uniquely serious—even in his most irresponsible phase. Many other American writers also served the revolutionary cause, but almost always as dilettantes who put little on the line and who consequently added almost nothing, despite their earnest efforts, to the literature of politics; in the radical Thirties political engagement meant, by and large, what it means today—signing petitions, attending rallies, joining committees, squabbling in the pages of journals. Not so for Chambers, who sojourned in the dark world of aliases, stolen documents, and orders sent from the Kremlin. It is commonly said that his motives were personal rather than political, that he embraced revolution not as a practical plan but as a species of romantic adventure. The same could be said of John Reed, or, for that matter, of Trotsky. And Chambers's political role did not end with his thirteen years of radicalism. It was he, more than any other intellectual, who awakened the American public to the dangers of totalitarianism, and his anti-Communist doctrine, spelled out as early as 1945, shaped the worldview of many post-war conservatives, including that of Ronald Reagan, his long-time admirer.

The real problem is that our culture has no tradition of men who meaningfully reconcile the claims of politics and art, and on this count Chambers, whose career was a sustained attempt at just such a reconciliation, stands convicted of un-American activity. Indeed he possibly inherited less of the native literary tradition than any other American writer of his time. His heroes were Dante, Dostoevsky, and Kafka. The book that opened his mind in childhood was *Les Misérables*. His favorite modern poet was Rilke, his favorite novelist Arthur Koestler (who reciprocated Chambers's esteem.) A quick glance at his published letters shows how steeped he was in the political and literary legacy of Europe, a legacy enriched by writers who translated their interior struggles, especially political and spiritual struggles, into the universal language of fable and allegory. It was not a coincidence that during the controversy that surrounded *Witness*, his strongest support came from abroad. "You are one of those," said one of his champions, André Malraux, "who did not return from Hell with empty hands."

The Hell was Stalinism, and Chambers's *Inferno* remains the best account of it written in the United States. Yet this major book has long been shunned like bad magic—alien in tone, anomalous in form, dangerous in meaning. Even the acclaim that greeted it on its publication in 1952 was mixed with abhorrence. Chambers saw what he famously termed the "tragedy of history" as a test of faith and the Manichaean rhetoric he used to describe it, though acceptable to a later generation, placed him outside the charmed circle of enlightened opinion forty years ago. "The most remarkable thing about *Witness*," wrote Irving Howe, "is that as a work of ideas it should be so raggedy and patchy. In all its 800 pages there is hardly a sustained passage of, say, 5,000 words devoted to a serious development of thought: everything breaks down into sermon, reminiscence, self-mortification, and self-justification." Chambers's prose was equally queer. Arthur Schlesinger, Jr., writing in *Saturday Review*, praised its vividness but shuddered at its "un-Anglo-Saxon intensity." In *The New Republic*, Merle Miller called *Witness* "sick." This distaste found its definitive expression two decades later when Lionel Trilling remarked that after the 1920s "something went soft and 'high' in [Chambers's] tone and I was never again able to read him either in his radical or in his religiose conservative phase without a touch of queasiness."[2] Just as certain lurid adjectives ritually cling to descriptions of Chambers's physical presence (drab, disheveled, soiled), so do their equivalents adhere to assessments of his prose style (apocalyptic, portentous, maudlin). In truth, Chambers's writing is rarely as overblown as people often suppose, and when he's carried away it's usually for a good reason. "Fear," he wrote in *Witness*,

> makes [ex-Communists] strident. They are like breathless men who have outrun the lava flow of a volcano and must shout down the smiles of villagers at its base who, regardless of their own peril, remember complacently that those who now try to warn them once offered their faith and their lives to the murderous mountain.

More than an explanation, this is a parable. And it's not surprising that so few critics acknowledge the parabolic essence of *Witness*, for to do so they must acknowledge, as well, the moral authority of a self-styled counter-revolutionary who repudiated one of the hallowed intellectual projects of his day—the attempt to extricate a viable liberalism from the wreckage of the Popular Front. Pundits find it easier to assail Chambers's arguments ("Faith in God or Faith in Man?") than to wrestle with the implications of his narrative and its irrefutable message: "I am the man, I suffer'd, I was there." In 1952 it fell to Rebecca West to marvel, in *The Atlantic*, that Chambers the memoirist "makes the further discoveries about reality, pushing another half-inch below the surface, which writers hope to make when they write." And it fell to West, who had herself "endured rough weather" in childhood, to point out how unwelcome certain "reminiscences are, and how likely to be greeted with impatient suggestions that they are exaggerated or are the figments of self-pity."

Irving Howe, for instance, dismissed Chambers's reminiscences as "a needless act of masochism." Needless, one wonders, for whom? Certainly not for anyone hoping to understand Chambers's passionate pilgrimage from hopelessness to belief. His family was the first Hell he knew. It "represented in miniature," as he put it, the crisis of the middle class. And it made him a candidate for other Hells. If we blanch at times during the course of Chambers's confessions—if we want to avert our eyes from his domestic *mises en scène*—it is because their plausibility fills us with dread: the lunatic grandmother stabbing the air with scissors; the cold, thwarted father secretly building his tiny toy theater in a room barred to his wife and sons; the shopkeeper cruelly leaning over a countertop to sneer (at the young Chambers), "Your mother is a broken down stagecoach." It was, as West said, "intricate and ambitious misery," and Chambers dredged up every detail. Was he masochistic? Perhaps, but so was Proust, the author of another "sick" book, another prodigious feat of recollection. Chambers, after all, had come before the public as an official rememberer, a witness summoned against his will. No wonder he often brooded on the fate of another reluctant bearer of bad news:

> I have, for years [he wrote William F. Buckley, Jr.] been fascinated by the Book of Jonah, and I said to a few at the time that that was the pattern of the Hiss Case. Therefore, in a sense, I fled to Tarshish with the dread words in my ears: "Go up unto Ninevah, that great city, etc." But, when the tempest arose, and it became a question of myself or the crew, I had also to say: "Take me up and cast me into the sea, because it is for my sake that this trouble is come upon you." . . . But, in the end, I did go unto Ninevah, and when nothing really happened . . . and others had eaten up the cucumber vine, and God had asked: "Do you well to be angry?" I answered and still answer: "I do well to be angry, even unto death."

. . .

In his later years, Chambers lumped together all his early writing as the noxious by-product of a misspent youth. He was born in Philadelphia in 1905, and grew up in Lynbrook, Long Island, the elder son of a commercial artist and a sometime actress. At an early age he acquired an appetite for literature and exhibited a rare gift for languages; but when he graduated from high school, in 1919, he put off going to college and instead went on the road, intent on reaching Mexico. Four months later—after a stint of vagabondage and day labor—he was stranded in a New Orleans flophouse and had to wire home for money. He returned to Lynbrook, toiled briefly in the Manhattan ad agency where his father did layouts, and then enrolled at Columbia. Morningside Heights was an exceptionally lively place, with an undergraduate population that included World War I veterans and, unusual for the Ivy League in the Twenties, many products of the local public schools. Chambers fell in with a group of city boys, most of them Jews, most of them inflamed with intellectual aspirations: Mortimer J. Adler, Clifton Fadiman, Meyer Schapiro, Louis Zukofsky, and others. They initiated him into the charms of skeptical humanism, and he moved among them as a magnetic presence, often silent, sometimes oracular, prone to sudden outbursts of hilarity.

Like the others, Chambers joined Boar's Head, a kind of "Conversazione Society," and tagged after Mark Van Doren, the "master of sunny influence," as Chambers later called him. In 1920, Van Doren was twenty-six, an English Department rookie assigned as Chambers's adviser; in this capacity he steered the gifted freshman away from the reflexive Republicanism he had inherited from his parents (Chambers's themes were sprinkled with quotations from Calvin Coolidge) and also, Chambers wrote in *Cold Friday*, "infected me with the idea that the literary life is the best in the world and that to be a poet is among the higher callings known to man." Better yet, Van Doren encouraged

Chambers to believe "that I was to be a poet." This belief was shared by others. "We were convinced he would leap into instant fame," recalled Jacques Barzun, a younger Columbia man. Another, Lionel Trilling, allowed that "Chambers had a very considerable college prestige as a writer. This was deserved. My undergraduate admiration for his talent was recently confirmed when I went back to the poetry and prose he published in a student magazine in 1924–25. At that time he wrote with an elegant austerity." The magazine was *Morningside*. Chambers made his debut in it as a sophomore with a story called "The Damn Fool," a somewhat clotted narrative inspired by Joseph Conrad's "Heart of Darkness."[3] Its hero, a young sailor flushed with idealism, ships to Russia and dies there in battle after leading a charge against the Bolsheviks. The plot alone is prophetic. But consider some clairvoyant remarks tossed off by secondary characters:

> "He wasn't a Bolshevist. He was a Puritan, perhaps. That is radical, of course. He was an extremist."

> "What he did gives weakness a false appearance of glory. He wasn't glorious. How many weary miles did he tramp to escape himself."

> "Probably he could have been a writer if he hadn't been so interested, after all, in life."

"The Damn Fool" contains the hard kernel of the sensibility that exfoliated thirty years later in *Witness*. Already we see Chambers's fascination with revolution, his flare for self-dramatization—tempered with self-appraisal—and his intuitive grasp of what his opponents are thinking. And there is that elegant austerity. Not quite twenty-one, Chambers writes disturbingly mature sentences, few of undergraduate artifice. Words for him are an instrument, and he puts them to the task of finding remedies for "the incurable sickness of the world." The young Chambers is often represented as a nihilist. In fact, he was already embarked on the search for a sustaining faith. A quatrain from this time pointedly borrows the rhyme scheme of Tennyson's great elegy, "In Memoriam":

And we on whom its shadow falls—
A sober and containing air—
Feel it as tired and late despair
Between enfolding iron walls.

From confession Chambers advanced to controversy. This was in 1922, a year of bold literary statements; Chambers read "The Waste Land" in *The Dial*. His own *succès de scandale* appeared that autumn in *Morningside*. He was now a junior, the magazine's editor in chief and the author of the lead piece in the November number, "A Play for Puppets." In it Jesus arises from the tomb to refuse the burden of divinity. This blasphemy—perceived as a prank despite its earnest attempt to humanize Christ—became an issue during the Hiss trial. So did it in 1922, as Chambers suspected it might: he published it, in fact, under a pseudonym, "John Kelly." Faculty members clamored for Chambers's expulsion, there was a fuss in the New York newspapers, and the offending author was summoned to the office of Dean Herbert E. Hawkes, a stern disciplinarian whose father had led a Union regiment in the Civil War. Chambers was ordered to retract his playlet and to collect all copies of the magazine. He demurred and was stripped of his editorship. But he was not expelled, as is often alleged. He quit Columbia of his own accord and announced the decision in a note he sent Hawkes in January 1923. The episode set the pattern for other, Jonah-like performances: Chambers learned early that unseemly utterances carry a price. This would be confirmed when he wrote "The Ghosts on the Roof" (1945), which outraged *Time* staffers with its dire warnings about Soviet expansionism, confirmed again when he testified before HUAC, and yet again when, in the pages of *Na-*

tional Review, he defended Alger Hiss's right to a passport. Once an idea—atheism, in this early instance—took hold of Chambers, he had to state it loudly. Polite aestheticism could only mock, not raze, the enfolding iron walls. Many years later Chambers put the case this way: "the natural habit of Mark [Van Doren]'s mind (like that of many academic liberals) was to treat ideas as having an existence apart from life; their delight was in their multiplex play; ideas never implied acts. The natural habit of my mind was the exact opposite. Ideas as intellectual game scarcely interested me at all. For me, an idea was the starting point of an act."

And writing was just such an act. Chambers's near expulsion proved to him that words could rock with seismic force. But they must serve a cause. Atheism wouldn't do. He was by nature a believer, not a skeptic; he needed something to argue for, not against. He found it in the summer of 1923, when he and Meyer Schapiro travelled abroad and got an eyeful of Weimar Germany, then on the brink of anarchy. This was months after French troops had brutally occupied the Ruhr valley and months before Hitler's Munich putsch. The two Americans went to Berlin, where purse-snatching was mirthless sport and marching Communists sent up an ominous chant: *Blut muss fliessen, Blut muss fliessen, Blut, Blut, Blut.* Chambers returned to New York wrapped in Spenglerian doom. The *Abendland* would sink under its own corrupt weight. The answer was revolution. He read Lenin and Sorel while he held down a night job in the Newspaper Division of the Forty-second Street Library (he remained in its employ, on and off, till April 1927.) He enrolled again at Columbia in September 1924, promptly cut classes, and in February 1925 joined the Communist Party, feeling "joy and exultation in the thought of surrendering one's self to the wash of the wave, of being carried higher on the sun-touched crests of wild billows than one could ever be by a dry, lonely effort of one's own."

Chambers didn't write those words. Henry James did, in *The Prin-*

cess Casamassina (1886). Its protagonist, Hyacinth Robinson, cannot choose between the rival imperatives of art and revolution and ends up a suicide. Chambers, in the middle Twenties, strove to satisfy both claimants. He adopted the unsmiling guise of the young Bolshevik but at the same time honed his poetic skills. The November 1923 *Morningside* includes his tender narrative "Braun." A sailor has returned home to Long Island after many years at sea and now wants to make amends with his father. He ambles along the shore and there meets another solitary walker, a poet, who strikes an uncannily Wordsworthian tone:

> Filled by the sun,
> Moved, as by the tide, as slowly,
> I prolonged the hour of my intention,
> And heard the whistles blow
> Noon in the meadow villages,
> And heard them cease.

Records at Columbia list Chambers as a student until June 1925, but in name only. He was consumed by extracurricular activity. He studied "the law of social revolution" under Scott Nearing at the Rand School, was a go-fer for *The Daily Worker*, travelled to the Far West, and wrote poetry. He sent lyrics to Van Doren, now the poetry editor at *The Nation*, who accepted them for publication. In May 1926 Chambers contributed "Railroad Yards (Long Island City)" to the inaugural issue of *New Masses*. Here his considerable feeling for nature succumbs to an ideal vision of "the workers" rising toward collective strength:

> . . . swing of motion thru the darkness
> without stay or let:
> With only the delicate human hands set
> Motionless above the controls, as a threat.

This was written at a time of intense personal anguish. Chambers's brother, Richard, who had passed untouched, it seemed, through the "rough weather" of childhood, had suddenly become despondent. He dropped out of college, drank incessantly, and talked of suicide. In September 1926, after repeated attempts foiled by Whittaker, Richard succeeded at taking his own life, at twenty-three. Chambers, devastated by the loss, felt the waters closing over his own head, but "[d]eep within me," he wrote, "there was a saving fierceness." He clambered aboard the life raft of the party and busied himself at *The Daily Worker* with editorial and organizational tasks, pausing only to compose lines like these, which appeared in the March 1927 issue: "For the dead, the dead, the dead/we march, comrades, workers." The poem is called "March for the Red Dead" and it is so defiantly unpoetic that it amounts to a proclamation: from now on Chambers's words will be conscripted into the service of, in James's phrase, "the great grim restitution."

But the party, it turned out, was not a safe haven. Chambers had enlisted during a particularly chaotic time, the so-called Third Period, marked by Stalin's brutal and despotic ascent. Party watchdogs in the United States mounted a purge, thinning the ranks of *The Daily Worker*. Chambers quit in disgust in 1929. His literary energy had already found a new channel, thanks to his chum Clifton Fadiman, now an editor at Simon & Schuster. The firm had started up a high-toned imprint, the Inner Sanctum, that was bringing out foreign novels; in 1928 Chambers prepared for it the first English-language edition of Felix Salten's *Bambi*. A Book-of-the-Month Club selection, it was released in a printing of 75,000 copies, complete with a puff from John Galsworthy (who had been bowled over by the galleys of Chambers's translation). The reviews were rhapsodic, and Chambers was instantly in demand. Between 1928 and 1931, he Englished three more books by Salten, Heinrich Mann's *Mother Mary*, Kasimir Edschmid's *The Passionate Rebel* (a fictionalized life of Byron) and

Franz Werfel's *Class Reunion*.[4] During the Hiss trial, Werfel's novel, the story of a destructive friendship, was ingeniously though erroneously cited as the inspiration for Chambers's "plot" to destroy Hiss.

. . .

This early work remains tucked away in more or less obscure places, and for many years Chambers's journalism was also hard to find. But an important chunk of it has now been exhumed by Terry Teachout and issued as *Ghosts on the Roof: Selected Journalism of Whittaker Chambers, 1931–59*.[5] Teachout includes in his collection four short stories written by Chambers in 1931 and published in *New Masses*. The magazine was presided over by Michael Gold, the author of *Jews Without Money* (1930) and a bleak exemplar of literary Stalinism—a sort of switchman who alertly changed his ideological track as new semaphores were flashed from Moscow. *New Masses* bore Gold's stamp but not his alone. It is a startling experience to examine antique issues of this publication—filled with jejune caricatures of obese capitalists and emaciated workers—and see the illustrious names on its masthead: Sherwood Anderson, Eugene O'Neill, Edmund Wilson, Lewis Mumford. John Dos Passos was a regular contributor—sections of *U.S.A.* originally ran in *New Masses*. Katherine Anne Porter reviewed fiction in it.

Chambers, the renegade "Lovestonite," reached a truce with party regulars and reemerged as a radical writer, though not of verse, "for as soon as I began to shake off the influence of authentic poets, I found myself writing prose." He began with agitprop short stories. On one level, they were flummery; yet Teachout rightly calls them, in his incisive introduction, "the product of a writer of considerable technical skill and a genuinely poetic sensibility." Each story doles out a different morsel of Communist dogma. The message of the first, "Can You Make Out Their Voices?," is "Organize!" Chambers based his story on news reports of a small insurrection in Arkansas, where five hundred destitute farmers had stormed a Red Cross station. It happened in January 1931, the nadir of the Depression, and it heralded the coming revolution, at least in Chambers's treatment. His pious rebels seemed lifted from the movies, not from the sod:

> "What did you say you called yourself?"
> "A Communist."
> "That's like a Red, Russians, huh?"
> "No, workingmen and poor farmers, like you and me."

There are, however, taut descriptions of the blighted landscape and its suffering inhabitants, human and animal: "A red-headed woodpecker lay on the front path, its wings spread out. The boys took it into the house. In the shade it revived. They gave it a drop of water; it uttered its single sharp scream." "Can You Make Out Their Voices?" was published in March 1931, and *New Masses* proudly announced a thick drift of fan mail. Hallie Flanagan, of Vassar's Experimental Theater, secured permission for a stage adaptation. She and her collaborator, Margaret Clifford, expanded the original by adding a subplot built around a debutante and her political coming of age. The result, entitled *Can You Hear Their Voices?*, became a staple of the radical repertory. News of Chambers's talent widened on the Left and rippled all the way to Moscow. A Soviet literary journal extolled him for "rais[ing] the image of the Bolshevik." His other stories are more experimental. "The Death of the Communists" concludes with a Brechtian peroration:

> The Communists were obviously men of courage, single-minded no doubt, but capable of a kind of fanatical calm in the face of death, on the basis, however difficult for one of us to comprehend, of certain convictions arrived by means of an intelligence no matter how limited. Were possessed, I mean, of intelligence, conviction, courage. Were, therefore, men, gentlemen, men. Men! Men, do you hear me, you beasts, men!

"The Death of the Communists" appeared in December 1931. Soon Chambers was placed on the editorial board of *New Masses*. But in the spring of 1932, in the wake of his first literary triumph, he was recruited to undertake more useful, clandestine work—work that would lead him, in 1934, to Washington, D.C. and the Communist cell set up there by Harold Ware. When the call came, Chambers, age thirty-one, was the author of several published poems, four stories, and eight translations—hardly the marginal flop who dominates accounts of the Hiss case.

. . .

The bulk of *Ghosts on the Roof* consists of articles, reviews, and essays written by Chambers after he arose from the Communist netherworld in 1938. It took him a year to find a steady job, but it was a good one, on the staff of *Time*. (The man who hired him, T. S. Matthews, had reviewed *Class Reunion*, favorably, in *The New Republic*.) Chambers shared an office with James Agee, with whom he formed a close friendship, especially after Chambers discovered God (Agee was a tormented Episcopalian.) They also led their section—book and film reviews—to the top of the reader polls. For a man who had struggled up to daylight from the bottom rungs of Hell, the corporate ladder of Time Inc. was not insurmountable. Chambers scaled it nimbly. It helped that he had a wife and two children to support and that his party salary had peaked at $165 a month (in the Thirties spies rarely were in it for the money). At *Time* Chambers routinely worked forty-eight-hour shifts, and in 1942 he suffered the first of several heart attacks (the last would kill him). By his own estimation, he wrote a thousand articles for Henry Luce—news stories, features, reviews, occasional essays. None, as a rule, was signed. Hence, Teachout and his research assistant, Patrick Swan, have had to do some detective work. Luckily, not even the lacquer of Timese can entirely obscure an original style.

It is undoubtedly Chambers that Teachout has given us—the rounded phrases, the wide learning. Sidney Hook was right to call Chambers an autodidact, despite all those semesters at Columbia. He had the autodidact's fondness for making big connections and the autodidact's fingertip command of everything he's read.

Time Inc. was not just a publishing company. It was the prototype of today's corporation, a pretend empire. Its monarch, Luce, noticed Chambers right away—first his prose, then his manner. Chambers was a potent presence. People smiled at his glum countenance, portly figure (loosely bagged in oversize suits), and enigmatic air. Not many smiled at his politics: these were the days when "right-wing" meant Trotskyist, and as Chambers evolved toward anti-Communism, he undertook to reorient the political views of his colleagues. "The driving force of my work at *Time*," he wrote Luce in a letter quoted by Teachout, "has been a sense of mission, of calling." He was girding for Ninevah. He polarized the local chapter of the Newspaper Guild, regaled colleagues with tales from the underground, and campaigned for the editorship of *Time*'s "Foreign News" section. He got the job in 1944. The war was ending, and Luce, who agreed with Chambers that the Soviet Union loomed as the next global threat, gave him license to promote this worldview, even if certain writers did not share it. There were mutinous showdowns with John Hersey, Theodore White, and others. In 1945, after Chambers blacked out on a train, he was relegated to the culture desk. There partnered again with Agee, he produced his celebrated cover stories on Reinhold Niebuhr, Arnold Toynbee, Rebecca West, and Marian Anderson—each an example of oratorical journalism raised to a standard that would never be surpassed at *Time*.

Chambers was Luce's pet writer. Few begrudged him his special status. His copy was legendary for its "flow" and he had an infallible eye for the striking image. His skills were shown to best advantage in literary portraits, such as "Silence, Exile & Death" (1941), a haunting précis of James Joyce's flight, his last, from Nazi-occupied Paris: "Every afternoon at 4 sharp, Joyce and [Paul] Léon reread *Finnegans Wake*. Joyce would sit with his long thin legs wrapped inextricably around each other while he held the book close to his eyes, studied it through a thick lens. Léon read aloud. They would then make corrections."

The attacks on *Witness* created an impression—still with us—that Chambers had a weak mind. This wasn't so. True, he sanitized Toynbee (and made him, in the process, a household name), but it was a feat that demanded mental agility and that earned him the admiration of college professors. Those who have avoided *Witness* will be surprised to discover that Chambers could be epigrammatic and astringent: "Fundamentally benevolent and humane, [American intellectuals] loved their fellow countrymen in distress far more than they could ever love them in prosperity." He had, as well, the ability to carve a shapely thesis from an inchoate mass of details: George Santayana, wrote Chambers,[6] had

> an integrity of Catholic suppleness and irrefragability, enriched by the deep experience of two cultures (one rock-bound, Protestant and New England, the other Catholic and Mediterranean), international yet intensely local (for most of Santayana's life has been passed in the Spanish provincial city of Avila and the American provincial capital of Boston). It had been lent fluency by his necessity of thinking in two languages, Spanish and English, and tempered by the age's ultimate test of individualism, the discipline of preserving the classic mind, smiling and ascetic, in a world of technological uniformity. It is an integrity in which there is room for humor, for it has traveled in the world and looked upon the Woolworth Building as well as the Dome of St. Peter's. And it has been matured by overcoming a duality of experience that was both geographic and psychic—a divided family, the alternating influences of a Spanish father and a Spanish boyhood, and a Spanish mother and a New England boyhood.

Chambers closed out his days at Time Inc. with a series of brief historical Baedekers published in *Life* in 1947–48. He wrote on, among other subjects, "The Middle Ages," "The Glory of Venice," and "The Protestant Reformation." It was his turn at the public lectern manned variously by Adler, Barzun, Fadiman, and Trilling, all veterans like himself of Columbia's innovative Great Books courses. Chambers's *Life* essays were immensely popular, though he badly overshot his deadlines. He was distracted, I suspect, by certain events taking place in the House Committee on Un-American Activities. "The Tranquil Years," as Chambers fondly characterized his decade at *Time*, were in fact fraught with anxiety. He feared violent reprisal from his ex-comrades and was troubled by the faltering signals sent from Washington, which seemed curiously indifferent to Soviet infiltration. As early as September 2, 1939—ten days after Hitler and Stalin became blood brothers and the day after the Nazis invaded Poland—Chambers gave a thorough run-down on the Washington spy apparatus to Adolf A. Berle, Assistant Secretary of State. But nothing came of it. FBI interviewers visited Chambers's office in 1942 and again in 1945 and both time left convinced that everything he had to tell them was 'history hypothesis or deduction." Not until 1946 was there a glimmer of genuine interest: the Bureau had targeted Hiss, and agents alerted Chambers to stand by. On July 31, 1948, Elizabeth Bentley, "the Blonde Spy Queen," told HUAC a fanciful tale about Washington officials passing on secret documents to Soviet operatives, and two days later Chambers, who had begged the Committee not to summon him, was served with a subpoena. His vassalage at *Time* was over and his public trauma began.

• • •

Prophecy erupts in concentrated bursts, and the two-year paroxysm of writing *Witness* left Chambers drained. He started another book, but it kept changing shape; finally it became an albatross. He repeatedly assured Bennert Cerf, his publisher, that he was at work, and he was—contributing essays to *National Review* and polishing the reminiscences and meditations issued posthumously as *Cold Friday*. He preferred shorter forms. All the more remarkable that he saw *Witness* through to completion. In some respects, it was his most taxing ordeal. It was lightened, though, by moments of optimism. In December 1950 he informed David McDowell, his editor at Random House, that he had at last found a suitable opening line. He meant the first sentence, not of his foreword, "Letter to My Children," but of "Flight": "In 1937, I began, like Lazarus, the impossible return." Of course it was the example of another resurrection, Jonah's, that Chambers was fated to follow. For, like all true writers, he could not escape the burden of his eloquence.

NOTES

[1] *Witness*, the autobiography of Whittaker Chambers, was published in 1952; a paperback edition, with a preface by Robert Novak and a foreword by Milton Hindus, is available from Regnery Gateway. *Cold Friday*, a posthumous collection of memoirs and fragments edited by Duncan Norton-Taylor, was published in 1964. *Odyssey of a Friend: Whittaker Chambers's Letters to William F. Buckley, Jr., 1954–61*, was published in 1969.

[2] From Trilling's introduction to the 1975 reissue of *The Middle of the Journey* (1947). Gifford Maxim, the pivotal character of this, Trilling's only novel, was based on Chambers.

[3] "The Damn Fool" was published in the March 1922 *Morningside*. Copies of this and the other issues of *Morningside* mentioned in this article are in the Columbiana Collection, Columbia University.

[4] Chambers translated two more books after he left the party. One was about the Red Cross; the other, which he co-translated with Barrows Mussey, was Gustav Regler's *The Great Crusade* (1940), a novel about the Spanish Civil War.

[5] *Ghosts on the Roof: Selected Journalism of Whittaker Chambers, 1931–59*, edited and with an introduction by Terry Teachout; Regnery Gateway, 361 pages.

[6] In "Santayana, Poet of Dissolution," a review of *Persons and Places: The Backgrounds of My Life*, *The American Mercury*, March 1944.

21

SAM TANENHAUS

Sifting through the Evidence

APPENDIX TO *WHITTAKER*
CHAMBERS: A BIOGRAPHY, 1997

T O THIS DAY, THE HISS case remains one of the great
controversies of the postwar era, especially as new evidence, real and
alleged, has surfaced.

The first strong challenge to the guilty verdict came in Hiss's
motion for a new trial, filed on January 24, 1952, and denied (by
Judge Goddard) six months later. The motion rested on two major
contentions.

The defense argued that Chambers had testified falsely at the
trial (and earlier) about the date of his defection from the underground. Chambers had initially said he broke "in late 1937 or very
early 1938." But after producing the spy papers, some of which dated
from April 1938, he pushed the date back to April 15, about the
time he had begun work on the *Dunant* translation for the Oxford
University Press.

But the defense, in its motion, cited as evidence correspondence
from Oxford's files that indicated Chambers had been in touch with
Oxford in March 1938. How, then, to explain documents in
Chambers's possession dating several weeks later?

The confusion was easily solved when FBI agents questioned

Chambers on the events leading up to and culminating in his break. Rethinking the sequence of moves he had made in those weeks of high anxiety, Chambers realized the defense was partly right. He had received the manuscript from Paul Willert in March 1938 and promptly translated some chapters. Then he had set the job aside while he saw to the next, definitive stage of his defection, his physical separation from the underground and his flight to Daytona Beach. It was there, in mid- to late-April, that he seriously began work on the translation, racing to meet Oxford's May 1 deadline. This chronology was borne out by his correspondence with Willert, by Esther's letters to the Park School, and by the timing of the flight to Florida and back.

The centerpiece of the defense's appeal was a charge of conspiracy, first broached by Hiss at his sentencing when he declared himself the victim of "forgery by typewriter." The 1952 motion theorized that Woodstock 230009, the machine produced so dramatically at the first trial by Lloyd Stryker, was a fake built by Chambers (and un-named accomplices). To demonstrate the feasibility of the theory, Hiss hired a wizard of typewriter construction, Martin K. Tytell, who de-vised a type face that closely duplicated Woodstock 230009. Accord-ing to the defense's document expert, Elizabeth McCarthy, Tytell's copy was so good she herself would "find it difficult if not impossible" to tell apart samples typed on the two machines. Thus, the defense argued, a phony machine *could* have been built.

But if the Woodstock was a fake, who had manufactured it and how had he—or they—succeeded in planting it on the Hiss defense? Here the defense was hard put to supply plausible answers.

Martin Tytell's experiment seemed to establish the feat was pos-sible. But he was an outstanding technician with years of experience customizing typewriters. Even so, he struggled mightily to build a replica. His first effort, five months in the construction, was a failure that came nowhere near duplicating Woodstock 230009. Only when

Elizabeth McCarthy joined in, checking weekly on Tytell's progress, did the results improve. The final product was the outcome of more than a year's careful labor, and kinks still remained. McCarthy noted imperfections. FBI analysts found more. It was hard to imagine how Chambers could have produced a flawless copy in a far narrower period, the three-month interval between August 17, 1948 (when Hiss had first dared him to risk a slander suit), and November 17, 1948, when Chambers had walked into the Baltimore deposition with a sheaf of typed documents. As for his mechanical aptitude, it was best summed up by Laha, who, when told of the theory, laughed. "Why, Beadle couldn't even pound a nail in the wall," she said. "He was all thumbs." What was more, he would have had to accomplish this feat at a time when his schedule was filled with interrogations and trial preparations.

The only answer, then, was that the FBI and possibly HUAC had been the true authors of a conspiracy to frame Hiss. The bureau, at least, had the technical wherewithal to build a typewriter. But even if this had happened—and not one document in the massive FBI archive suggests it did—how had the fraudulent Woodstock wound up in the hands of Hiss's attorneys, who were following their own leads? And what of the two dozen or more FBI agents who "shook the City of Washington down to a fare-thee-well" in a frantic search for the Woodstock? Had that been an act, a phony hunt complete with mountainous paperwork? Or had J. Edgar Hoover sent his foot soldiers in one direction while he subtly guided the Hiss team through the winding path of inquiry that eventually led them to a Washington junk dealer?

This theory also required a redefinition of Chambers's role. He was no longer the depraved mastermind of Hiss's ruin, driven by "motives of revenge or hatred," but, in the defense's new rendition, a pawn manipulated by the true conspirators, Hoover and possibly Nixon.

Besides being improbable, the theory did not account for two important facts: (1) The government's case against Hiss had never rested on the authenticity of the recovered Woodstock, but on the similarity of the type face on the two sets of documents, evidence not linked to any particular typewriter, and (2) Chambers had also been in possession of handwritten notes whose authorship Hiss acknowledged.

Meanwhile, even as the Hiss defense mounted its appeal, a new witness had come forward: Nathaniel Weyl, sometime AAA economist and Ware Group wunderkind. Weyl had quit the unit in July 1934, finding the pressure of secrecy intolerable. He had lasted just a few weeks longer, he would doubtless have been introduced to Carl, the courier from New York. As it was, the two did not meet, so Weyl could not testify to any relationship between Chambers and Hiss, although he could have said whether he remembered Hiss as a cell member.

But Weyl had been silent all during the case. More curious still, in *Treason*, a book he had written in 1949 on the Communist conspiracy, he had implied the charges against Hiss were false. "I had to write about the Hiss case," he later explained. "But the matter was still in court . . . the first trial was a hung jury. So as far as I was concerned the matter of espionage was still an open question." Besides, Weyl himself had not participated in espionage and knew nothing about it. As for the activities he did know about, "I was not going to reveal my involvement . . . I did not desire any career as a former Communist. So I approached [the subject] as if I had no personal knowledge of Communist Party membership."

Finally, in the fall of 1950, ten months after Hiss's conviction, Weyl had gone to the FBI and confessed his membership in the Ware unit. He repeated his testimony before the McCarran Committee in February 1952, a month after Hiss had filed his appeal. As a charter member of the Ware Group, Weyl had attended "fifteen to twenty" unit meetings at Helen Ware's violin studio and was able to name his other accomplices. They included Alger Hiss, whom Weyl recalled as a dues-paying and doctrinaire Party member, "a true believer, a deeply committed Communist."

. . .

One last fling at establishing Hiss's innocence came in 1992, when selected Moscow archives were unlocked and opened to researchers. At the request of Alger Hiss, then aged eighty-eight, General Dmitri A. Vokogonov, chairman of the Russian government's military intelligence archives, authorized a search of the KGB files and then sent Hiss a letter exonerating him on the basis of available files, none of which indicated Hiss had ever spied for Soviet intelligence. Within weeks, however, Vokogonov sheepishly admitted his search had been cursory and many relevant files had been destroyed. He did not offer to check again. Other Russian researchers, diligently combing intelligence files, privately reported that after Vokogonov's blunder, officials had scoured the archives and removed all files pertaining to Chambers and Hiss.

But documentation on Hiss did turn up in a Communist archive. In 1993 Maria Schmidt, a Hungarian historian working in the files of the Interior Ministry, in Budapest, came upon the dossier of Noel Field, who had been imprisoned in Budapest in 1949 after his defection behind the Iron Curtain. Released in 1954, Field was debriefed by the Communist police, to whom he gave a detailed accounting of his secret work in the United States and of his close relationship with Alger Hiss, a fellow agent. According to Field, Hiss had tried to recruit him into the underground in 1935—the same incident Hede Massing had recalled. "I knew from what Hiss told me that he was working for the Soviet secret service," said Field. Surprised by Hiss's overture, Field "carelessly told him I was already working for Soviet intelligence." When Field reported his blunder to Hede Massing, "I received a stern rebuke from her . . . A little later she told me I had done greater damage than I would believe and that because of me the whole network had to be reorganized."

Not long after this, new revelations emerged from the U.S. government. First, in 1993, the State Department declassified documents relating to a security investigation in 1946 that disclosed Hiss had procured top secret reports he was not authorized to see—on atomic energy, China policy, and other matters relating to military intelligence. The investigation was concluded in late November 1946. Two weeks later Hiss notified John Foster Dulles he was available, after all, to head the Carnegie Endowment.

Then, in the summer of 1995, the National Security Agency began to release the Venona traffic, a total of more than two thousand cables sent from U.S.-based Soviet agents to the home office in Moscow. The messages had been intercepted in the 1940s by American counterintelligence officers and in the next years were painstakingly decoded. The more important batch of cables, released on March 5, 1996, confirmed that there had been a large espionage network centered in the federal government. Among those implicated were Harry Dexter White, Victor Perlo, Laurence Duggan, and Alger Hiss, who was implicated in a single cable, dated March 30, 1945.

In the cable Anatoly Gromov, the NKVD *rezident* in Washington, reports on a conversation with another Soviet handler, Ishkak Akhmerov, "the leading NKVD illegal" in the United States. Akhmerov had recently interviewed a well-placed unnamed GRU agent within the State Department. The official told Akhmerov he had attended the Yalta Conference and then flown on to Moscow, where he was thanked by Soviet diplomat Andrey Vyshinsky for his devoted service.

The Yalta delegation included only four members of the State Department, all of whom flew on to Moscow. The four were Secretary of State Stettinius; his assistant, Wilder Foote; the director of the Office of European Affairs, H. Freeman Matthews; and the deputy director of the Office of Special Political Affairs, Alger Hiss. In Moscow, the contingent met with Vyshinsky. Only Hiss was ever suspected of being a Communist.

The American agent further told Akhmerov he had been working with Soviet intelligence since 1935 and "for some years . . . has been the leader of a small group" of agents, "for the most part consisting of [family] relations."

All of this led American counterintelligence officers to conclude that the agent, identified only by his code name Ales, was "probably Alger Hiss." Thus Hiss remained a Soviet agent long after Chambers's defection and possibly up until the moment he was forced out of the State Department. Chambers had made a thoughtful surmise, not a wild accusation, when, under threat of a lawsuit, he declared, "Alger Hiss was a Communist and may be [one] now."

22

R O N   R O S E N B A U M

My Lunch With Alger: Oh No, Not Hiss Again!

N E W   Y O R K   O B S E R V E R ,
A P R I L   1 6 ,   2 0 0 1

"GOOD LORD DELIVER US," the incomparable Murray Kempton once wrote. "Everyone seems to be talking about Alger Hiss again."

That was 1978. That was after three decades of interminable, tendentious arguments over the Alger Hiss case. And now, a quarter-century later, *good Lord deliver us* (and this time for real, please), they're *still* talking about Alger Hiss.

I've tried to stay away, I really have—but like Al Pacino in *Godfather III* (underrated, I think), *they're pullin' me back in.* It's one of the eternal schisms in American culture—and I think I have a new perspective on that to add.

It's been more than a half century now since Hiss—the brilliant, patrician Harvard Law protégé of Oliver Wendell Holmes and Felix Frankfurter, rising star in F.D.R.'s State Department, architect of the U.N.—found himself accused of being part of a Soviet spy ring. Convicted of lying to a grand jury, sent off to Lewisburg federal penitentiary, Hiss spent the rest of his life trying to prove his innocence. And when he died in 1996, he left behind a loyal cadre of true believers who've devoted their lives to trying to prove that he was framed by his chief accuser, Whittaker Chambers; framed by his chief Congressional prosecutor, Richard Nixon; framed by the F.B.I., which "forged" a typewriter to somehow fix the case against him (I never could follow that one).

But Hiss is still with us. Hiss will not go away—because, of course, Hiss has become larger than the Hiss case. Hiss has become a pawn in the debate over the Cold War and American communism: Was the Party just a front for a Soviet spy ring? Is there no way to distinguish the domestic arm of Stalinism from, say, the domestic arm of Hitlerism? Or is it not possible to conceive that some who joined the Party to fight for civil rights and labor rights were unaware of the spying and the slave-labor camps?

But yes, the debate about Hiss still rages: The recent debut of an N.Y.U.-sponsored pro-Hiss Web site prompted an anti-Hiss attack in *The Weekly Standard* which framed the debate in very contemporary terms:

> The Hiss case, it becomes clear [from the N.Y.U. Web site], was part of some tremendous and sinister effort—a vast right-wing conspiracy, you might say—designed to frame Hiss, and led by that 1950s Kenneth Starr, a young congressman named Richard Nixon.

And so the ancient war of words goes on and on. It's a war I've tried to stay a million miles away from lately. I've come to think that the cumulative weight of the evidence from Hiss' own colleagues (the Noel Field story!) makes it hard to escape the conclusion that Hiss was a spy, although I respect the efforts of certain of Hiss' more intelligent defenders, such as Victor Navasky, to poke holes in the evidence, and I distrust some of the blanket generalizations drawn from the Hiss case by those who believe he was guilty.

For many on the right, Alger Hiss represents the true face, the *only* face of the American Communist Party, which they see less as a domestic party than a front for an international spy ring whose members' main purpose was to serve the ends of Stalinism, making them morally indistinguishable from the guards in the gulags. But I think it's possible to believe that many who joined the American Communist Party during the Depression—before the purge trials and the Hitler-Stalin pact—did so out of genuine, if naive, idealism. It was a time when the capitalist nations were kowtowing to Hitler, and when the major political parties in America tolerated a vicious, racist system in the American South that was morally indistinguishable from apartheid.

Of course, it is these people who were the collateral victims of Hiss and those elements in the Communist Party leadership who undeniably *were* aiding and abetting Soviet espionage, thereby discrediting the idealists in the field who risked their lives to defend sharecroppers against lynch mobs. Hiss and his fellow Communist Party moles made them vulnerable to the lynch mobs of McCarthyism.

But there's no profit in such a mixed perspective on the Hiss case and the Communist Party; you just make yourself a target of lynch mobs of both left and right. And I wouldn't be venturing back into the briar patch of the Hiss case if the recent revival of the controversy hadn't recalled to me an afternoon I'd once spent with Alger Hiss. Recalled an intimation I had then of a perspective on the case that has not, to my mind, been articulated. One unrepresented in the clash of left and right over Hiss' dead body—a perspective, I suspect, that Alger Hiss himself may have shared, but one that he could never express while alive. A better way of defending him than the denial his most vocal defenders have locked themselves into. One that offers Hiss at least a semblance of dignity, that rescues him from being made to seem, in effect, the real Richard Nixon—the Richard Nixon of the left.

The position Hiss' defenders take is that he didn't do it—didn't collude with other Communist Party members to spy for the Soviets as he rose from minor New Deal functionary to major figure in the State Department, a key player in the creation of the U.N. and the diplomacy of that crucial postwar moment when the wartime alliance between the U.S. and USSR shifted to Cold War confrontation.

He didn't do it, and it's important to absolve him of the charge because—and this is implicit in the rhetoric of almost all of Hiss' defenders—it would have been irredeemably shameful if he *did*.

What I began to suspect about Hiss during my long-ago lunch with him was that he did do it, that he was secretly *proud* rather than ashamed of having done it, that part of having done it was maintaining his innocence—and the Party's deniability in regard to espionage—and that part of maintaining that deniability was stringing along his well-meaning defenders, encouraging them to become unwitting collaborators in a cover-up he believed was a principled necessity, a cover-up of a secret he would carry to his grave.

But now that he's dead, now that extensive revelations from the files of the former Soviet Union have documented the Party's complicity in espionage, now that the Soviet Union *is* "former," perhaps it's time for some of Hiss' defenders to give him credit for—even to defend—the reality of what he did.

Let me briefly outline my own evolution in regard to the Hiss case before my lunch with Alger. I was not a red-diaper baby; my parents were relatively apolitical F.D.R. Democrats. But as an impressionable 12-year-old, I'd come across a copy of Hiss' post-prison memoir, *In the Court of Public Opinion*, in my local suburban library. It was my first exposure to the case, and it shaped my view of it for some time. As, of course, did the key role of Richard Nixon and the House Un-American Activities Committee. Something about the ugliness of that epithet "un-American" had fired me up as a kid about HUAC; as a ninth-grader, I'd gone to a showing in my high school of the pro-HUAC documentary, *Operation Abolition*, and stood up alone to protest the crude McCarthyite tactics of the committee. With enemies like Nixon and HUAC, I was sure Hiss had to be a victim of a frame-up.

That was the problem with the Hiss defense: so much of it depended on the creepiness of those pursuing him. Consider Horace Schmahl, a world-class creep if ever there was one. It was an effort to investigate the shadowy role in the Hiss case played by this shady character that led to my lunch with Alger. Back in the late 70's, a researcher had approached me about doing a story based on some recently declassified intelligence-agency files on Schmahl, a German-American private investigator who had played a highly suspect role in the Hiss case.

Schmahl had initially volunteered to help Hiss' defense lawyers prepare for his perjury trial in 1949. After worming his way into the counsels of the Hiss defense, Schmahl then switched sides and fed information to the prosecution. Many Hiss-case followers believe he was not a defector but a deliberate infiltrator, a spy trying to frame Hiss as a spy. A Hiss-case mole. Hiss' Hiss (if you believe Hiss was a mole). A call to longtime Hiss advocate Jeffrey Kisseloff, who helped design the N.Y.U. Hiss Web site (www.nyu.edu/hiss), refreshed my memory about further sinister aspects of Schmahl's files: He'd been under considerable suspicion for his involvement in the kidnap-murder of Jesus de Galindez, a democratic opponent of the Dominican dictator Trujillo. And most significantly, Mr. Kisseloff believes, Schmahl may have boasted that he'd fabricated a typewriter for the O.S.S.—possible corroboration for the longtime belief by Hiss defenders that the typewriter evidence against Hiss had somehow been forged.

Whether or not you believe that, there's no doubt Schmahl was a major-league scuzzball, a window into the James Ellroy–like underside of McCarthyite culture in the 50's. But he also epitomizes the problem: It isn't hard to find any number of creeps and snitches and liars among Hiss' opponents, but that in itself is not evidence of Hiss' innocence. And so much of the rhetoric of the Hiss defenders has relied on sneering at his accusers, sneering at all anti-Communists as if they were all McCarthyites, sneering at Whittaker Chambers for his bad teeth and his cheap suits and his sexuality. It's also true that Hiss' opponents on the right have relied on deductive generalizations: The fact that Chambers was more accurate in his assessment of Stalinism than Hiss—and most left liberals at the time—is not *dispositive* evidence that Chambers was right about Hiss' guilt.

And it's also worth remembering that there were a number of savvy observers on the left who believed that Whittaker Chambers was telling the truth about Hiss. Check out the Hiss-Chambers chapter in *Part of Our Time*, Murray Kempton's brilliant and invaluable memoir of Communists pro-, ex- and anti- from the 30's to the 50's. Kempton, who had briefly joined the Party in the 30's, and who came from the same shabby-genteel precincts of Baltimore as Hiss, wrote in 1978 that he always thought the "[Hiss] jury was correct."

"The terrible conflict between [Hiss'] private self [the strains of his shabby-genteel class origins] and his public conduct is the most compelling reason why he could have joined the Communist Party," Kempton wrote in 1955's *Part of Our Time*, "for the Communists offer one precious, fatal boon; they take away the sense of sin. It may or may not be debatable whether a man can live without God; but if it were possible, we should pass a law forbidding man to live without the sense of sin."

I don't know whether Alger Hiss had a sense of sin, but he certainly didn't seem to have a sense of guilt. Which is not to say he wasn't, well, guilty. So many of Hiss' supporters who became close to him in his struggle have cited his innocent-seeming demeanor as if it were somehow convincing evidence. I, too, was struck by it when I met him: the absolute, unruffled serenity of his composure, the aura of faintly world-weary innocence he radiated.

Pale, ethereal, almost priest-like, Hiss appeared virtually transparent, like someone who hasn't a thing to hide. But, of course, one could just as easily cite this as evidence of how skillful a mole he'd been, how skillful an actor he was. Almost everyone who'd been fooled by the century's supreme mole, Kim Philby, spoke of *his* unflappable composure both before and after the mole accusations (before he fled to Moscow, of course), the way he too seemed transparent, without the slightest sense of something guilty to hide.

Certainly Hiss evinced no sense of guilt about encouraging generations of researchers, volunteers and true believers—a small army of amateur investigators—to devote a good part of their lives to him and his cause. And, in fact, almost all of them will cite this fact to you as further evidence of his innocence: "You don't think," they'll say, "that he would have gotten all these people to work on the case for him if he *wasn't* innocent?"

Well, of course he would have. If he *was* a mole, the same political convictions that led him to deceive the people close to him when he was active might just as well have led him to deceive those defending his innocence in "retirement."

Still, there must have been a price for him—if he was a mole—to maintain the position that it would have been *deplorable* to do what he did. To agree, in effect, with his accusers about the indefensibility of what he was accused of in order to maintain his denial of it.

There must have been a price at some level, one imagines, in not being able to say to *someone* what he couldn't say to his earnest defenders: *I did it, and I'm proud of what I did.*

I'm not sure what it was about the afternoon I spent with Hiss— lunch at an Irving Place restaurant, then up to his apartment to go through some files. But I came away thinking (well, *wondering*, anyway) whether that wasn't what was going on behind his faint, world-weary smile: *I did it, and I'm proud of it.*

It was a memorable afternoon for me. I mean, innocent or guilty, here was a guy who had become the singular focus of nearly a half-century of bitter debate over one of the great questions of the century. A question that went beyond Hiss' guilt or innocence: He had become a symbol of what Alistair Cooke called, in a book of that title, "a generation on trial." One of the great enigmas of American history.

He had survived trial, conviction and jail, had been forced to eke out a living as a small-time stationery salesman for two decades, virtually forgotten—only to see his chief accuser, Richard Nixon, driven from the White House for lying and covering up. The logic of if-Nixon-was-guilty-Hiss-is-innocent was winning Hiss a new audience for his crusade to clear his name. All of which may have further locked him away from ever defending—taking credit for—what he really did.

Kim Philby, after all, had gone through a similar denial-limbo period. From 1951, when he was fired from the British intelligence service under suspicion of being the so-called "Third Man" in the Cambridge spy ring, until 1963, when definitive evidence forced him to flee to Moscow, Philby had maintained the same posture of injured innocence that Hiss had. Philby, too, accumulated defenders in and out of government who thought he'd been framed by a McCarthyite witch hunt.

But at last, after he turned up in Moscow, he could revel in the truth, boast of his achievements (as he did in *My Silent War*, the memoir of his mole career that supposedly inspired alleged F.B.I. mole Robert Hanssen). He could receive decorations from a grateful government and explain himself as having been deceived out of noble, idealistic convictions.

In a peculiar way, history has denied Hiss ever having that satisfaction, that *recognition*, and his well-meaning defenders continue to deny it to him after his death. (Their posture is *moles are bad and of course Alger wasn't one.*) But I think it's somehow the final sadness of Alger Hiss' life that his defenders seem committed to the idea that, if he did it, there's no defense for it. They've adopted the values of Hiss' accusers!

No one is making the kind of defense for Hiss that Graham Greene made for Kim Philby: the "secret Catholic" analogy that Greene drew in his famous, and famously controversial, introduction to Philby's memoir.

Greene had worked with Philby in British intelligence during World War II and may well have suspected there was more to Philby than met the eye at the time. Greene seems to have refused a promotion that would have had him working directly under Philby, but he also refused to rat on him—a conflicted situation he seems to have been meditating on in his novella *The Third Man*.

Anyway, in that controversial introduction, Greene compared Philby's secret Communist allegiance to that of the secret Catholics in Elizabethan England who risked torture to work for a restoration of Catholic rule. They believed they were working for the salvation of mankind, despite the unappetizing Inquisitional culture of the Popes they risked their lives for.

Similarly, Greene suggested, Philby could be seen as a true believer, someone aware of the Inquisitional culture of the Stalinist regime he served, but one who, like the secret Catholics, persevered in the hopes that someday communism would produce the kind of figure Pope John XXIII had been for Catholicism. (Philby died before Gorbachev—his John XXIII figure—was rudely shoved off the stage of history along with Soviet Communism.)

One can reject this defense as fatally flawed; one can loathe Philby and loathe Hiss; but I'd suggest that it's not impossible that Hiss viewed *himself* in this way: as a man of principled idealism, one who kept the faith and kept his silence to protect not just himself but a salvific future he still believed in. Even if it meant deceiving his own most active and self-sacrificing loyalists.

Perhaps Hiss loyalists should consider whether they are in fact no longer defending Hiss at this point, but rather perpetuating a cover story he no longer needs—at the cost of denying him a truly principled defense, a defense, at least, of the person he really was.

23

HILTON KRAMER

Thinking about Witness

NEW CRITERION, MARCH 1988

Almost all of the prophecies of Marx and his followers have already proved to be false, but this does not disturb the spiritual certainty of the faithful, any more than it did in the case of chiliastic sects: for it is a certainty not based on any empirical premises or supposed "historical laws," but simply on the psychological need for certainty. In this sense Marxism performs the function of a religion, and its efficacy is of a religious character. But it is a caricature and a bogus form of religion, since it presents its temporal eschatology as a scientific system, which religious mythologies do not purport to be.

— Leszek Kolakowski, *Main Currents of Marxism*, 1978

At this distance in time the mentality of the Communist-oriented intelligentsia of the Thirties and Forties must strain the comprehension even of those who, having observed it at first hand, now look back upon it, let alone of those who learn about it from such historical accounts of it as have been written. That mentality was presided over by an impassioned longing to believe.

— Lionel Trilling, in the Introduction to *The Middle of the Journey*

Human societies, like human beings, live by faith and die when faith dies.... Economics is not the central problem of this century. It is a relative problem which can be solved in relative ways. Faith is the central problem of this age.

— Whittaker Chambers, in *Witness*

THE PUBLICATION, LATE LAST YEAR, of a new paperback edition of Whittaker Chambers's *Witness*[1] did not, so far as I am aware, cause even the smallest ripple of attention to be paid to this important book. This should not have come as a surprise to anyone. Although *Witness*—a stout volume of some eight hundred pages—was hailed as an event of immense consequence upon its original publication in 1952, the book has in recent decades virtually disappeared from our historical consciousness. It is rare—in my experience, anyway—to meet anyone under the age of forty who has actually read it.

The book has never been without its isolated devotees, to be sure, but these have tended to be readers with special interests either in the history of the radical movement or in the literature of anti-Communism or in the activities of the Soviet espionage apparatus, about all of which, of course, *Witness* has much to tell us. But as a work of more general interest for readers who make a point of keeping themselves informed about the political and cultural world they inhabit and most particularly, as literature of "a high order," which is how John P. Marquand described it in 1952, *Witness* was long ago consigned to oblivion. The critics never speak of it, the writers of the Eighties have never heard of it, and the older generation with certain honorable exceptions has been content to leave its obscurity undisturbed. One can hardly imagine a professor anywhere assigning it to a class as required reading even in a period when the study of autobiography has come to enjoy something of a vogue on American campuses. Yet the truth about *Witness* is that it is one of the classic American autobiographies, and at the time of its publication it was clearly seen to be one even by many of the critics who found much to disagree with in its author's political views.

Since ours seems now to have become a chronically amnesiac culture, it may be worth recalling what the nature of this critical reception was in 1952. And the first and most fundamental thing to be recalled, I suppose, is the great uproar that the publication of *Witness* created not only on the political scene, where Chambers's role in the Alger Hiss case could be expected to generate enormous interest in anything he might write about this fateful event in our history, but in the world of literary and intellectual debate as well. That was, as a matter of fact, the world—or one of the worlds—that Chambers had come from.

Long before the Hiss case came to dominate the nation's headlines and insinuate itself into the political life of the 1950s, Chambers had been known to virtually everyone on the literary Left as a familiar and problematic figure. In the early Thirties he had been—albeit briefly—one of the literary stars of the *New Masses*. In more recent years he had become a controversial figure at *Time* magazine, first as a book reviewer and then as a senior editor, and a well known contributor to *Life*. His long sojourn in the Communist Party "underground" seems to have been an open secret to many of his former associates on the literary Left. Most of them knew nothing very specific about what his Party work actually entailed, of course, but they knew it was clandestine and they also knew that the Party served the interests of the Soviet Union. Neither in his Party days nor during his tenure at *Time* was Chambers universally admired among those who knew or knew about him. But he seems always to have had something of an aura—to have been a man with a talent for commanding attention, causing uneasiness, and dividing opinion. It was, in any case, to his friendships in the literary world, where his skills as a writer and translator were known to be considerable, that he owed his survival when he made his decision to break with the Party, and it was through one of those friendships that he got his job at *Time*. Given this history, it was inevitable that Chambers and his views would become a hotly debated issue in the literary intellectual world when, in 1948, he found himself in the political limelight as Hiss's accuser. Indeed, owing to the use that Lionel Trilling made of Chambers in creating the character of Gifford Maxim in his novel *The Middle of the Journey*, he had become an issue—though a much smaller one—even in advance of the Hiss case. For Trilling's novel was published in 1947, and anyone who read and really understood *The Middle of the Journey* at that time was more or less prepared for much of what followed when, a few months later, Chambers named Hiss as an underground Communist before the House Un-American Activities Committee. In the somewhat sour critical reception accorded Trilling's novel, we can now see that we were given a polite preview of the far more noisy, hostile, and indeed vicious press that Chambers received when he began his long ordeal of public testimony against Hiss and the Party apparatus they had both served so efficiently.

By the time that he came to write *Witness*, in the immediate aftermath of Hiss's conviction on two counts of perjury, Chambers had ample reason to know that one of his worst fears had been realized. He knew that as far as liberal opinion was concerned—and in the literary and publishing world at least, it was liberal opinion that dominated all discussion—Hiss, though sent to jail for criminal acts that publicly identified him as a Soviet espionage agent, was firmly established as a political martyr. By the same token, Chambers, who had risked his hard won career and indeed his life by exposing a Soviet spy network at the very heart of the Washington bureaucracy, stood condemned as a turncoat, and a villain. In the court of liberal opinion, informing on a fellow conspirator was deemed to be a far greater crime

than belonging to a clandestine Communist spy apparatus and stealing government documents for a foreign power.

Thus, in the crazy logic of the case, Hiss—convicted of crimes
that showed him to be a liar, a thief, and a traitor—was judged to be
innocent even if guilty, and Chambers—the self-confessed renegade
who recanted his treachery—was judged to be guilty even if he was
telling the truth. For what mattered to liberal opinion was that Hiss
was seen to have remained true to his ideals—never mind what the
content of these "ideals" proved to be—whereas Chambers was seen
to have betrayed them. (It was on this note that Alistair Cooke concluded his hastily written but very influential book on the case—*A
Generation on Trial*—in 1950.) Exactly why Chambers had chosen
to do this was never clearly established in the frightful campaign of
vilification that was mounted against him. Was he simply a liar?
But in two trials, in which Hiss was represented by some of the
most illustrious legal talent in the country, twenty out of twenty-
four jurors believed that Chambers spoke the truth about Hiss. Was
Chambers then an opportunist? But his action against Hiss cost
Chambers his job at *Time* and brought the prospect of ruin for him
and his family. Was he a psychopath and a forger, as Hiss continued
to claim? But the repeated attempts of the Hiss defense attorneys to
make those charges stick always turned to ashes. Yet none of this
counted against Hiss except with the jurors, of course. Whatever
the court decreed, liberal opinion had rendered its own irreversible
verdict in the case: Chambers, whatever his motives, was found to
be a monster, whereas Hiss—whatever his actions—was a man who
had been wronged. In 1988, as we approach the fortieth anniver-
sary of Chambers's historic testimony before the House Un-American Activities Committee, the evidence against Hiss is even more
definitive than it was in the perjury trials—it has been especially so
since the publication of Allen Weinstein's *Perjury: The Hiss-Chambers Case* in 1978—yet liberal opinion has not been significantly

altered in the interim. Which is the main reason, of course, why *Witness* has remained a buried classic.

. . .

It has to be remembered, then, that even before the publication of *Witness*, Chambers had emerged as a despised, emblematic figure—the archetypal ex-Communist and counter-revolutionary who was not to be trusted, who was to be feared in fact, even when he was telling the truth, and most to be feared, perhaps, when it was no longer possible to deny that he was telling the truth. No doubt there are many reasons that could be adduced to explain this strange situation, and not the least of them was Chambers's own personality. Philip Rahv, who knew him in the early Thirties before Chambers went into the underground, noted that there was "something in his talk and manner, a vibration, an accent, that I can only describe as Dostoevskyean in essence."

> I thought at the time [Rahv wrote] that he was far from unconscious of the effect he produced. He had the air of a man who took more plea-sure in the stylized than in the natural qualities of his personality. Still, whether aware or not, it was distinctly the Dostoevskyean note that he struck, that peculiar note of personal intensity and spiritual truculence, of commitment to the "Idea" so absolute as to suggest that life had no meaning apart from it, all oddly combined with a flair for mystification and melodrama.[2]

Lionel Trilling had met Chambers even earlier, in 1924–25, when Trilling was a senior at Columbia and Chambers, also at Columbia, had just joined the Communist Party. According to Trilling, they had never been friends, but they had friends in common—"young men of intimidating brilliance"—and, as Trilling later reported, "I observed [Chambers] as if from a distance and with considerable irony, yet accorded him the deference which my friends thought his due." When, toward the end of his life, Trilling came to write a new introduction for the re-issue of *The Middle of the Journey*, he gave us a very vivid account of what the basis of that "deference" had been. It was not only that "Chambers had a very considerable college prestige as a writer," and, as Trilling added, that "this was deserved." There was the man himself:

> The moral force that Chambers asserted [Trilling wrote] began with his physical appearance. This seemed calculated to negate youth and all its graces, to deny that they could be of any worth in our world of pain and injustice. He was short of stature and very broad, with heavy arms and massive thighs; his sport was wrestling. . . . His eyes were narrow and they preferred to consult the floor rather than an interlocutor's face. His mouth was small and, like his eyes, tended downward, one might think in sullenness, though this was not so. When the mouth opened, it never failed to shock by reason of the dental ruin it disclosed, a devastation of empty sockets and blackened stumps. . . . [T]hat desolated mouth was the perfect insigne of Chambers' moral authority. It annihilated the hygienic American present—only a serf could have such a mouth, or some student in a visored cap who sat in his Moscow garret and thought of nothing save the moment when he would toss the fatal canister into the barouche of the Grand Duke.
>
> Chambers could on occasion speak eloquently and cogently, but he was not much given to speaking—his histrionism, which seemed unremitting, was chiefly that of imperturbability and long silences. Usually his utterances were gnomic, often cryptic. Gentleness was not out of the range of his expression, which might even include a compassionate sweetness of a beguiling kind. But the chief impression he made was of a forbidding drabness.[3]

In later life, however much Chambers may have changed in other respects, all of the characteristic qualities observed by Rahv and Trilling (and many others) became even more marked in the personality and appearance of this complicated figure. They led many of his associates—including, it is said, the Hisses—to believe that he might be "foreign," maybe even Russian. The fact that he spoke several languages, and even seemed to speak English with an "accent," also contributed to the impression that he was somehow not an American, though in fact he was born in Philadelphia and grew up on Long Island. The Dostoevskyean note became, if anything, an even more ingrained element of Chambers's outlook and manner of utterance as he grew older. The forbidding drabness, too, the unremitting histrionism, the imperturbability and long silences, as well as the eloquence and beguiling sweetness all came to be remarked upon, though they inspired differing responses in different quarters, by the friends and the enemies who came to know Chambers as an editor of *Time*, as a figure in the Hiss case, as the author of *Witness*, and in the years that remained to him after the publication of *Witness* when, among other things, he was involved in the early development of *National Review*.

In the matter of appearances, at least, Chambers himself was acutely aware of the fact that he was woefully miscast for the hero's role in the Hiss case, and he was not without a certain grim humor on the subject. "You know what the trouble with this case is?" he once asked Bennett Cerf, the publisher of *Witness*. And he answered:

> We're cast wrong. I look like a slob, so I should be the villain. Hiss, the handsome man who knows all the society people, is the born hero. It's bad casting. If it was the other way around, nobody would pay any attention to the story; but because of the way we look, all of you people think he must be telling the truth. That's what has made him so valuable to the other side.[4]

. . .

But as Chambers well understood, it was more than a matter of appearances, of "bad casting," however much appearances and, indeed, his own problematic personality may have contributed to the overall atmosphere of hostility and suspicion. There was a whole view of the universe at stake in the belief that had been vested in Hiss's innocence, and it was because of the force with which Chambers placed that issue at the center of *Witness* that the book caused the furor that it did. For *Witness* fundamentally altered the terms of the political and intellectual debate that had been raging within the liberal camp at least since the Moscow Trials in the Thirties: the debate about the relation in which liberalism stood not only to Communism and Stalinism but to socialism and other modalities of Marxist and "progressive" thought. That debate—essentially a debate among disabused liberals over the future of liberalism—had reached what seemed to many a kind of watershed in the fierce divisions and acrimonious quarrels caused by the Hiss case and the other revelations of spying, treason, and disloyalty in the late Forties and early Fifties. The "innocent" liberalism of the Thirties was now seen to be hopelessly compromised by its inability (or refusal) to resist the corruptions of Communist influence. Something else—a "new" liberalism—was needed to take its place.

Liberals had entered upon a vast effort to set their own intellectual house in order, and it was proving to be a formidable task. Liberalism, it turned out, was not to be so easily dislodged from the whole morass of illiberal doctrines and beliefs in which, under the influence of Marxism, it had become so deeply embedded, and every attempt to effect such a separation raised the question of whether, in what survived this process of political surgery, there was still something that could legitimately be called liberalism. Over the whole of this worthy enterprise, moreover, there hovered a great fear—the fear of being thought "reactionary," the fear of being relegated to the Right. Even the most disabused liberals believed in their hearts that they still belonged to the Left. The very thought of being accused of collaborating with "reaction," as it was still called, was a liberal nightmare, and there was no shortage of Stalinist liberals (as I believe they must be called) to bring the charge of "reaction"—which might mean anything from outright fascism to perfectly respectable political opposition to certain New Deal initiatives—at every infraction, or suspected infraction, of "progressive" doctrine.

Among the revisionist liberals I speak of, conservatism in this period did not loom as a viable alternative. This was the period, after all, in which Lionel Trilling, in his Preface to *The Liberal Imagination* (1950), famously observed that "in the United States at this time liberalism is not only the dominant but even the sole intellectual tradition."

> For it is the plain fact [Trilling continued] that nowadays there are no conservative or reactionary ideas in general circulation. This does not mean, of course, that there is no impulse to conservatism or to reaction. Such impulses are certainly very strong, perhaps even stronger than most of us know. But the conservative impulse and the reactionary impulse do not, with some isolated and some ecclesiastical exceptions, express themselves in ideas but only in action or in irritable mental gestures which seek to resemble ideas.[5]

In the same year that *The Liberal Imagination* appeared, Diana Trilling published an important essay called "A Memorandum on the Hiss Case" in *Partisan Review,* which was one of the principal journals—the others were *Commentary* and *The New Leader*—in which the revisionist liberal debate was conducted. Of the several significant points that Mrs. Trilling was concerned to make in this essay, the following now seem especially notable both in themselves and for the light they cast on the reception of *Witness* (whose publication still lay two years into the future).

1. Of the duties that now devolved upon anyone who, as Mrs. Trilling wrote, "thinks Hiss guilty but would still think of himself as a liberal," the first, she argued, was "that he separate himself from his undesirable allies." She was quite specific about what this meant.

> In the Hiss case, [the] enforced alignment between anti-Communist liberals and reactionaries is particularly open and distasteful [she wrote]. Who brought Hiss's perfidy to public issue, except the one agency in

Washington most suspect for its political motive, the Un-American Activities Committee? What is the anti-Hiss press, except the usual rabble rousers and Redbaiters? What party has most to gain from his conviction, except the Republican Party, and the Republican Party in its most retrograde wing? It is scarcely an attractive company, and the liberal must make a clean break with it.

In this respect, it is worth noting that Mrs. Trilling's essay was, in part, a review of *Seeds of Treason* by Ralph de Toledano and Victor Lasky, who were certainly writing from the Right, and not of *A Generation on Trial* by Alistair Cooke, who was writing from the liberal Left. Mrs. Trilling left her readers in no doubt that she was appalled to find that de Toledano and Lasky regarded Chambers as "a hero of our times, a martyr to principle and to the security of the nation," and she condemned such a judgment as "an unthoughtful and dangerous attitude."

2. About the relation that had obtained between liberalism and Communism, Mrs. Trilling was perfectly clear and properly troubled, and she well understood that the challenge of separating the liberals from their disbelief in Communism's malevolent character would be immense. "But the task of persuading the liberal who is not afraid of Communism," she wrote, "that he should be afraid of it is a gigantic one, and one which involves changing a climate of opinion and feeling over the whole of our culture." Yes, we might add, and the task is no less gigantic in 1988, alas, than it was in 1950. The great difference, of course, is that in 1988 are no Trillingesque liberals left to aid in the task.

3. Then there was the reflection that Mrs. Trilling offered on the source of the "idealism" that Hiss was believed by so many to have represented.

If we can say, as I think we can, that before this century the source of all political idealism was (however remotely) religion, I think we can also say that in our own century the source of all political idealism has been socialism, and, since the Russian Revolution, specifically the socialism of the Soviet Union. I do not mean that whoever has worked for political progress has necessarily been a socialist. I mean only that it has been from socialist theory that political progress has chiefly taken its inspiration, and from socialist example its practice.[6]

What Mrs. Trilling wrote in this passage is largely true, but what is striking about it in retrospect, and especially in relation to *Witness*, is its bland, untroubled acceptance of the momentous event it speaks of. Socialism had indeed supplanted religion as the source of "political idealism," and from that fateful shift there have flowed many of the horrors of the modern age. This was to be one of the philosophical issues that Chambers placed at the center of *Witness*; it had already served, on a more modest scale, as a key element in Lionel Trilling's portrayal of Gifford Maxim in *The Middle of the Journey*. Yet in her "Memorandum on the Hiss Case," Mrs. Trilling did not pause to consider its implications. It clearly did not impress her as a subject that needed to be addressed on that occasion. It might even have seemed that, in addressing it, she would have been in danger of appearing to have something in common with "undesirable allies." She turned instead to a criticism of President Roosevelt for his failure "to see the reality of the Red threat and its menace to democracy."

Mrs. Trilling then went on to express the hope "that if this case is to serve any purpose in our lives there must be salvaged from it a better notion of liberalism." One of the things this meant, she insisted, was that "the case will have been useful, I think, if it helps us to detach the wagon of American liberalism from the star of the Soviet Union." In what ways the wagon of American liberalism remained firmly attached to the idea of socialism, however, and what that meant, was nowhere discussed. It obviously did not occur to Mrs. Trilling or to the anti-Communist liberals who shared her views that if socialism remained the source of "political idealism," then liberalism itself might be doomed.

This, I believe, is what we have seen happen in the decades since Mrs. Trilling wrote her essay: liberalism—in substance, if not in name—has, in our political institutions, our governmental policies, and in what Mrs. Trilling called the "climate of opinion and feeling over the whole of our culture," ceded more and more ground to the kind of political outlook that is anchored in the socialist vision. You can observe the results in our universities, you can see it in the media, you can hear it in the speeches of the Democrats who run Congress and who are running for the Presidency. In many respects it is now the liberal impulse that expresses itself "only in action and in irritable mental gestures which seek to resemble ideas," for as an intellectual tradition liberalism is bankrupt. Liberalism dares not openly acknowledge, even to itself, its surrender to socialist ideology, for everybody knows that the American voter will not elect a frankly socialist government. And so the rhetoric of liberalism, no matter how threadbare and transparent, must be continually repaired and refurbished and made re-usable until the prize can be won.

. . .

I have focused on Mrs. Trilling's essay because it encapsulates so many of the ideas and fears that characterized the most enlightened liberal minds of her generation—those that came to be identified as liberal anti-Communists. It was that sector of the liberal community—staunch in its opposition to Communism and very knowing not only about its underground operations but about the spell it had cast over the whole of our culture—that played a crucial role in the critical reception of *Witness*.

The intellectual uproar over *Witness* occurred on two principal fronts. It was to be expected that the "progressive" Left—those still under the sway of Stalinism and the Popular Front mentality—would attempt to bury the book with the same vicious methods that had been employed in the campaign to discredit Chambers's testimony and render Chambers himself a moral leper. (The term "leper" was actually used in court by Hiss's most celebrated defense counsel, Lloyd Paul Stryker, one of the famous liberals of his day.) As Chambers wrote in *Witness*: "This personal assault upon me was the only real defense that Alger Hiss and his supporters ever developed," and the assault was renewed with added venom when his book was published. If, in the short run, this effort on the part of the orthodox Left failed to impede the immediate success of *Witness*—it was a Book of the Month Club selection and a big best-seller in its day—the long run effect was nonetheless to keep the book from having much of a literary afterlife. In the world of *The New Yorker*, which was solidly pro-Hiss,[7] *The New Republic*, whose editor in those days was subsequently revealed to have been a member, earlier on, of another underground Soviet apparatus,[8] and other such staunch liberal journals, the barriers were erected and Chambers was stripped of his literary standing.

The response of the liberal anti-Communists to *Witness* was very different—and far more honorable, of course—yet the effect was also in the end to place Chambers outside the boundaries of enlightened intellectual opinion. Because they believed that Chambers was telling the truth about Hiss—and indeed about Communism—it became the primary task of the liberal anti-Communists in dealing with *Witness* not to defend Hiss but to rescue liberalism from Chambers's sweeping attack on it. And because they recognized that the author of *Witness* was, as even Philip Rahv acknowledged, a "born writer," and that the book itself was, as Bennett Cerf said, "superbly written," the liberal anti-Communists were concerned, above all, not to challenge Chambers's literary gifts but to diminish the impact which his powerful testament might have on the political and moral status of liberalism. The whole effort of the liberal anti-Communists in regard to *Witness* thus became an exercise in what we would now call damage control.

Rereading the criticisms of *Witness* that were written by some of the outstanding liberal anti-Communists of the early Fifties, what is particularly remarkable in retrospect is the way they managed to combine a genuine admiration for Chambers's achievement with a fundamental rejection of his views. Take, for example, the review article written by Arthur Schlesinger, Jr., in the *Saturday Review* ("Whittaker Chambers & His '*Witness*,'" May 24, 1952). Schlesinger was full of praise for *Witness* as a contribution to American literature:

> Whittaker Chambers has written one of the really significant American autobiographies. When some future Plutarch writes his American Lives, he will find in Chambers penetrating and terrible insights into America in the early twentieth century. Nor need he search long for a parallel life; just as Henry L. Stimson's *On Active Service* is the powerful counterstatement to Henry Adams's *Education,* so Whittaker Chambers's *Witness* is the counterstatement to that book so influential twenty years ago, the *Autobiography of Lincoln Steffens.*

Nothing could have been better calculated to impress upon the readers of the *Saturday Review* the idea that *Witness* was a book of immense importance than to have placed Chambers in the company of Adams, Stimson, and Steffens at that particular moment in history. But there was more:

> In part, *Witness* is an extraordinary personal document—a powerful and compassionate story of a middle-class family broken on the shoals of life in middle class America, until the surviving son rejects his class and enlists in the ranks of the proletarian revolution. But, like the other great autobiographies, *Witness* is much more than a personal document. It is also a political document and a philosophical document. Its weight and urgency as a personal document are likely to win acceptance for its politics and its philosophy. But the politics and the philosophy, in my judgment, raise basic issues which deserve independent and critical examination.

Schlesinger then went on to belittle the role that espionage and Communist influence might have played in American foreign policy in the Roosevelt era and, what was even more important in his view, to defend the New Deal against the harsh and categorical criticisms that Chambers had made of it in *Witness*.[9]

This was no surprise, of course. Schlesinger was writing less as a disinterested historian than as a partisan of the Democratic Party and a pillar of the "new" liberalism, and it was impossible—philosophically as well as politically impossible—for any champion of the New Deal who also aspired to a position of influence in the Democratic Party to accord any real importance either to Chambers's charges of Communist influence or to his strictures on the vast changes that the Roosevelt administration has brought to the governing of the nation.[10] Given this disposition to reject and condemn Chambers's political analysis on partisan as well as philosophical grounds, it must also be noted that in those days liberals like Schlesinger conducted this debate in a rather higher minded intellectual style than was later to be the case. There hadn't yet occurred that coarsening and softening of the mind that has been so evident in Schlesinger's writings—and not his alone, alas—since the emergence of the Kennedy machine in the Sixties.

. . .

Another important review of *Witness* by a leading liberal anti-Communist was Sidney Hook's in *The New York Times Book Review* ("The Faiths of Whittaker Chambers," May 25, 1952). This, too, described Chambers's book as "one of the most significant autobiographies of the twentieth century."

> It is not among the hundred great books [Hook wrote]. Yet it throws more light on the conspiratorial and religious character of modern Communism, on the tangled complex of motives which led men and women

of goodwill to immolate themselves on the altars of a fancied historical necessity, than all of the hundred great books of the past combined... . [*Witness*] contains interesting vignettes of the Communist movement, a record of religious conversion, the saga of a farm, an account of desperate courage alternating with moods of spiritual despair, all knit together by the essentially mystical and romantic personality of the author.... The literary quality of the writing is impressive.

Hook also said of *Witness* that "this book, even more than the verdict of the [Hiss] trials, may well be called the vindication of Whittaker Chambers."

Its pages [he continued] show that [Chambers] has long since atoned for his own complicity in conspiratorial work by his suffering at the hands of Hiss's friends, whose outrageous smears against his personal life and that of his wife surpassed in virulence anything known in recent American history.

Still, Hook too was adamant in voicing the most categorical rejection of Chambers's political and philosophical interpretation of his own experience. About the New Deal, in Hook's case, there was plenty of political sympathy but no partisan defense—he wasn't writing with a view to an appointment in some future Democratic administration. Yet the best explanation that Hook could come up with to explain how it had happened that the Communists had had such a free ride in the Roosevelt administration—in *Witness*, Chambers quotes J. Peters, his boss in the Soviet spy apparatus, as saying that "even in Germany under the Weimar Republic, the party did not have what we have here"—was not very persuasive. "Most of Chambers' facts are rendered intelligible by a less sinister hypothesis than the one he offers," Hook wrote. "It is that stupidity is sometimes the greatest of all historical forces."[11] Now, stupidity certainly played its part in this story; it usually does in human affairs. But to elevate it to the status of one of "the greatest of all historical forces" as a way of accounting for the New Deal's failure to take the Communist issue seriously is tantamount to abandoning the whole question. Mrs. Trilling's analysis of the relation in which the New Deal liberals stood to the kind of Communist "idealism" which Hiss represented had at least the merit of placing the question firmly in the realm of political reality.

What bothered Hook the most about *Witness,* of course, were its author's religious views. These he condemned in toto, declaring that "it is not unlikely that the [secular] humanistic spirit may be the best defense on a world scale against the Communist crusade because it can unite all human beings who, despite their religious differences about first and last things, value truth, justice, kindness and freedom among men." Now, over a third of a century later, I think it would be accurate to say that the "spirit" so fondly invoked by Sidney Hook in his review of *Witness* has not proven to be much of a defense at all. However problematic Chambers's religious views may still be for those readers of *Witness* who are non-believers, he wasn't wrong in his diagnosis that "faith is the central problem of this age." The liberal mind, so comfortable in its own articles of faith, shied away from such an idea, as if from the most dreaded of heresies, and went merrily to its doom in the Sixties when that "impassioned longing to believe," which Lionel Trilling spoke of as the presiding impulse of the Thirties and Forties, reasserted itself in even more virulent forms and with more lasting consequences.

History, as a matter of fact, has proved Whittaker Chambers to have been right about many things, and *Witness* remains not only one of the few indispensable autobiographies ever written by an American—and one of the best written, too—but the very thing that Sidney Hook said it wasn't: "an intelligent guide" to the victory of freedom over Communist tyranny. It is the only great book on the Communist experience to have been written by an American, and it deserves to be recognized as a first-class achievement. Yet there is no reason to believe that this new edition of so important a book will succeed in winning the readers or in exerting the influence it should have. On the contrary, over the whole of our cultural and intellectual life today there reigns an atmosphere that is deeply inimical not only to Chambers's ideas but to his moral gravity—the sense he had that it was not only our political future but our whole civilization that was at stake in the momentous issues he lived through and wrote about so eloquently. Forty years after he brought his first public charges against Alger Hiss, Chambers remains in the liberal mind—which is more than ever the mind that dominates the universities, the media, and the literary world—the monster that Hiss's defenders shamelessly made him out to be. And he remains, too, a writer denied his proper literary standing. And Hiss? Well, among other things, he has been given the distinction of having an academic chair named in his honor at Bard College—a chair in, of all things, the humanities. And as far as I know, it hasn't been funded by the KGB, either. It is, I suppose, supported by that same brand of "idealism" that inspired Alger Hiss. *Plus ça change . . .*

NOTES

[1] *Witness*, by Whittaker Chambers. Preface by Robert Novak. Foreword by Milton Hindus. (Washington, D.C.: Regnery Gateway, 1987.)

[2] "The Sense and Nonsense of Whittaker Chambers," by Philip Rahv; *Partisan Review*, July-August 1952.

[3] The edition of *The Middle of the Journey* with Trilling's new introduction was published by Charles Scribner's Sons in 1976. It should be said that Trilling clearly disliked Chambers and came to dislike his writing, too. Yet at the time of the Hiss case, Trilling supported Chambers and exhibited remarkable courage in doing so. Approached by one of Hiss's lawyers who, as Trilling wrote, "tried to induce me to speak against [Chambers] in court," he not only refused but shocked this attorney by asserting that "Whittaker Chambers is a man of honor." He could still recall, Trilling wrote, "the outburst of contemptuous rage [my remarks] evoked from the lawyer who had come to call on me to solicit my

testimony."

⁴ Bennett Cerf, in *At Random*, published by Random House in 1977. In this memoir Cerf, who considered himself a liberal (and was), tells the story of how he came to publish—and believe in—*Witness*.

⁵ *The Liberal Imagination* was published by The Viking Press in 1950. Since he believed himself, with just reason, to be writing as a liberal, Trilling was said to have been considerably shaken when Joseph Frank wrote an article in *The Sewanee Review*, in 1956, entitled "Lionel Trilling and the Conservative Imagination." The article was occasioned by the publication of Trilling's *The Opposing Self.*

⁶ "A Memorandum on the Hiss Case," by Diana Trilling, *Partisan Review*, May-June 1950.

⁷ A. J. Liebling, *The New Yorker*'s celebrated press columnist, served as an unpaid volunteer for the Hiss defense while pretending to write about the case as an objective reporter. See Allen Weinstein's account of this unlovely episode in *Perjury* (Alfred A. Knopf, 1978), pages 166-167.

⁸ I refer to Michael Straight. His later role in identifying Anthony Blunt as a Soviet spy is described in *Conspiracy of Silence: The Secret Life of Anthony Blunt*, by Barrie Penrose and Simon Freeman (Farrar, Straus & Giroux, 1987).

⁹ "Whittaker Chambers & His 'Witness,'" by Arthur Schlesinger, Jr., *Saturday Review*, May 24, 1952.

¹⁰ The appalling record of the Roosevelt administration in dealing with charges of Communist influence and spying is still almost unbelievable. In the immediate aftermath of the Hitler-Stalin pact in 1939, Chambers had taken his information about Hiss and other Soviet spies to Adolf A. Berle, who is described in a new book—*Liberal: Adolf A. Berle and the Vision of an American Era* by Jordan A. Schwarz (The Free Press, 1987)—as the man "who then administered State Department intelligence." "For reasons he never felt he needed to give," writes Schwarz, "Berle did nothing with Chambers' information until he turned it over to the FBI in 1941 for an investigation of Chambers' charges. While Chambers' list surfaced in the State Department in 1943 again, nothing was done until Chambers showed up once more in 1948 to repeat his charges to the House

Committee on Un-American Activities." Berle regarded the whole subject, according to Schwarz, as "not really important."

[11] "The Faiths of Whittaker Chambers," by Sidney Hook, *The New York Times Book Review*, May 25, 1952.

— Some Autopsies Never Die   *Tues 8/13/13*

— Eternal Sleep Is Not For Everyone

— [Mostly Dead People Are Laid To Rest

Some Corpses Are Raised To Unrest

A Hiss-Chambers Bibliography

Because
—/Some Corpses Are Exhumed & Re-Autopsied
So Frequently, An Eternal Sleep
Aid Pill Is Being Developed

— No Rest For the Dead

SIGNED PIECES IN JOURNALS AND PERIODICALS

Altman, George T. "The Added Witness," *Nation*, 1 October 1960, 201–09.

Ambrose, Stephen E. "Letter to the Editor," *New York Times*, 3 September 1989, 7:4.

Anderson, Susan Heller. "Chronicle," *New York Times*, 16 February 1990, B6.

Ascoli, Max. "Lives and Deaths of Whittaker Chambers," *Reporter*, 8 July 1952, 5–8.

Atkins, Ollie. "The Pumpkin Papers," *Saturday Evening Post*, January 1976, 40.

Authur, Robert Alan. "Hanging Out," *Esquire*, July 1972, 26, 29.

Bath, Oliver. "Wa rm Friday," *National Review*, 4 May 1984, 41–44.

Bendiner, Robert. "The Ordeal of Alger Hiss," *Nation*, 11 February 1950, 123–24.

Berg, Louis. "The Odyssey Was Ended," *Harper's*, July 1970, 98–101.

Bingham, Robert K. "The Case Does Not Rest," *Reporter*, 29 September 1953, 46–47.

B reindel, Eric M. "Alger Hiss: A Glimpse Behind the Mask," *Commentary*, November 1988, 55-58.

Brogan, Colm. "The Comfort of Cold Friday, *National Review*, 29 December 1964, 1153–54.

Brown, Mike and Robert T. Garrett. "Ford Aide Defends Farm as Landmark for Father," *Louisville (Ky.) Courier-Journal*, 19 February 1989, 4B.

Buckley, William F. "The Assault on Whittaker Chambers," *National Review*, 15 December 1964, 1098–1102.

———. "Counselor Hiss," *National Review*, 29 August 1975, 955.

———. "The End of Whittaker Chambers," *Esquire*, September 1962, 77–82, 162–172.

———. "Good-bye Hiss," *National Review*, 28 April 1978, 548.

———. "Hiss Again," *National Review*, 3 December 1971, 1374.

———. "The Prophet," *National Review*, 6 July 1979, 879.

———. "Whittaker Chambers' Medal," *National Review*, 6 April 1984, 63.

Cerf, Bennett. "Witness," *At Random*, 1977, 242–244.

Chambers, Whittaker. "Il Faut le Supposer Heureux," *National Review*, 29 July 1961, 47.

———. "Whittaker Chambers on Money," *Saturday Review of Literature*, 20 May 1950, 26.

Clark, Charlie. "The Pumpkin Papers Caper: How Donald Hodel Gave America a Commemorative Mud Patch," *Washington Post*, 9 April 1989, B5

Cogley, John. "Witness: Whittaker Chambers." *Commonweal*, 23 May 1952, 176–77.

Cohen, Carl. "Checking up on Peter's Smile," *Nation*, 6 May 1978, 525–26.

Cook, Fred J. "Alger Hiss: A New Ball Game," *Nation*, 11 October 1980, 340–43.

———. "Freedom Medalist," *Nation*, 10 March 1984, 277.

———. "The Ghost of a Typewriter," *Nation*, 12 May 1962, 416–21.

———. "The Hiss Case and the American Conscience," *Nation*, 21 September 1957, 141–80.

———. "Nixon Kicks a Hole in the Hiss Case," *Nation*, 7 April 1962, 296.

Cooke, Douglas O. "The Critics Maligned," *Saturday Review of*

Literature, 17 January 1953, 21–22.

Cooney, Thomas E. "Alger Hiss' Story," *Saturday Review of Literature*, 11 May 1957, 14, 45–46.

Cort, David. "A Dedicated Madness," *Nation*, 16 February 1970, 185–86.

———. "Of Guilt and Resurrection," *Nation*, 20 March 1967, 373–74.

Countryman, Vern. "One Small Step for Alger Hiss," *New Republic*, 30 August 1975, 14–17.

Davis, Elmer. "History in Doublethink," *Saturday Review*, 28 June 1952, 8-9.

de Toledano, Ralph. "The Alger Hiss Story," *American Mercury*, June 1953, 13–20.

———. "Let Only a Few Speak of Him," *National Review*, 29 July 1961, 49–51.

———. "Ten Years Dead," *National Review*, 21 July 1971, 793.

———. "Whittaker Chambers Remembered: 'Imperatives of the Heart,'" *National Review*, 1 August 1986, 31–32.

DiBacco, Thomas V. "Eras Contrast Spy Cases of Bloch, Hiss," *Washington Times*, 25 July 1989, A4.

Douglas, Ann. "Whittaker Chambers, a Biography," Undated, <http://www.english.upenn.edu/~afilreis/50s/chambers-review.html>.

Dos Passos, John. "Mr. Chambers' Descent into Hell," *Saturday Review of Literature*, 24 May 1952, 11.

Downing, Francis. "Man Is the Measure of History," *Commonweal*, 29 February 1952, 514–15.

Edwards, Lee. "Whittaker Chambers: Man of Courage and Faith," Heritage Foundation Executive Memorandum, 2 April 2001, <http://www.heritage.org/library/execmemo/em735.html>.

Feeney, Mark. "Alger Hiss Is Dead at 92; Allegations That He Spied Put a Generation on Trial," *Boston Globe*, 16 November 1996, A1.

Fielder, Leslie A. "Hiss, Chambers, and the Age of Innocence: Who Was Guilty—And of What?" *Commentary*, August 1951, 109–119.

Finn, James. "Whittaker Chambers," *Commonweal*, 26 February 1965, 696–97.

Fitzgibbon, William.. "The Hiss-Chambers Case: A Chronology Since 1934," *New York Times*, 12 June 1949, E8.

Friedman, David D. "Déjà Vu: The New Alger Hiss," *Liberty Magazine*, January 1992, 19.

Folkenflik, David. "Hiss, From Humble Beginnings; Assessment: Native Son Alger Hiss," *Baltimore Sun*, 16 November 1996, 7A.

Galbraith, John Kenneth. "Alger Hiss and Liberal Anxiety," *Atlantic Monthly*, May 1978, 44–47.

———. "A Revisionist View," *New Republic*, 28 March 1970, 17–19.

Gelber, Jack. "A Son's Own Story," *Nation*, 22 November 1999, 26

Gelman, David. "A Medal for Chambers," *Newsweek*, 5 March 1984, 39.

Givens, Ron. "The Pumpkin Papers Landmark," *Newsweek*, 30 May 1988, 8.

Goldstein, Amy. "Pumpkin Papers' Farm . . . ," *Washington Post*, 18 May 1988, B1–B4.

Green, Gil. "Forgery by Typewriter," *Nation*, 10 November 1984, 468–469.

Greenberg, Paul. "On the Beach," *Arkansas Democrat-Gazette*, 10 May, 1998, J4.

———. "The Writer as Minority of One," *Seattle Post-Intelligencer*, 14 March 1990, A7.

Griffith, Robert. "A Victim of McCarthy and the Cold War," *Progressive*, May 1975, 40–41.

Gross, Robert A. "'History Hit Us,'" *Newsweek*, 2 February 1970, 79–80.

Harris, Mark. "The Accuser and the Accused," *Saturday Review of Literature*, 11 February 1967, 34–35.

Hickey, Jennifer G. "Romerstein Documents Soviet Espionage in U.S.," *Insight on the News*, 27 November 2000, 37.

Hicks, Granville. "The Final Search for Meaning," *Saturday Review of Literature*, 2 January 1965, 25–26.

———. "Whittaker Chambers's Testament," *New Leader*, 25 May

1952, 19–22.

Higgins, B.H. Letter, *New Republic*, 23 January 1965, 38.

Hiss, Alger. "Letter to the Editor," *New York Times*, 21 January 1986, A30.

Hitchens, Christopher. "A Regular Bull," *London Review of Books*, 31 July 1997, 15.

Hook, Sidney. "The Case of Alger Hiss," *Encounter*, August 1978, 48–55.

———. "The Faiths of Whittaker Chambers," *New York Times Book Review*, 25 May 1952, 1, 34–35.

———. "On the Couch," *New York Times Book Review*, 5 February 1967, 4, 40.

Howe, Irving. "Alger Hiss Retried," *New York Times Book Review*, 9 April 1978, 1, 24–26.

———. "God, Man and Stalin," *Nation*, 24 May 1952, 502–504.

——— "Madness, Vision, Stupidity," *New Republic*, 28 November 1964, 22–24.

Howe, Mark DeWolfe. "The Misfortune of a Nation," *Nation*, 18 May 1957, 442–444.

Hutchinson, Paul. "The Works of God?" *Christian Century*, 11 June 1952, 700–01.

Hyde, Douglas. "Earl Jowett on the Hiss Case," *America*, 11 July 1953, 375–77.

Jeffreys-Jones, Rhodri. "Weinstein on Hiss," *Journal of American Studies*, April 1979, 115–126.

Johnson, Gerald W. "By Hook or Crook," *New Republic*, 12 April 1962, 16.

Judis, John. "The Two Faces of Whittaker Chambers," *New Republic*, 16 April 1984, 25–32.

Kazin, Alfred. "Why Hiss Can't Confess," *Esquire*, 28 March 1978, 21–22.

Kempton, Murray. "A Narodnik from Lynbrook," *New York Review of Books*, 29 January 1970.

Kennedy, John S. "The Witness of Whittaker Chambers," *Catholic World*, July 1952, 260–65.

Kenner, Hugh. "Chambers' Music and Alger Hiss," *American Spectator*, June 1979, 7-11.

Koestler, Arthur. "The Complex Issue of the Ex-Communists," *New York Times Magazine*, 19 February 1950, 10, 49–50.

Kramer, Hilton. "Thinking About 'Witness,'" *New Criterion*, March 1988, 1–10.

Judgment

———. "Whittaker Chambers: The Judgment of History," *New Criterion*, February 1997, 13–17.

Krauthammer, Charles. "Alger and O.J.," *Time*, 30 December 1996 / 6 January 1997, 174.

Krvine, David. "Political Justice," *Jerusalem Post*, 30 May 1989, 5.

Kutler, Stanley I. "The Shame of Joe McCarthy's Defenders; An Unsettling Settling of Scores," *Capital Times* (Madison, Wisc.), 14 February 2000, 11A.

Langer, Elinor. "The Great Pumpkin," *Nation*. 17 February 1997, 27.

Lankford, Ronald D. "Another Side of Alger Hiss," *Roanoke Times & World News*, 3 October 1999, Books, 4.

Lasky, Victor. Letters, *Saturday Review of Literature*, 12 July 1958, 21–22.

———. "Special Pleading, Tricky," *Saturday Review of Literature*, 31 May 1958, 16–17, 29–30.

Lumpkin, Grace. "The Law and the Spirit," *National Review*, 25 May 1957, 498–99.

Maloff, Saul. "Tommy and Vivian," *Newsweek*, 30 January 1967, 92–93.

Martin, Kingsley. "The Witness," *New Statesman and Nation*, 19 July 1952, 60–61.

McManus, Otile. "Finding the Right Place for Change: By Design," *Boston Globe*, 6 September 1990, 77.

McWilliams, Carey. "Battle of the Book Reviews," *Nation*, 1 May 1976, 517–19.

———. "Will Nixon Exonerate Hiss?" *Nation*, 20 September 1975, 229–31.

Melvern, Linda. "Obituary: Alger Hiss: In the Shadows of the Cold War," *Guardian* (London), 18 November 1996, 13.

Miller, Merle. "Memoirs From Sanctuary," *New Republic*, 26 May 1952, 19–20.

———. "The Trial of The Age," *New Republic*, 3 August 1953,

17–18.

Millis, Walter. "Was Alger Hiss Framed? A Debate," *Saturday Review of Literature*, 31 May 1958, 14–15.

Millis, Walter and Assorted. Letters, *Saturday Review of Literature*, 22 June 1958, 27–28.

Milton, Joyce. "The Old Left," *New Republic*, 4 November 1996, 12.

Moore, Thomas. "'By 80, I'll Be a Respected Man,'" *Life*, 7 April 1972, 78A.

Morris, Richard. "Chambers' Litmus Paper Test," *Saturday Review of Literature*, 24 May 1952, 13.

Morrow, Lance. "Alger, 'Ales' and Joe," *Time*, 3 June 2001, 66-67.

Navasky, Victor. "The Case Not Proved Against Alger Hiss," *Nation*, 8 April 1978, 393–401.

———. "New Republic, New Mistakes," *Nation*, 6 May 1978, 523–25.

———. "Waiting for Weinstein," *Nation*, 22 April 1978, 453–54.

Navasky, Victor and Allen Weinstein. "On Dasher On Dancer On Prancer and Vixen," *New Republic*, 13 May, 1978, 5–38.

Nixon, Richard. "Lessons of the Alger Hiss Case," *New York Times*, 8 January 1986, A23.

———. "Plea for an Anti-Communist Faith," *Saturday Review of Literature*, 24 May 1952, 12–13.

Nobile, Philip. "The State of the Art of Alger Hiss," *Harper's*, April 1976, 67–76.

Norton-Taylor, Duncan. "Wisdom Is the Most Terrible Ordeal," *National Review*, 29 July 1961, 49–61.

O'Brien, Conor Cruise. "Whittaker Chambers, Perjured Saint," *New York Review of Books*, 19 November 1964, 1, 3–4.

O'Hara, James. "Witness from the Past," *Commonweal*, 26 February 1965, 687.

Olasky, Marvin N. "Liberal Boosterism and Conservative Distancing: Newspaper Coverage of the Chambers-Hiss Affair, 1948–1950," *Continuity*, spring 1992, 31–44.

Osborne, John. "Alger Hiss: The True Story," *New Republic*, 17 April 1976, 27–29.

Peterson, Clarence. "Hiss Remains True to Himself in Memoir,"

Orange County Register, 18 November 1990, M26.

Rahv, Philip. "The Sense and Nonsense of Whittaker Chambers,"
Partisan Review, July-August 1952, 472–82.

Rees, Goronwy. "The Psyche and the Typewriter," *Atlantic
Monthly,* August 1967, 54–57.

Renshaw, Patrick. "Obituary: Alger Hiss," *Independent* (London),
18 November 1996, 16.

Reuben, William. "New Development," *Nation,* 10 November
1984, 469.

Roazen, Paul. "The Strange Case of Alger Hiss and Whittaker
Chambers," *Queen's Quarterly,* December 1999, 518–533.

Robberson, Tod. "War, Politics and Other Obsessions," *Washington
Post,* 8 April 1990, X10.

Rodell, Fred. "Phony, Fabricated Evidence," *Saturday Review of
Literature,* 31 May 1958, 15, 28–29.

Rosenbaum, Ron. "My Lunch with Alger: Oh No, Not Hiss
Again!" *New York Observer,* 16 April 2001, 23.

Sancton, Thomas. "The Case of Alger Hiss." *Nation,* 4 September
1948, 251–52.

———. "Hiss and Chambers: A Tangled Web." *Nation,* 18
December 1948, 691–92.

Schlesinger, Arthur. "Espionage or Frame-up?" *Saturday Review of
Literature,* 15 April 1950, 21–23.

———. "The Truest Believer," *New York Times,* 9 March 1997.
7:5.

———. "Whittaker Chambers and His 'Witness,'" *Saturday
Review of Literature,* 24 May 1952, 8–10, 39–41.

Scott, Janny. "Alger Hiss, 92, Central Figure in Long-Running
Cold War Controversy," *New York Times,* 16 November
1996, 1-2.

Shapiro, Meyer. "Dangerous Acquaintances," *New York Review of
Books,* 23 February 1967, 5–9.

Sheerin, John B. "Chambers Provokes the Reviewers," *Catholic
World,* July 1952, 241–45.

Sklar, Robert. "The Tolerant Tiger," *Nation,* 5 May 1956, 374–
76.

Smith, John Chabot. "The Debate of the Century (Cont.),"

Harper's, June 1978, 81–85.

Smith, John Chabot and James Aronson. Letters, *Nation*, 22 April 1978, 450–53.

Sobran, Joseph. "Spy Story," *National Review*, 19 August 1988, 42–44.

Stember, Sol. "Letter to the Editor," *New York Times*, 21 January 1986, A30.

Strachey, John. "The Absolutists," *Nation*, 4 October 1952, 291–93.

Tanenhaus, Sam. "Misreadings," *New Republic*, 5 April 1999, 46.

———. "Whittaker Chambers, Man of Letters," *New Criterion*, April 1990, 11–19.

Taylor, John H. "Letter to the Editor," *New York Times*, 3 September 1989, 7:4.

Teachout, Terry. "The Man Who Heard Screams," *National Review*, 5 February 1982, 121–22.

———. "Thoughts on a Secondhand Ghost," *National Review*, 1 August 1986, 32, 45.

Thompson, Craig. "The Whittaker Chambers I Know," *Saturday Evening Post*, 15 November 1952, 24–25, 116–21.

Trilling, Diana. "A Memorandum on the Hiss Case," *Partisan Review*, May-June 1950, 484–500.

Trilling, Diana and Hilton Kramer. "Whittaker Chambers and 'Witness': An Exchange," *New Criterion*, May 1988, 1–5.

Trilling, Lionel. "Whittaker Chambers and *The Middle of the Journey*," *New York Review of Books*, 17 April 1975, 18-24

Tytell, Cook. Letters, *Saturday Review of Literature*, 14 October 1958, 21–22.

van den Haag, Ernest. "Psychoanalysis and Fantasy," *National Review*, 21 March 1967, 295–298, 321.

Waldrop, Frank C. Letter, *National Review*, 29 December 1964, 6.

Wanniski, Jude. "Re: A Good Book," *Polyconomics.com*, 15 May 1997.

Weiner, Lauren. "'Ghosts' Shows Misery, Mastery of Chambers," *Washington Times*, 25 December 1989, E5.

———. "Hiss, Chambers and 'Polite Liberalism,'" *Investor's Business Daily*, 26 August 1998, A32.

———. "Hiss' Suit Against Chambers: On the Case's 50th Birthday; the American Intellectual World Is Still Bedeviled by the Residue of the 'Stylish Stalinism' of the Cold War Era," *Baltimore Sun*, 27 September 1998, 12G.

Weinstein, Allen. "The Alger Hiss Case Revisited," *American Scholar*, winter 1971, 121–132.

———. "Allen Weinstein Statement," *New Republic*, 7 June 1978, 11.

———. "The Hiss and Rosenberg Files," *New Republic*, February 14, 1976, 16–21.

———. "Was Alger Hiss Framed?" *New York Review of Books*, 1 April 1976, 14-20.

———. "The Witness," *Commentary*, June 1970, 85–88.

Weisberg, Jacob. "Cold War Without End," *New York Times*, 28 November 1999, 6:116.

Werchen, Raymond and Fred J. Cook. "New Light on the Hiss Case," *Nation*, 28 May 1973, 678–84.

West, Rebecca. "Whittaker Chambers," *Atlantic Monthly*, June 1952, 33–39.

Whalen, Robert G. "Hiss and Chambers: Strange Story of Two Men," *New York Times*, 12 December 1948, E6.

Wheatcroft, Geoffrey. "Inside Story: Boo, Hiss," *Guardian* (London), 6 August 1998, 8

———. "Why Does BBC News Exonerate a Traitor?" *Sunday Telegraph* (London), 17 November 1996, 17.

Will, George. "The Myth of Alger Hiss," *Newsweek*, 20 March 1978, 96.

———. "Whittaker Chambers: Up a Winding Staircase," *National Review*, 31 December 1985, 65–67.

Williams, C. Dickerman. "Let Bygones Be Bygones?" *Saturday Review of Literature*, 18 May 1957, 27–28, 45.

Wills, Gary. "The Hiss Connection through Nixon's Life," *New York Times Magazine*, 25 August 1974, 8, 40.

———. "Plato and the Hiss Case," *Bergen (New Jersey) Record*, 23 June 1989, B11.

Wolfert, Ira. "Strange Hiss Case," *Nation*, 18 July 1953, 46–48.

Wright, Charles Alan. "A Long Work of Fiction," *Saturday Review of Literature*, 24 May 1952, 11–12.

———. "Turning Point of Our Time, *Nation*, 18 July 1953, 54–56.

Wrong, Dennis H. "The Rest of Him," *New York Times Book Review*, 7 August 1988, 7:18.

Younger, Irving. "Was Alger Hiss Guilty?" *Commentary*, August 1975, 23–37.

Zeligs, Meyer and G. Rees. Letters Debate, *Atlantic Monthly*, December 1967, 47–48.

unnamed Authors
Authorless

UNSIGNED PIECES IN JOURNALS AND PERIODICALS

Associated Press. "Site in Hiss-Chambers Case Now a Landmark," *New York Times*, 18 May 1988, A20.

Assorted. "Arguments (New and Old) about the Hiss Case," *Encounter*, March 1979, 80–90.

———. "The Hiss Maneuver," *National Review*, 25 May 1957, 496–97.

———. Letters, *Nation*, 5 October 1957, inside cover.

———. Letters, *Nation*, 2 November 1957, inside cover.

———. Letters, *National Review*, 12 January 1965, 4, 26.

———. Letters, *Saturday Evening Post*, 15 March 1952, 4–6.

———. Letters, *Saturday Evening Post*, 29 March 1952, 6.

———. Letters, "Concerning Witness," *Saturday Review of Literature*, 14 June 1952, 31–33.

———. Letters, *Saturday Review of Literature*, 29 June 1958, 23–24.

Book Editor. "Cause Celebre," *Atlantic Monthly*, July 1957, 87–88.

———. "Hegel's Road to Walden," *Time*, 6 November 1964, 108.

Editors. "Alger Hiss; Dead at 92: Accused of Spying for the Soviets, He Always Proclaimed Innocence," *Baltimore Sun*, 16 November 1996, 10A.

———. "Chambers and His Critics," *Life*, 9 June 1952, 36.

———. "Chambers' Choice of God Looks Odd to the Liberals," *Saturday Evening Post*, 12 July 1952, 10.

————. "The Critics and the Absolutes," *Saturday Review of Literature,* 20 June 1952, 259–60.

————. "Death of the Witness," *Time,* 21 July 1961, 16–17.

————. "Footnotes to History," *Nation,* 17 March 1984, 309, 320.

————. "Footnotes to the Hiss Case," *Nation,* 27 April 1974, 515–16

————. "Fraternal Twins," *National Review,* 10 June 1988, 15–16.

————. "The Hiss File," *Nation,* 18 December 1972, 613–14.

————. "The Hiss File," *Nation,* 21 December 1974, 645.

————. "Jury Still Out," *National Review,* 14 April 198, 453–54.

————. "The Legacy of Alger Hiss," *St. Louis Post-Dispatch,* 19 November 1996, 10C.

————. "Man and Wife," *Time,* 20 June 1949, 19–20.

————. "Memo to Charles Alan Wright," *Nation,* 22 October 1973, 389–90.

————. "Nixon and the Hiss Case," *Nation,* 15 May 1974, 644.

————. "No Rest for the Innocent," *National Review,* 28 April 1978, 512.

————. "Overcame Many Struggles to Become One of the Shining Lights of the New Deal," *Baltimore Sun,* 17 November 1996, 1B.

————. "Pitfalls of Partisanship," *Nation,* 8 April 1978, 386–88.

————. "Slander of a Dead Man," *Time,* 10 February 1967, 102–03.

————. "A Strange Silence about Alger Hiss," *Sunday Telegraph* (London), 21 October 1990, 23.

————. "A Verdict: 'Hiss Has Been Lying,'" *Time,* 29 March 1976, 30–31.

————. "Weinstein Fires Back," *National Review,* 12 May 1978, 577.

————. "Whittaker Chambers' Farm Is Proposed for Landmark," *National Review,* 5 April 1988, 21–22.

————. "Words from the Center of Sorrow," *Time,* 9 March 1970, 67, 69.

Editors and Allen Weinstein. "'Perjury,' Take Three," *New Republic,* 29 April 1978, 16–21.

Richmond News-Leader Editors. "Death Deceived," *National Review,* 29 July 1961, 51.

"Envoy as Spy: Rare in U.S.," *New York Times,* 24 July 1989, A6.

"Whittaker Chambers-Alger Hiss Spy Case Timeline," *New York Times.* 12 June 1949, E8.

SELECT BOOKS BY OR ABOUT
ALGER HISS OR WHITTAKER CHAMBERS

Andrews, Bert, and Peter Andrews, *A Tragedy of History: A Journalist's Confidential Role in the Hiss-Chambers Case.* Washington, D.C.: R.B. Luce, 1962.

Chambers, Whittaker. *Cold Friday,* ed. and intro. Duncan Norton-Taylor. New York: Random House, 1964.

———. *Witness.* New York: Random House, 1952.

———. *Ghosts on the Roof: Selected Journalism of Whittaker Chambers, 1931-1959,* ed. Terry Teachout. Washington, DC: Regnery: 1989.

———. *Odyssey of a Friend: Whittaker Chambers' Letters to William F. Buckley, Jr., 1954-1961,* ed. William F. Buckley, Jr. New York: Putnam, 1969.

Cook, Fred J. *The Unfinished Story of Alger Hiss.* New York: Morrow, 1958.

Cooke, Alistair. *A Generation on Trial: U.S.A. v. Alger Hiss.* New York: Knopf 1950.

De Toledano, Ralph, and Victor Lasky. *Seeds of Treaton: The True Story of the Hiss-Chambers Tragedy.* New York: Funk & Wagnalls, 1950.

———. *Notes from the Underground: The Whittaker Chambers-Ralph de Toledano Letters, 1949-1960.* Washington, DC: Regnery, 1997.

Hiss, Alger. *In the Court of Public Opinion.* New York: Knopf, 1957.

———. *Recollections of a Life.* New York: Arcade, 1988.

Hiss, Tony. *The View From Alger's Window: A Son's Memoir.* New York: Knopf, 1999.

Smith, John Chabot. *Alger Hiss: The True Story.* New York: Holt,

1976.

Tanenhaus, Sam. *Whittaker Chambers: A Biography*. New York: Random House, 1997.

Trilling, Lionel. *The Middle of the Journey*. New York: Harcourt, 1975.

Weinstein, Allen. *Perjury: The Hiss-Chambers Case*. New York: Knopf, 1979.

Zeligs, Meyer A., M.D. *Friendship and Fratricide: An Analysis of Whittaker Chambers and Alger Hiss*. New York: Viking, 1967.

Notes on Contributors

LESLIE A FIEDLER was the author of numerous important critical books on twentieth-century literature. In his analysis, Fiedler examines the Hiss case in relationship to the political and moral history of America at mid-century. "American liberalism has been reluctant to leave the garden of its illusion, but it can dally no longer: the age of innocence is dead.... We who would still like to think of ourselves as liberals must be willing to declare that mere liberal principle is not in itself a guarantee against evil." He calls for a movement forward from "a liberalism of innocence to a liberalism of responsibility."

DIANA TRILLING, wife of Lionel Trilling, was the fiction critic for the *Nation* during the 1940s. Her books include *We Must March*, *My Darlings*, and *Reviewing the Forties*. In this piece, a review of *Seeds of Treason*, Trilling articulates the dilemma created by the Hiss case for liberals. "Just as the pro-Hiss liberal claims his right not to be smeared as a Communist just because the Communists agree with him in this case, so the anti-Hiss liberal must insist on his right not to be labeled a reactionary just because reactionaries agree with him in this case.... [I]f this case is to serve any purpose in our lives there must be salvaged from it a better notion of liberalism. . . . The case will have been useful, I think, if it helps us detach the wagon of American liberalism from the star of the Soviet Union and if it gives liberals a sounder insight into the nature of a political idea."

ARTHUR KOESTLER was a prominent left-wing journalist during the 1930s who became an equally prominent anticommunist during the 1940s and afterwards. His most famous book is *Darkness at Noon*, a novel about the Stalinist purges. He was a close friend of Whittaker Chambers. Koestler struggles with the question of how society should treat informers. "People don't mind if you betray humanity in the name of some particular cause; but if you betray your club or party, they will turn from you in contempt. . . . The public is entitled to feel attracted or repelled, but it is not entitled to let its bias interfere with its judgment: to talk of betrayal where loyalty would mean persistence in crime: to talk of persecution; to defend an evil regime on the grounds that those who denounce it are no saints. The greatest danger to liberalism today lies in such starry-eyed confusion."

GRANVILLE HICKS was one of the most notable American Communist literary intellectuals of the 1930s and 1940s. Like Chambers, he wrote for the *New Masses* and broke with the Communist Party, although he remained a man of the Left. Calling *Witness* a "testimony to the spirit of man," Hicks concludes that the West's best hope is not to oppose communist dogma with some other dogma, but to meet rigidity of mind with flexibility of mind. "If we are in danger of losing the battle, that is in part because we are in danger of giving up not so much the freedom as the activity of the mind."

SIDNEY HOOK was a socialist, an anticommunist, and a distinguished philosopher. His books include his autobiography, *Out of Step*. Here, Hook repudiates Chambers's choice between faith in God on the one hand, and intelligence and scientific method on the other. "In the war for human freedom ... Chambers is a tragic casualty. Instructive to the last about the mortal threat of the Communist movement ... [*Witness*] does not offer us an intelligent guide to victory or even survival."

IRVING HOWE, a prominent socialist intellectual, was the editor of *Dissent*. His books include *A Margin of Hope*. In reviewing *Witness*, a skeptical Howe notes that "[t]hose who abandon a father below ... are all too ready for a father above. . . . This shift of faith . . . gives the opponents of the totalitarian state no strategy, no program with which to remake the world; it makes our situation appear even more desperate than it already is. For if Chambers is right in believing the major bulwark against Stalin to be faith in God, then it is time for men of conviction and courage to take to the hills."

ELMER DAVIS was a classicist, novelist, essayist, political analyst, and commentator whose radio news summaries early in World War II won him the job of director of the Office of War Information. In this article, Davis rhetorically asks, "How long will these ex-Communists and ex-Sympathizers abuse the patience of the vast majority which had sense enough never to be Communists or sympathizers at all?" A pox on both houses, Davis seems to say.

KINGSLEY MARTIN, a British journalist of the Left, was editor of the *New Statesman and Nation*. For Whittaker Chambers, Martin writes, "The world is divided into Good and Evil; reason as understood since the Renaissance leads a man logically step by step through liberalism to Communism, and Communism is the final evil. . . . Thus, all the people we call liberals ... are enemies of society. Hiss must be a symbol, the representative of evil men, liberals, intellectuals, New Dealers, graduates of the Harvard Law School. These are the unconscious allies of Communism, servants of the Devil."

DAME REBECCA WEST was one of the most distinguished British journalists, feminists, anticommunists and literary critics of her time. Her books include *The Meaning of Treason*. West calls the Hiss-Chambers case "the most recent manifestation of a recurrent threat to society, which recurs because it is the work of mischievous human tendencies which appear to be ineradicable. It was yet another dervish trial. . . . It is one of the great jokes of history that the dragnet of a Washington committee should have fetched up this man [Chambers] of all men to take part in a dervish trial." West recites a history of such trials, including the famous Dreyfus Case in France.

MARK DEWOLFE HOWE was a distinguished legal scholar and historian who edited the papers of Supreme Court Justice Oliver Wendell Holmes Jr. (for whom Alger Hiss clerked in the 1920s.) In reviewing Alger Hiss's autobiography, Howe claims that Hiss's conviction was dependent upon the spongy word of a notorious sinner. That American jurors could give credence to such a man as Chambers in preference to such a man as Hiss is to Howe incredulous. Howe believes that history will ultimately "condemn the action of those who converted an investigating committee of the Congress into a prosecuting agency of the government."

WILLIAM F. BUCKLEY JR. is the founder of *National Review* and author of numerous books, including *God and Man at Yale* and *Odyssey of a Friend: Letters of Whittaker Chambers to William F. Buckley, Jr., 1954–1961*, which he edited. He was a close friend of Chambers during the last decade of Chambers's life. By quoting extensively from Chambers's correspondence with him, Buckley weaves a compelling, revealing narrative of the final years of Chambers life. Buckley quotes Chambers: "I came to communism . . . above all under the influence of the Narodniki . . . , those who went with bomb or revolver against this or that individual monster. . . . I remained under the spiritual influence of the Narodniki long after I became a Marxist. In fact, I never threw it out. It has simply blended with that strain in the Christian tradition to which it is akin."

DAVID CORT, was a frequent contributor to the *Nation* who went to Columbia University with Whittaker Chambers and worked with him at Time, Inc. He was the author of *The Sin of Henry Luce*. Calling Chambers a "walking swindle from childhood," Cort accepts psychoanalyst Meyer Zeligs's thesis, in *Friendship and Fratricide*, that Chambers "somehow conspired in his younger (and more attractive) brother's suicide . . . and thus inaugurated a life pattern of death, guilt, resurrection." Cort writes that the book is important as a compilation of significant data about Chambers and Hiss, while noting that "it would be easy to find fault with it as literary psychoanalysis." (Indeed, Lionel Trilling remarked that "no other work does as much as this psychoanalysis in absentia to bring into question the viability of the infant discipline of psychohistory.") Cort concludes that "Zeligs has started something. . . . Alger Hiss must be vindicated. . . . And Chambers, with that cute dimpled chuckle and the sly, friendly gleam, is laughing in the grave at his 'friends,' the priceless butts who believed in him."

MURRAY KEMPTON was a columnist for *Newsday* and a regular contributor to the *New York Review of Books*. He was the author of *Part of Our Time*, an important history of the American Left during the 1930s and 1940s, *Rebellions, Perversities, and Main Events*, and *The Briar Patch*. He won the Pulitzer Prize in 1985. This selection is something of a sequel to Buckley's *Esquire* essay. In a review of the posthumous collection of letters from Chambers to William F. Buckley Jr. (*Odyssey of a Friend*), Kempton finds that "it has been Chambers's general fate to have struggled to be an historical presence and to end up [instead] being treated merely as an historical object, to be offered for notice only when it can be presented as current." He adds, "The gap between Chambers and the persons most outraged by him is that great: they condemn him to the degradation of having lied, while he writhes in the degradation of having told the truth."

LIONEL TRILLING, husband of Diana Trilling and for many years a professor at Columbia University, was one of America's most distinguished and prominent literary critics. He went to Columbia with Chambers and based the character of Gifford Maxim in *The Middle of the Journey* on him. His other books include *The Liberal Imagination*. Trilling here details how Chambers became a model for an essential character in his novel. Writing less than a year after Richard Nixon's presidential resignation, Trilling finds that "partisans of Hiss's innocence were encouraged to revive their old contention that Hiss had been the victim of Chambers and Nixon in conspiracy with each other.... The tendentious association of the two men does Chambers a grievous injustice." Trilling concludes, "In Whittaker Chambers, there was much to be faulted, but nothing I know of him has led me to doubt his magnanimous intention."

PHILIP NOBILE, a former media critic for *New York* magazine, authored *Judgment at the Smithsonian: The Bombing of Hiroshima and Nagasaki*. Nobile conducts an informal poll of intellectuals and finds that, as Chambers himself once wrote, "the best people were for Alger Hiss and were prepared to go to almost any length to protect and defend him." And despite his acceptance of the damaging evidence revealed in *Perjury*, Nobile nonetheless votes Hiss innocent as well, because as Lillian Hellman wrote, "Nothing else makes sense." Nobile's argument turns on psychology. "I cannot conceive of a sane person perpetuating a quarter-century of deceit, jeopardizing the welfare of his family and the reputation of his friends, in a doomed attempt to reverse what that person well knows to be the truth. . . . If this inner harmony is simply a routine repeated by a deranged player since 1948, then Hiss has deluded me and a large audience of fools." Or, one might say, "the best people."

A distinguished liberal literary critic, ALFRED KAZIN's books include *On Native Grounds* and *New York Jew*. Kazin finds Allen Weinstein's "devastatingly complete and detailed *Perjury: the Hiss-Chambers Case*" to be a "revelation of how politicized, partisan and hallucinated most of the pro-Hiss (and even a little of the anti-Hiss) literature has been." Kazin suggests that, "If Alger Hiss has been telling the truth for thirty years, as many American liberals believe, then he is a victim of the most outrageous injustice. . . . If he was guilty as charged, . . . what are we to make of a man whose character was defended by the secretary of State, two Supreme Court justices, two Democratic nominees for the Presidency, some of the most famous newspapers, publicists and writes in the land, but who has held to lie after lie for thirty years?"

HUGH KENNER is a distinguished conservative literary critic originally from Canada. He specializes in "difficult" twentieth-century literature (e.g., James Joyce, Ezra Pound). His books include *The Pound Era* and *A Colder Eye*. Kenner analyzes the phenomenon of "cadences." . . Everyone's habits with language have a characterizing cadence, what we recognize when we recognize a 'style.' Its gestures mime his sense of how the world goes, how he goes. Alger lives yet, to a rhythm of his own. It is the rhythm of the sewing-machine, busily piecing and stitching; the parts glinting, the motor humming, the needle hopping, the pieces of material lapped and fed: no thread in the bobbin, none in the needle."

JOHN JUDIS, a senior editor of the left-of-center magazine *In These Times*, is a biographer of William F. Buckley Jr. Judis notes that Chambers's importance to American political history did not end when Hiss was finally pronounced guilty in January 1950. After *Witness*, Chambers spent "the remainder of his life working with a new generation of American right-wingers trying to develop an American conservative movement. Chambers's contribution to that movement was immense." But it was also problematic, in his view. Judis claims that "conservatives would have done well to recall that it was not George Bush, nor James Baker, but Whittaker Chambers, ruminating in the basement study of his farm, who condemned America's conservatives to wander between theology and pragmatism, between dreams of redemption and the intractable complexities of politics and diplomacy."

ERIC M. BREINDEL was senior editorial-page editor of the *New York Post* and a syndicated columnist. Taking a view opposite that of Philip Nobile, Breindel writes that in Hiss's autobiography, *Recollections of a Life*, it becomes easier and easier to understand how, in spite of everything, Hiss stood his ground, held to his absurd story, and never cracked. Breindel guesses that Hiss was still a communist and that at every turn in his life he served the cause as best he could. "In the Roosevelt administration, this meant passing documents. From 1948 on, it meant posing as an American Dreyfus. Now it means he must stand fast, which is exactly what he does in this book."

SAM TANENHAUS, a contributing editor at *Vanity Fair* and a former editor at the *New York Times* op-ed page, has written for the *New York Review of Books*, the *New York Times Magazine*, and the *New Republic*, and he is author of the biography, *Whittaker Chambers*. He is currently writing a biography of William F. Buckley Jr. In an review of a published collection of Chambers's journalism (*Ghosts on the Roof*), Tanenhaus writes that the attacks on *Witness* created "an impression—still with us—that Chambers had a weak mind," which, he says "neatly fits the demonology of the Hiss case." Nevertheless, Chambers as "writer manqué" is a false characterization, Tanenhaus concludes, noting instead that Chambers could not "escape the burden of his eloquence." As for Hiss, in light of the evidence of his espionage provided by the release of the formerly top secret Venona cables, Tanenhaus writes, "Hiss remained a Soviet agent long after Chambers's defection and possibly up until the moment he was forced out of the State Department. Chambers made a thoughtful surmise, not as a wild accusation, when under threat of a lawsuit, he declared, 'Alger Hiss was a communist and may be [one] now.'"

RON ROSENBAUM writes for the *New York Times Magazine*, the *New York Observer*, and *Esquire* and teaches a course on literary journalism at the Columbia Graduate School of Journalism. He is the author of several books, including *Travels with Dr. Death and Other Unusual Investigations* and *Explaining Hitler: The Search for the Origins of His Evil*. Rosenbaum writes that "Hiss is still with us. Hiss will not go away. . . . [I]nnocent or guilty, here was a guy who had become the singular focus of nearly a half-century of bitter debate over one of the great questions of the century." He speculates that Hiss may have viewed himself as a "man of principled idealism, one who kept the faith and kept his silence to protect not just himself, but a salvific future he still believed in, even if it meant deceiving his most active and self-sacrificing loyalists." Rosenbaum argues provocatively that "perhaps it's time for some of Hiss's defenders to give him credit for—even to defend—the reality of what he did."

HILTON KRAMER is the editor of the *New Criterion*, a neoconservative arts magazine. He was formerly art critic for the *New York Times*. His books include *The Revenge of the Philistines* and *The Age of the Avant-Garde*. Kramer writes that there is a "crazy logic" in the Hiss-Chambers case. "Hiss, convicted of crimes that showed him to be a liar, a thief, and a traitor was judged to be innocent even if guilty, and Chambers, the self-confessed renegade, who recanted his treachery, was judged to be guilty even if he was telling the truth. For what mattered to liberal opinion was that Hiss was seen to have remained true to his ideals, never mind what the content of these 'ideals' proved to be, whereas Chambers was seen to have betrayed them." Kramer laments, "Forty years after he brought his first public charges against Alger Hiss, Chambers remains in the liberal mind, which is more than ever the mind that dominates the universities, the media, and the literary world, the monster that Hiss's defenders shamelessly made him out to be."

Index

Aberdeen Proving Grounds, 71, 72

Abt, John, 18, 259

Acheson, Dean, 22–23, 205, 218, 256

Adams, Charles. *S e e* Chambers, Whittaker

Adler, Mortimer J., 270

Agee, James, 142, 278

A Generation on Trial (Cooke), 209, 307

Agriculture Department, 11

Akhmerov, Ishkak, 290, 291

Aksakov, Sergei, 113(n)

Alexander VI, 174

Alger, Horatio, 14

Alger Hiss: The True Story (Smith), 201, 208–9

Almereyda, Miguel, 174

America

    communism in, 47–48, 72–75, 103–4, 294–96

    conservatism in, 244–51

    liberalism in, 6–7, 25, 43–45, 314–15

    politics in, 18

    Soviet Union and, 36–37, 112

    Spanish War and, 35

American Dream, 11

Americanism, 36, 42

American Scholar, 207

American Student Union, 23

Anderson, Marian, 279

Anderson, Sherwood, 276

Anti-Comintern Pact, 72(n)

Aquinas, Thomas, 162–63

Asia, 83

Associated Press, 154

The Atlantic, 268

Atlas Shrugged (Rand), 152–53, 248

Atom Spy. *S e e* Fuchs, Klaus

Augustine, Saint, 57

Australia, 108

Austria, 157

Baker, James, 251

Baltimore News-American, 221

Baltimore Sun, 221

Bambi (Salten), 275

Barzun, Jacques, 271

Beaconsfield, Lord, 244

Bedacht, Max, 16

Bentley, Elizabeth, 3, 20, 281
Berle, A. A., 22–23, 180, 260, 281
Boatner, Haydon L., 96(n)
Bob. *See* Chambers, Whittaker
Boehme, Jakob, 117
Bolshevik Party, 63–64
Bowden, Mark, 221–23
Brandt, Carl, 149
Breen, David. *See* Chambers, Whittaker
Browder, Earl, 19–20
Buber, Martin, 157
Buber-Neumann, Greta, 157
Buckley, William, 205, 215
    Chambers and, 136, 165–78
    National Review and, 242–43
Bukharin, Nikolai Ivanovich, 88(n)
Bullitt, Ambassador, 22
Bundy, William, 205
Burnham, James, 156, 175, 243
Bush, George, 251
Bykov, Colonel, 5, 10, 86, 87–88, 165
Byron, Lord, 275

Camus, Albert, 161
Canada, 218
Cantwell, George. *See* Chambers, Whittaker
Can You Hear Their Voices?, 16, 277
capitalism, 65
Carl. *See* Chambers, Whittaker
Carnegie Foundation, 33
Cerf, Bennett, 282, 310, 316
Chamberlain, John, 155, 239
Chambers, Esther, 154
Chambers, Jay David. *See* Chambers, Whittaker

Chambers, Jay Vivian. *See* Chambers, Whittaker
Chambers, John, 140–41, 149, 163
Chambers, Richard, 225, 275
Chambers, Whittaker
    aliases of, 8, 135, 226, 231
    character of, 144, 160, 177–78, 309–10
    communism and, 58–66, 232–33, 238–42
    Communist Party and, 11–18, 27, 92–93
    confession of, 6, 31, 51–52
    conservatism of, 244–51
    death of, 163–64
    health of, 143–44, 156, 158
    Hiss and, 7–10, 15, 27, 221–34, 253–58, 305–6
    history and, 1
    HUAC and, 7, 13, 21, 62
    as informer, 101–3, 170, 196–97, 202–3, 253–54, 306–7
    The Middle of the Journey and, 171–73, 179–99
    National Review and, 144–45, 150–56, 158–60, 165–66, 243–45
    New Masses and, 15, 60, 61, 146
    Nixon and, 165–70
    personal history of, 27, 114–17, 140–41, 238
    psychology of, 133–38, 149–50
    religion and, 75–79
    science and, 160–63
    Seeds of Treason and, 31
    as Soviet agent, 235–40
    Soviet Union and, 10
    Time and, 14, 62
    as writer, 265–83
    See also Witness

Chiang Kai-shek, 11
China, 83, 104, 250
Choate, Hall and Stewart, 206
Chodorov, Frank, 240
Christianity, 62
Christie, Agatha, 229
Clark, Grenville, 218
Class Reunion (Werfel), 276,
    278
Clifford, Margaret, 277
Cockburn, Alexander, 206
Cold Friday (Chambers), 183, 232,
    248, 265, 270
Collazo, Oscar, 3(n)
Colliers, 105
Collins, Henry, 18, 258, 259
Colson, Charles F., 96(n)
Columbia University, 135
Commentary, 151, 312
communism
    in America, 47–48, 72–75,
    103–4, 294–96
    Chambers and, 58–66, 69–
    75, 232–33, 238–42
    in China, 83, 104, 250
    fascism and, 63
    God and, 105–6, 120,
    240–41
    Hiss and, 259–61, 294–96
    idealism and, 38
    images of, 226–27
    liberalism and, 30–31, 34, 36,
    46–47, 64, 242, 311, 312
    Marx and, 241–42
    New Deal and, 64, 319
    religion and, 75–79
    Roosevelt and, 314, 319
    roots of, 64
    Soviet Union and, 43–45, 305
    Stalin and, 62–63, 66
    See also Communist Party
Communist International, 73
Communist Manifesto (Marx), 64

Communist Party
    Chambers and, 11–12, 15–
    17, 18, 27
    changes in, 18
    ex-members of, 49–56, 91–
    100
    Germany and, 35
    Hiss and, 6–9, 11–14,
    46–47
    New Deal and, 19
    Popular Front and, 24
    Third Period of, 15–17
    underground of, 16
    See also communism
Confessions (Augustine), 57
Confessions (Rousseau), 57
Conrad, Joseph, 271
conservatism, 244–51
The Conservative Mind (Kirk), 242
Conservative Political Action Con-
    ference, 236
Cooke, Alistair, 2, 6, 93, 203, 209,
    300
Coolidge, Calvin, 270
Coplon, Judith, 1
Cousins, Norman, 204
Covington & Burling, 261
Croom, Arthur, 182, 184–85
Croom, Nancy, 182, 184–85
Crosley, George. *See* Chambers,
    Whittaker

Daily Worker, 18, 189, 260, 274,
    275
"The Damn Fool" (Chambers),
    271
Dante, 267
Darkness at Noon (Koestler), 145–
    46
Deals and Dreamers (Lash), 258
"The Death of the Communists"
    (Chambers), 277–78

Debevoise and Plimpton, 261
Democratic Party, 20–21, 37
dervish trials, 108–12
Dewey, John, 77, 99
The Dial, 272
Dilke, Sir Charles, 108–9
Diogenes, 162
Disraeli, Benjamin, 244, 248
Djerjinsky, Felix, 119(n)
Djilas, Milovan, 151
Dodd, Francis T., 96(n)
Dollard, Charles, 255
Dos Passos, John, 95, 276
Dostoevsky, Fyodor, 17, 76, 267
Douglas, William O., 203
Dreyfus, Alfred, 4, 109–11, 210
Duggan, Laurence, 290
Dulles, John Foster, 290
Dwyer, David. *See* Chambers,
    Whittaker

Eastman, Max, 238, 242
Eckhart, Johannes, 117
Edschmid, Kasimir, 275
Eisenhower, Dwight, 147–48,
    150, 167
Elistratova, 60
Ellroy, James, 297
Emerson, Thomas, 206
England, 35, 108–9
Enlightenment, 85
Europe, 41

Fadiman, Clifton, 270, 275
Family Chronicle, 113(n)
fascism
    Americanism and, 36
    communism and, 63
    European, 41
    liberalism and, 34–35
    Spain and, 35

Stalinism and, 86
Federal Bureau of Investigation
    (FBI), 205, 208
    Hiss and, 294
Fiedler, Leslie, 204
Field, Noel, 18, 258, 259, 289
Flagstad, Kirsten, 164
Flanagan, Hallie, 277
Foote, Alexander Allan, 71, 72(n)
Foote, Wilder, 290
Foreign Affairs, 204–5
Fortas, Abe, 206, 207
Fourteenth Amendment, 98
France, 53, 109–10
Franco, Francisco, 35, 77
Frankel, Max, 204
Frankfurter, Felix, 218
Franklin, Benjamin, 99
Freedom of Information Act, 216
Freeman, 88
French Revolution, 85
Freud, Sigmund, 7, 231
Fuchs, Klaus, 24, 45(n)

Galindez, Jesus de, 297
Galsworthy, John, 275
Gentleman's Agreement (Hobson),
    205–6
German-Japanese Pact, 72(n)
Germany
    Communist Party and, 35
    Hitler and, 43
    Nazi, 19
    Soviet Union and, 35,
    193–94
"The Ghosts on the Roof" (Cham-
    bers), 272
Ghosts on the Roof (Teachout), 276,
    278
Ginsberg, Allen, 237
The Glory and the Dream
    (Manchester), 211

God
  communism and, 105–6, 120, 240–41
  man and, 99–100
  mystic and, 117–18
  nature and, 116
  Stalinism and, 82, 85, 89
Goddard, Judge, 285
Go East, Young Man (Douglas), 203
Gold, Harry, 45(n)
Gold, Michael, 276
Goldstein, Emmanuel, 94
Goldwater, Barry, 243, 248
GPU, 14, 22
Greene, Graham, 300–301
Gromov, Anatoly, 290
Gromyko, Andrei, 260

Hall, Gus, 206, 207
Hamilton, Alexander, 100
Hanssen, Robert, 300
Harden, Maximilian, 110
Harvard Law School, 22
Hawkes, Herbert E., 272
Hayek, Frederick Von, 242
Hearst, William Randolph, Jr., 205
"Heart of Darkness" (Conrad), 271
Hellman, Lillian, 206, 207, 211
Hentoff, Nat, 206
Herald-Tribune, 208
Herbst, Josephine, 218, 258
Hersey, John, 279
Hield, Hermann, 259
Hiroshima, 84
Hiss, Alger
  appeal of, 285–91
  as Bolshevik, 18–21
  career of, 30, 32–33, 37–43, 215
  Carnegie Foundation and, 33
  Chambers and, 9–10, 15, 27, 221–34, 253–58, 305–6

character of, 219–20, 261
communism and, 259–61, 294–96
Communist Party and, 6–9, 11–14, 46–47
confession of, 24–25, 213–20
In the Court of Pubic Opinion, 127–32
credibility of, 128
death of, 293
defense of, 2–3, 38–39, 203–11, 296–301
friendships of, 32–33
HUAC and, 7, 20–21
idealism and, 33, 313–14
innocence of, 1–26, 27–32, 254–58, 293–94
liberalism and, 25, 32, 43
Nixon and, 209, 213–14, 229, 255, 295, 300
perjury of, 1, 7–9, 201–3
personal life of, 208–10, 263–64
politics of, 257–61
Popular Front and, 18
right to passport of, 246, 273
Roosevelt and, 21–23
Soviet Union and, 3, 5, 10–11
treason of, 1–2, 4, 11
as victim, 4
Hiss, Donald, 23, 205
Hiss, Priscilla, 206, 209–10, 256
Hitchcock, Alfred, 139
Hitler, Adolf, 77, 86
  appeasement of, 6
  Germany and, 43
  rise of, 34
  Stalin and, 194
Hitler-Stalin Pact, 226–27
Hobson, Laura Z., 205, 205–6
Hobson, Thayer, 206

Hobson, Timothy, 206, 209, 256
Holmes, Oliver Wendell, Jr., 22, 202, 215
Hook, Sidney, 204, 228, 265–66, 279, 318
Hoover, J. Edgar, 216, 287
Hopkins, Harry, 37
House Committee on Un-American Activities (HUAC)
    Chambers and, 7, 13, 21, 62
    criticism of, 31
    Hiss and, 7, 20–21
    New Deal and, 13
Howe, Irving, 266, 267, 269
HUAC. *See* House Committee on Un-American Activities

I Chose Freedom (Kravchenko), 53(n)
idealism
    communism and, 38
    Hiss and, 33, 313–14
    religion and, 40
    socialism and, 40
    imperialism, 15
Inferno (Chambers), 267
"In Memoriam" (Tennyson), 272
Institute for Policy Studies, 206
International Military Tribunal, 53(n)
International Publishers, 65(n)
In the Court of Pubic Opinion (Hiss), 127–32, 254, 296

Jackson, Andrew, 20
James, Henry, 116, 184, 273–74
Janeway, Eliot, 205
Janeway, Elizabeth, 205
Japan, 72, 262
Jefferson, Thomas, 20, 86, 100
Jews Without Money (Gold), 276

John Birch Society, 248
John XXIII, 301
Johns Hopkins, 215
Joyce, James, 280
Justice Department, 216

Kafka, Franz, 267
Kelly, John. *See* Chambers, Whittaker
Kempton, Murray, 204, 293, 298
Kennedy, John Fitzgerald, Jr., 140
Kenner, Hugh, 142
Kepler, Johann, 161
Khrushchev, Nikita, 245
Kierkegaard, Soren76
Kirk, Russell, 205, 242, 243
Kisseloff, Jeffrey, 297
Koestler, Arthur, 65, 145–46, 157, 160, 161, 267
Kolakowski, Leszek, 303
Kravchenko, Victor, 53(n), 54
Krivitsky, Walter, 63(n), 95
Kronstadt Rebellion, 63(n), 83

Land, John. *See* Chambers, Whittaker
Lash, Joseph P., 258
Laskell, John, 184, 188
Lasky, Victor, 27, 31, 32
Laval, Pierre, 53(n)
League against War and Fascism, 35
League of Nations, 19, 259
Lenin, Vladimir, 15–16, 19, 63, 85–86
Leviné, Eugene, 119
Levitt, Morton and Michael, 255
Lewis, Anthony, 204
Lewis, Wyndham, 143
The Liberal Imagination (Trilling), 312

liberalism
    in America, 43–45, 314–15
    communism and, 30–31, 34,
    36, 46–47, 64, 242, 311, 312
    fascism and, 34–35
    Hiss and, 25, 32, 43
    Marx and, 311
    modern, 33–34
    socialism and, 311
    Stalinism and, 311
    weakness of, 34
Liberty League, 96
Lieber, Maxim, 218
Life, 143, 192, 281
Lincoln, Abraham, 20, 100
Litinov, Maxim, 19
London, Jack, 15
Luce, Boothe Clare, 205
Luce, Henry R., 137, 148, 151,
    239–40, 278, 279, 165

Macdonald, Dwight, 151, 161, 204
Mailer, Norman, 204
Main Currents of Marxism
    (Kolakowski), 303
Malraux, André, 267
Manchester, William, 211
Manhattan Project, 45(n)
Mann, Heinrich, 275
Mao Tse-tung, 83
Marbury, William, 255–56
Marquand, John P., 304
Marx, Karl, 16, 241–42, 303, 311
Massing, Hede, 289
Matthews, H. Freeman, 290
Matthews, T. S., 278
Maxim, Gifford, 171–72, 179–82,
    187
Mazlish, Bruce, 206
McCarran Committee, 288
McCarran Internal Security Act,
    91

McCarthy, Elizabeth, 286–87
McCarthy, Joseph, 47–48, 142,
    143, 165, 197
McCarthy and His Enemies
    (Buckley and Bozell), 246
McDowell, David, 282
McGohey, John F. X., 165
McLean, Edward, 255–56
McWilliams, Carey, 24, 206
"A Memorandum on the Hiss
    Case" (Trilling), 312
Menorah Journal, 171
Meyer, Frank, 175
The Middle of the Journey
    (Trilling), 137, 171–73,
    179–99
Miller, Arthur, 206
Miller, Merle, 205, 267
Molotov, Vyacheslav, 37
Mooney, Tom, 4
Morningside, 271, 274
Morris, Professor, 94
Moscow-Berlin Pact, 157
Moscow trials, 7, 10, 77, 311
Moses, 231
Mother Mary (Mann), 275
Muenzenberg, Willi, 157
Muenzenberg Trust, 157
Mumford, Lewis, 276
Mundt, Karl E., 17
Murphy, Thomas, 82–83
Mussolini, Benito, 77
My Silent War (Philby), 300
mystics, 117–19
Myth of Sisyphus, 151

Narodniki, 146
The Nation, 206, 228
National Emergency Committee
    on Civil Liberties, 261
National Labor Relations Board,
    258

National Lawyers Guild, 261
National Review, 136, 140, 148
    Chambers and, 144–45,
    150–56, 158–60, 165–66,
    243–45
    conservatism of, 159,
    244–46
    founding of, 174–75,
    242–43
National Security Agency, 290
nature, God and, 116
Navasky, Victor, 206, 294
Nazi Germany. *See* Germany
Nazism, 43
Nearing, Scott, 274
Neumann, Heinz, 157
The New Class (Djilas), 151
New Deal
    American politics and, 18
    communism and, 64, 72–73,
    319
    Communist Party and, 19
    HUAC and, 13
New Leader, 312
New Masses, 15, 16, 60, 146, 189,
    276, 305
New Republic, 20, 205, 263, 267,
    278, 316
Newspaper Guild, 279
New Statesman, 176
Newsweek, 27, 154
New York, 140, 155
New York Post, 6
New York Times, 154, 204, 208
New York Times Book Review, 318
New Yorker, 316
Niebuhr, Reinhold, 279
1984 (Orwell), 94
Nixon, Richard, 17, 150, 197, 202
    Chambers and, 136–37,
    139–40, 165–70
    Hiss and, 209, 213–14, 229,
    255, 294, 295, 300

NKVD, 88(n), 157–58
Nuremberg, 53(n)
Nye Committee, 11, 22, 83–84

O'Brien, Conor Cruise, 232
O'Neill, Eugene, 276
Odyssey of a Friend (Chambers),
    265
Office of European Affairs, 290
Office of Special Political Affairs,
    291
Official Secrets Act, 124
Operation Abolition, 296
Operation Barbarossa, 72(n)
Oppenheim, E. Phillips, 5
Orton, Arthur, 108
Orwell, George, 94, 161
Osborne, John, 205
Out of Step (Hook), 265
Oxford University Press, 285

Partisan Review, 312
Part of Our Time (Kempton), 298
The Passionate Rebel (Eschmid),
    275
Pasternak, Boris, 161
Patent Office, 71
patriotism, 2, 36
Pearl Harbor, 72(n)
Peguy, Charles, 125
*Perjury! The Hiss-Chambers Con-
    flict* (Weinstein), 201, 215,
    223, 227–31, 307–8
Perlo, Victor, 258, 259, 290
Peters, J., 60, 319
Philby, Kim, 299, 300–301
Philipp, Prince, 110
Picquart, Colonel, 125
Plain Speaking (Miller), 205
Poland, 262
Popular Front, 4, 18, 24

Porter, Katherine Anne, 276
Pressman, Lee, 18, 258, 259
Princess Casamassina (James), 274
Psychopathia Sexualis (Freud), 7
Puerto Rico, 3

Quakerism, 65

Ragozinikova, 147
Rahv, Philip, 308, 309, 316
Rand, Ayn, 152–53, 248
Random House, 160, 282
Rankin, 13, 17
Raskin, Marcus, 206
Rauschning, Hermann, 71(n)
Reagan, Ronald, 236–37, 249–51, 266
Recollections of a Life (Hiss), 253, 256, 257, 261
"Red-baiters," 22
Reed, John, 266
Regnery, Henry, 143
Reichstag trial, 111–12
religion
    Chambers and, 75–79
    communism and, 75–79
    idealism and, 40
Remington, William, 1, 3, 11
Republican party
    Chambers and, 159–60
    conservatism of, 248
    Hiss and, 20–21
Rilke, Rainer Maria, 267
The Road to Serfdom (Hayek), 242
Rogge, O. John, 84
Roman Catholic Church, 125
Roosevelt, Eleanor, 23
Roosevelt, Franklin, 86
    communism and, 100, 314, 319

Democratic Party and, 37
    Hiss and, 21–23
    Soviet Union and, 35–37, 40–41
Roosevelt, Theodore, 39–40
Rosenberg, Anna M., 13
Rosenberg, Julius and Ethel, 1, 3, 45(n)
Rosenwald, Harold, 84, 257
Rousseau, Jean-Jacques, 57
Rovere, Richard, 169
Rovinsn, Hyacinth, 274
Rusk, Dean, 204, 207
Russia. *See* Soviet Union
Russian Revolution, 5, 10

Sacco-Vanzetti trial, 4
Salten, Felix, 275
Santayana, George, 280
Saturday Evening Post, 142
Saturday Review, 94, 267, 317
Sayre, Francis B., 255, 261
Sazonov, 120–21, 147
Schacht, Hjalmar, 53(n)
Schapiro, Meyer, 270, 273
Schlamm, William S., 166, 175, 239, 242–43, 148
Schlesinger, Arthur, Jr., 94, 99, 204, 267, 317–18
Schmahl, Horace, 297
Schmidt, Maria, 289
science, 160–63
Scottsboro boys, 4
Seeds of Treason (Lasky), 27, 27–32, 140
Senate Committee on Internal Security, 165
Serge, Victor, 174
Service, John S., 205
Shannon, William, 205
Sherrill, Robert, 206
Silesius, Angelus, 117

Silone, Ingazio, 54
Silverman, Noel, 18
Simon & Schuster, 275
The Sleepwalkers (Koestler), 160, 161
Smith, Adam, 226–27
Smith, Gerald L. K., 240
Smith, John Chabot, 201, 208–9
socialism
    idealism and, 40
    liberalism and, 311
    rural, 244
    of Soviet Union, 40
    triumph of, 3
Society of Friends, 62, 124, 125
Sorge, Richard, 72(n)
Sorge ring, 71–72
Soviet-Nazi pact, 7, 36
Soviet Union
    America and, 36–37
    American and, 112
    Chambers and, 10
    communism and, 43–45, 305
    espionage and, 1–2
    Germany and, 35, 193–94
    Hiss and, 3, 5, 10–11
    Reagan and, 249
    Roosevelt and, 35–37, 40–41
    socialism of, 40
    Yalta and, 104
Spain, 35, 104
Spanish War, 35
Stalin, Joseph, 14, 86
    Chambers and, 81–89
    communism and, 62–63, 66
    Hitler and, 194
    Lenin and, 85–86
Stalin-Hitler Pact, 122
Stalinism
    fascism and, 86
    God and, 82, 89

Left and, 81
liberalism and, 311
Popular Front and, 18
problem of, 87
State Department, 2, 71
Stein, Gertrude, 156
Stevenson, Adlai, 218
Stone, I. F., 204
Strachey, John, 161
Straight, Michael, 263
Strasser, Otto, 71(n)
Strategic Air Command, 165
Stryker, Lloyd Paul, 66–67, 257, 286, 316
Supreme Court, 98, 203
Swan, Patrick, 278
Switzerland, 71

Taft, Robert, 71, 98, 240
Taylor-Norton, Duncan, 243
Teachout, Terry, 276
Teheran, 22
Tennyson, Alfred Lord, 272
"The Theory and Practice of Oligarchical Collectivism" (Goldstein), 94
The Third Man (Greene), 301
Third Period, 15
Tichborne, Sir Roger. *See* Orton, Arthur
Time, 14, 62, 154, 192
Time, Inc., 148, 279, 280–81, 137
A Tissue of Lies: Nixon vs. Hiss (Levitt and Levitt), 255
Toledano, Ralph De, 27, 31, 32, 140
Tomsky, Mikhail, 88(n)
Torresola, Griselio, 3(n)
Toynbee, Arnold, 65, 279
Trachtenberg, Alex, 65
treason, patriotism and, 2
Treason (Weyl), 288